Rural Society in France

Rural Society in France

Selections from the

Annales

Economies, Sociétés, Civilisations

Edited by

Robert Forster

and

Orest Ranum

Translated by

Elborg Forster

and

Patricia M. Ranum

The Johns Hopkins University Press
Baltimore and London

This book has been brought to publication with the
generous assistance of the Andrew W. Mellon Foundation.

Manufactured in the United States of America

The Johns Hopkins University Press, Baltimore, Maryland 21218
The Johns Hopkins Press Ltd., London

Library of Congress Catalog Card Number 76-47373
ISBN 0-8018-1916-4 (hardcover)
ISBN 0-8018-1917-2 (paperback)

Library of Congress Cataloging in Publication data
will be found on the last printed page of this book.

Contents

Introduction

Marc Bloch and Lucien Febvre, two historians of remarkable breadth, are probably best remembered for their pioneering work in rural history and collective mentalities. The *Annales,* in the forefront of French scholarship, has earned incontestable prestige in the field of rural history, so much so that a single volume of articles cannot begin to do justice to its range and depth. For many historians and cultural anthropologists, the most rewarding aspect of the French approach to the rural world has been the recreation of a vivid and concrete human existence; not merely the formal design of the fields, the state of technology, the production and distribution of the fruits of the land, and the juridical framework that accompanied economic activities but also the attitudes and values—*moeurs* and *mentalités*—of ordinary people in a preindustrial society. Agrarian history readily lends itself to the *longue durée* by the timeless rhythm of the countryside, the slow acceptance of innovation, and the semiliteracy and inescapable localism of people who even today compose the world's largest human mass. In the work of the *Annales*-school historians, we never lose sight of real human beings who toil and talk, feel and reflect. As Febvre said thirty years ago, there is another world, a world of peasant psychology that the historian must recapture in all of its complexity.

In this volume we have attempted to join the two areas that Bloch and Febvre espoused so well in their own work. We have selected not only those articles that treat the impact of the events of a decade or the secular trends of a millenium on the agrarian structure of France but also those that describe the peculiar combination of physical surroundings, traditions, habits, and "tone" that give the village its special character and durability. Hence, three of the eight selections treat specific villages. The essays are qualitative, despite their precision about acreages and occupations; interdisciplinary, relying heavily upon cultural anthropology and folklore; and, above all, subtle in performing the double role of describing in depth the activities and values of a restricted number of human beings and of evoking situations that reflect a timeless, human dimension—the *durable.* As Paul Leuilliot writes, "Here local history overflows into the history of mentalities, of attitudes toward life, death, money, and innovation."

Lucien Febvre's short essay, entitled "Man or Productivity," is perhaps even more appropriate to our own time than it was to his, three decades ago. Febvre was concerned that in our obsession with economic growth and the efficiency of labor and capital, we might lose sight of the village community as a special way of life in which "production" may not be the primary value. There is in Febvre's comment more than a warning about historical method; it contains a strong nostalgic sentiment for the countryside and the peasant outlook on life. Like so many of his generation—Marc Bloch, Georges Lefebvre, Gaston Roupnel, Henri Sée, Pierre de Saint-Jacob—Febvre had a deep feeling for the French countryside, the empathy of one who viewed its rows of poplar trees, meandering river valleys, tidy furrows, and creaking carts with a loving eye. And if these men all erred a little in the direction of an idealized bucolic harmony, their sympathy for the village community gave their work a powerful evocative quality that even an urbanite in another "world" can appreciate and share.

Paul Leuilliot wrote his "defense and illustration of local history" ten years ago. No doubt it contains a defensive quality that seems unnecessary today. One thinks immediately of Emmanuel Le Roy Ladurie's *Montaillou,* a village study that in a year has not only sold 100,000 copies to the lay public but has also captivated specialists—historians, sociologists, ethnographers—who can now listen to thirteenth-century peasants speaking about their intimate, every-day lives. Leuilliot defends local history with "seven principles," almost like a military engineer's system of entrenchments, aimed against the writers of traditional political history, of premature or speculative syntheses, of thesis subjects chosen by Parisian mentors who have too often looked down on local history as trivial and nonanalytical. Leuilliot emphasizes that local history is an indispensible corrective to the broad synthesis, yielding the necessary nuance and suppleness that aggregate statistics and national trends cannot provide. But even more important, the local study stands on its own, not as a discrete building block for some future synthesis, but as a coherent "world" in its own right, able to capture, as no other framework can, the psychological dimension of daily life. By this vehicle one can hope to identify the elusive links among many aspects of human activity, such as diet and disease, birth control and religious belief, self-esteem and deference, or to uncover a hierar-chy of loyalties to family, craft, seigneur, or village community. Sometimes one can even hope to detect more subtle indications of changing attitudes toward work, leisure, and deviance, or toward childhood, old age, and death. Leuilliot would surely have been pleased to see today's practitioners of local history, researchers propelled by fresh élan, armed with new sources, new approaches, and new allied disciplines, clearly on the "offensive."

A collection of articles on French rural history would be incomplete without at least one selection from the prodigious corpus of Georges Lefebvre's histor-ical writings. Despite the efforts of some recent interpreters to force his history into a narrow mold, Lefebvre defies easy categorization. Deeply respectful of empirical evidence, scrupulously honest in his interpretations, fully aware of the continuities as well as the "ruptures" in social history, he earned the respect of historians of all shades of political opinion and philosophical affiliation. Among his many scholarly endeavors, his most intense commitment was to peasant history, followed closely by the French Revolution. Thus, when Lefebvre joined the two subjects, one clearly belonging to the *longue durée,* the other to *histoire événementielle,* he was able to bring his keenest talents and most sympathetic inclinations to bear. In this article written in 1929 Lefebvre is at his best, demonstrating the complexity of the rural world, its many internal conflicts and regional variations, the subtle changes that have undermined the traditional village community, and the strong continuities of autarchy, small property, communal rights, and suspicion of innovation. Against these deeply rooted conditions, psychological as well as material, a revolutionary wave would break, surely bending the rural structure but hardly splintering it or sweeping it away. Lefebvre is too honest not to express his doubts and hesitancies, and the accidental and unexpected results of a conscious policy, action, or piece of legislation have their place. "It should be pointed out," he writes, "that the Revolution was much more moderate than it might have been." Failing to attain for the poor what it promised, slowing down rather than stimulating agricultural innovation, the Revolution nonetheless favored the small landholder and the craftsman. In short, once Lefebvre's description of agrarian society of the Ancien Régime is understood in all its complexity and durability, the limitations of the revolutionary "event" seem almost—if not quite—predictable.

If Lefebvre conveys a philosophical acceptance of the limitations of the social effects of a "great event" in history, Albert Soboul exhibits a certain frustration before the failure of the Revolution to root out thoroughly and completely both the fiscal reality and the psychological legacy of "feudalism." But with an equal intensity of commitment to the hopes raised by the Revolution, Soboul exposes the delays of legislation against seigneurial rights and the various legalistic subterfuges employed by parliamentary committees to frustrate complete abolition before definitive action was finally taken in the spring of 1793. But the story of the survival of "feudalism" does not end in 1793 or even with the *Code Civil* in 1801. Soboul explores the persistence of the church tithe and other dues under various guises well into the nineteenth century, usually in new leases and sharecropping contracts, verbal or notarized. Like Lefebvre, Soboul is aware of regional variations and the different rates of atrophy of these dues. He moves beyond the legal and material aspects of *feudalism* to embrace the state of dependence that the word suggested to Frenchmen in the last century. Most medievalists and some scholars of the Ancien Régime, among them Alfred Cobban, have objected to the application of the word *feudalism* to nonmilitary, essentially owner-tenant relationships. But Soboul demonstrates how the word was used in nineteenth-century rural France, and his article explains its context and connotations. The persistence he stresses is not so much an economic reality as a "collective memory" of personal dependence that colored much of peasant thinking in the first two-thirds of the nineteenth century. It is a credit to Soboul's craftsmanship and careful reading of the evidence that his avowed Marxist theory of history does not seem to have conditioned his conclusion that the "antifeudal reflex" and "myth" influenced the minds and actions of peasants independently of the material reality of seigneurial dues or church tithes. "The attitudes of the collective mentality are at least as important as the legal and economic aspects of the institution."

The substantial article by Emmanuel Le Roy Ladurie and Jean-Marie Pesez is a fine example of history over the *longue durée,* since it treats the survival and decline of villages of France from the late Middle Ages to the present. But beyond the scope in time, the most interesting aspects of this piece are its methodology, resourceful use of evidence, and open discussion of possible explanations for the desertion of villages at certain times and in certain regions. First, the authors know their geography; they map the distribution of abandoned village sites and relate them, where possible, to physical considerations including natural resources, defensible positions, proximity to disease-infested areas, and so on. They use archeological findings to help confirm locations indicated in the written documents. The regions are considered in the perspective of both cyclical and linear developments—for abandoned villages were often reoccupied—and these developments are related to secular trends in demography, food production, and major migrations as well as to more episodic influences, like natural catastrophe, epidemic, and war. The authors also consider local custom, types of agriculture, and the pull of the *villeneuve* or larger urban center. The rise of the monarchical state, the domain building of both urban and rural seigneurs, and the burden of taxes and debts on the average villager were particularly intense between 1560 and 1720, accounting for a spurt in the desertion of villages. However, Le Roy Ladurie and Pesez are careful to distinguish between "real villages," on one hand, and hamlets and outlying farms, on the other. Taking the millennium as a whole, French villages were remarkably tenacious, more so, it seems, than those of England and Germany and perhaps even Spain. The authors point out that even the best tax lists (*compoix*) cannot furnish explanations and that villages undergoing similar pressures may react in quite different ways. Although much weight is given to the secular trends, there is no rigid determinism here; human will counted for something.

This article marks a certain milestone in the history of the *Annales.* Part of a large project presented at the meeting of the International Economic History Association in Munich in 1965, "Deserted Villages" captures much of the boldness of the "school." Ambitious in scope and in the use of new sources and ancillary disciplines, it was able to build on a solid and proven tradition of rural history. Under the imaginative guidance of a new generation of historians such as Emmanuel Le Roy Ladurie and Georges Duby, French scholarship in agrarian history took another leap forward. And if more recent developments in the "history of mentalities" have redirected research to subjects more circumscribed in space and time, "Deserted Villages" remains a classic of its kind.

Alain Morel departs from a compartmentalized approach to village study—demography, production, social structure, and mentalities—in order to demonstrate how his nineteenth-century Picard village society was held together. His is a study of "social control" by the local families of notables that goes beyond economic power and even social preeminence based on access to educational advantages and contacts with the outside urban world and includes a code of normative behavior, an ideology. This code was one of reciprocal obligations between the patron-employer and those dependent on him, and it did much to mitigate, or at least disguise, a crass economic relationship. The villagers "behave more like commoners toward a seigneur than like proletarians toward management." But in Picardy, that relationship exhibited little of the "antifeudal hatred" described by Albert Soboul; it was much more a relationship of active paternalism on one side and social respect on the other. Morel suggests that the villagers, especially the very small farmers and the landless agricultural workers, might have opted for rural socialism, unionized, and fought collectively for a more favorable distribution of wealth. But instead, a pervasive work ethic gave them hope of improvement by individual effort. What is more, theirs was a highly competitive work ethic. Morel reviews a whole litany of epithets for those who failed to measure up, as well as those popular expressions—*vaillant, fameux, heuré*—that conferred public approval. Invidious distinctions were founded on sheer energy and a capacity for work rather than on achieved wealth or power in the community. The patron-employer in his turn practiced Christian paternalism—including private charity, of course—but there was also a bonus system, cheap housing, a religious school, and even "trousseaux" for the poorer girls of the village. The patron's relations with the villagers were direct and personal.

Morel's Picard village appears to be the fulfillment of the idealized seigneurialism of the Ancien Régime. The family in the château, albeit without any claim to noble ancestry, combined the leadership roles of employer, rich landowner, local erudite, mayor, and "notable." This personal clientage network was sustained by a whole package of values and attitudes that are only now, three-quarters of the way through the twentieth century, beginning to crumble, as more and more villagers leave their circumscribed world. New needs, inspired by the city, cannot be supplied by the patron-employer. "Individual "arrangements" will no longer do."

The last two articles share a certain resemblance. Both treat tensions in the village community that are based, not on the distribution of wealth, but on essentially nonmaterial cleavages. They serve to remind us that the village world is large enough to produce—and accommodate—a wide range of internal tensions. Tina Jolas and Françoise Zonabend have chosen to study Minot, a village situated in a heavily wooded region of northern Burgundy. In addition to endemic conflicts between the "rich" and the "poor" and between two families of notables, Minot exhibited a more fundamental cleavage, based on a relation to the land and livestock, between those who had "land and cows" and those who had only "a goat, a pig, and some chickens." The former were the "tillers of the fields" and lived in the village; the latter, "woodspeople," made their living as woodcutters, sawyers, charcoal burners, and day laborers; they lived most of the time in the woods. The remarkable part of this study is the manner in which the authors construct an outlook or mentality by a careful inspection of everyday chores and occupations, intimately related to physical environment and local custom and made immediate and compelling by personal interviews with the villagers.

"There was a certain way of doing things" is the constant refrain of the villagers. The tillers of the fields were bound by exacting laws and customs involving mutual aid, an etiquette of kinship, and marriage within the group, all of which relegated newcomers and "outsiders" to the outlying farms, "for a generation or two." The woodspeople were very different in their habits. Far from sedentary, they worked in the forest about half the year, but gleaned on the communal fields or worked as harvest hands in the summer. They produced a large number of "handymen," people who performed all sorts of "odd jobs"—which was not the same as "working" at a steady occupation or craft. They also appeared suspect to the villagers, who saw them as "shack people," who hunted or poached, ate differently (their staples were game and herring), and had no milk of their own. Above all, the woodspeople did not live regulated lives, either in their work or with regard to their property or in human relationships. Even their marriages were unregulated, and their kinship ties were loose. And, of course, there was almost no intermarriage between the two neighboring communities. But the cleavage of habits and outlook did not result in open conflict. The village festival, *Mardi Gras,* national holidays, and periods of communal labor in field or wood followed by the harvest banquet brought the two "worlds" together long enough to keep hostilities within bounds throughout the year. The authors end with a touch of envy for the way of life of the woodspeople, in whose "wild sphere" there is no place for hierarchies or even for the categories of space and time.

Lucienne Roubin's village is in sunny Provence, far from the wooded plateaus of North Burgundy and the wheat fields of Picardy. It is the land of *chambrettes* and clubs, of an advanced community life and a *sociabilité* that seem to be particularly strong in the south of France and in Mediterranean lands generally. The tension analyzed by Roubin is that between the sexes or, more precisely, between the two spheres of their assigned activity. "Male space" dominates field and municipality—*champs* and *place.* "Female space" is the "domestic universe"—house, especially kitchen, poultry yard, and kitchen garden, and the nave and the chapels of the church. Much of the male's free time is spent talking in the square or wine cellar or hunting, where a certain kind of physical endurance is often tested; the female is a less frequent participant in the *chambrette,* which in her case assumes the form of a sewing bee held in the stable or barn on winter nights. Roubin's description of the two spheres would have us first believe that sexual segregation is so complete that the spheres defy comparison. But in fact sexual segregation is not airtight; it is "tempered" by an elaborately organized and carefully executed array of saint's-day festivals, charivaris, banquets, community balls, games *(boules,* horseracing), and processions. Most of the essay is devoted to describing and dissecting the ceremonial aspects of these ritualized activities. As an anthropologist and folklorist, Roubin interprets these festivals as part of a timeless *constante fondamentale* in Provençal society. The rules involving precedence, for example, are indicators of notions of hierarchy; the masks worn on Mardi Gras, a momentary relief from hierarchical boundaries. Among many functions, the festival also consciously joins couples and, somewhat like the forest banquet of the woodspeople, reduces a tension in the local community that might otherwise become unbearable.

The varieties of rural history are hardly exhausted in this selection of articles from the *Annales.* They do reveal, however, at least three kinds of French rural history: the impact of a revolution on the rural community, the temporal endurance of the village, and the values and attitudes that hold the village community together. The *Annales* might use the shorthand of "event," *longue durée,* and *mentalité* to categorize them. Of course, one must resist facile classification; the richness of description and nuance is central to the recreation of milieu without which there can be no rural history. Yet considering the guiding themes of each article, it is impossible not to notice the impact of new sources and the new use of auxiliary disciplines (sociology, social psychology, and ethnography, among others). It is obvious that these newer approaches have led to greater sophistication and depth; in the field of rural history they have also led to a greater appreciation of the remarkable staying power of a certain form of social organization in the total environment of the countryside. If this suggests a kind of conservatism, it is one that Marc Bloch, Lucien Febvre, and Georges Lefebvre would endorse and share.

Robert Forster
Orest Ranum

Rural Society
in
France

1
Man or Productivity

Lucien Febvre

Spread out upon the desk before me lies the manuscript of a monograph, a good article on an Alpine valley. It is divided into three parts: the setting (physical conditions, patterns of land ownership); agriculture (the farm calendar, income, husbandry, dairy farming, colts and mules, produce, tools and buildings); manners and customs (secondary trades, relationships among farmers and their relationships with the outside world, daily life); plus a conclusion (prospects for the future). I repeat, this is an intelligently and carefully done article. Should it be published? That question often arises.

Should it be published? Yes and no. We need studies of this sort. Only they can and do raise certain questions. Only they can call our attention to certain problems. Yes, but—what approach does the study take? And above all, in what spirit was it conducted?

The approach of the study? Any work of this sort collects and presents two sorts of data. Some facts are already familiar and are common to an entire region, to everyone living in a specific region. These facts can be presented quickly, and they must be presented. For example, the phenomenon called "the mountains" has become a familiar thing ever since the fine work of Philippe Arbos and many other geographers. Few words are needed to show that the valley under discussion resembles other valleys. Simply add a few statistics applicable to that particular valley, and the picture is complete.

But there are also the facts that pertain to the group under consideration. Or, at least, the facts perceived by the observer, facts he did not find in books dealing with the region. Or else it appears to him that, in the area he is investigating, these facts seem to take on a certain unusual tinge of color. So he must of course stress them. Above all, he must explain them. Explain their individuality.

Annales, E.S.C. 1(January–March 1946):87–91. Translated by Patricia M. Ranum. Lucien Febvre is known for his unique style. Every effort has been made to retain the declamatory tone of the original French. Imagine Febvre reading this text from behind a lectern. Or better yet, imagine yourself in his office. Seated opposite you, behind his desk, Febvre carries on an animated monologue.—Trans.

Yet, here is the rub. The researcher will often say, "I am not a professional. Circumstances led me to become interested in a tiny area where I
happened to spend a few months. I tried to show the mechanisms governing
the lives of the men who live there. I had no library close at hand. Anyway, I
am not prepared to make the difficult diagnosis you seem to be expecting of
me. What is special? What is general? It is up to you professionals to say
that." That is true; the researcher is correct. So, how can we overcome the
difficulty? Very easily, I believe.

Researchers such as the individual I have in mind at the moment believe
they are correct—and indeed, in most cases their psychological make-up
compels them to believe this—when they lay down as guides certain excellent
rules.
    1. "From the facts that confront me, I am not going to choose, I must not
choose, those to be kept and those to be discarded. To do so would be contrary
to any good methodology. In a sense it would be dishonest."
    2. "But naturally I am not going to tell everything I know. Describe
everything I see. I am carrying on an economic and social study. I am
interested in a specific locality because I am a cultivated, intelligent, inquiring
man of 1946 and am primarily concerned with certain problems—say, economic and social problems."
    3. "Thus, I must assemble all the economic and social data available to
me. But watch out. Let's not be tendentious! Let's classify these data in a
manner that is both *intelligent* (in other words, that permits a "rational"
linking of facts) and *objective,* for I am not doing my research in order to
prove a theory. I am conducting it impartially. I am recording exactly what I
observe. It is up to the theoreticians to use the material I am presenting when
they build their constructions."
    All this is perfect. All this, where we see emblazoned the principal articles
of the intellectuals' faith in serene intelligence and in scientific truth, which is
one of the highest, purest, and worthiest manifestations of this relative perfec-
tion to which a high degree of culture permits one to accede.
    Yet, having said that?

Having said that, we must consider the study itself. About village Y in
Normandy; about canton Z in Provence, or about valley X in Savoy. Such a
study inevitably (whatever the researcher's talent, gifts, and efforts) runs the
risk of being looked down upon by the reader as a result of its very form—
because it is conceived exclusively as an analytical monograph. And anyway,
the reader is only waiting for his chance to carry out a similar investigation of
his own, based on the very same principles, whenever the opportunity arises.
An investigation he will be very enthusiastic about conducting, even though
reading the report of the study made by his neighbor left him quite unim-
pressed. An investigation that will share the same noble concerns and that, in

the end, will share the same weaknesses. Once again, how do we get out of such a tangle?

By providing an orientation for the study. That is all. And, to be even more frank, by stating a problem (I hesitate slightly to be so frank: I shall be accused openly of constantly repeating myself; but, if I constantly repeat myself, it is because...). Yet stating a problem is not enough. By correctly stating a problem. The problem.

The problem. Do you understand what I mean? A group of men living on a bit of land and using that land as a tool for earning their livelihood. This group of men constitutes more than one problem. It constitutes a group of problems. But one must be able to distinguish among them. Clearly. And not unwittingly change one's point of view in the course of the study.

To return to the article lying on my desk. It deals with an Alpine valley. Not one of the highest: the fields are located at altitudes varying between 1,000 and 2,000 meters. Not one of the most forbidding: the cold is not excessive, the amount of sunshine is considerable. Not one of the most isolated either, nor one of the most unsociable. Yet the study deals with one of those localities about which people are asking more and more frequently: will man desert the region or will he stay? A painful question, for will France eventually be emptied of her population? Will the French countryside revert to fallow fields and soon after to wilderness? Will the French peasant population become completely urban and industrial—even though we are continually being told that France has no industries? And, alas, in a sense (and even in several senses) this last statement is only too true!

Well. There you have the question. There you have the problem. So state it clearly. Don't provide me with an objective description of valley X, all the while boasting of your scruples. Go right to the heart of the problem posed by valley X—as by so many other regions of France. As by so many other regions of Western Europe. For in the end the problem is not solely a French one.

The problem. But there is also the methodology. Methodologies. To simplify matters, let me call it the conflict between two methodologies.

The depopulation of France is a serious national problem. A human one. A problem with a thousand different factors to be considered. Let me simplify: will valley X in Savoy be deserted? The dimensions of this problem are more limited. But it is still a human problem. Valley X will be deserted by its inhabitants if they decide to desert it and if no one appears to fill their places. So, let's question the inhabitants of valley X. Let's ask: "Why abandon—or not abandon—the bit of land where you have lived for so many generations?"

Why? "Well," some spokesman for these inhabitants will answer (and if need be some one will suggest this reply to them, will whisper it in their ear), "for economic reasons." Because they don't earn enough. Because productivity is too low. So let's devote our efforts to the problem of productivity. It is the heart of the problem. Let's increase productivity. Well-being will follow. And valley X will not be abandoned.

This is specious reasoning. Let's try to see why. Our researcher first of all carefully establishes the pattern of land ownership. He notes two trends: the municipality does not fiercely defend its communal land from usurpation, and individuals are rounding out their own private property at the expense of communal land. This is an important observation, because it prompts us, or should prompt us, to ask a very important question: What is the current conception of ownership among the people of valley X? A conception that from all appearances is no longer that held by their ancestors before 1789. A conception that has evolved, that continues to evolve. What are we dealing with here? An economic problem? No, a psychological problem grafted onto a juridical state of affairs. A frame of mind, a conception that the people of valley X have of ownership. Upon which the investigation should focus, chiefly by interviewing the notaries of the region, if they will allow themselves to be interviewed and if they are open-minded. Methodology: move from the material, concrete, and carefully observed *fact* to the duly analyzed *state of mind*. And then move back from the *state of mind* to the *fact*, which then becomes clear and assumes its meaning. Its true meaning.

Another thing: They tell us that people today will no longer accept the difficult working conditions of the past. Or rather, in a world that is preoccupied with not wasting time, that on the contrary organizes time so that it can be used with maximum efficiency in order to increase the worker's "productivity"—these people, these mountaineers, are time-wasters. They waste precious hours coming and going from one of their properties to the other; they do not know how to work and they do not work. Here the problem of "laziness" raises its head. And the problem of productivity, which is inadequate.

Granted. But since the problem involves learning why the people of valley X remain on their lofty perches, or why they leave, would it not be wiser to ask if what we call "laziness"—using the terminology of producers and employers—is not simply a prerequisite for acceptance of rural life and of all the sacrifices that life involves? That life whose activities—since they seem poorly organized to us—we instinctively would like to standardize. That life of low tides and still waters, following upon periods of raging, foaming, flood waters. We are tempted to turn the saw-toothed profile of peasant activities into a beautiful, harmonious curve. But should we yield to such a temptation? I understand the importance of productivity. And that it is inadequate. And that this underproduction gives rise to a whole series of unfortunate consequences. But in the end doesn't the problem boil down to striving above all else for high productivity, even if, as a result of our overwhelming concern for achieving this goal, we risk killing "country life"? If so, we should no longer deplore the depopulation of our countryside. If we believe the countryside remains a reservoir of vital strength for the nation (and *that* it must remain), we must remember that a reservoir contains still waters, waters that have to remain at rest long enough to give birth to those vital forces that the city will use up and waste.

Note that I am not claiming to solve in these few paragraphs, and in this simplistic fashion, a vast problem that should one day be treated in detail in this journal. No. My sole aim is to contrast two states of mind. First, the position of the engineer, who suffers from the wasted time he observes about him, just as he suffers from the poor quality of the equipment that is used in farm work and that is a prime cause of low productivity, whether it is a question of manufactured materiel such as plows or harrows or of living instruments such as cows or oxen of inferior breeds. So let the quality be improved! Let the amount of wasted time be reduced! Let the peasant be given a goodly number of supplementary activities to fill the hours he has thus regained. Let him be encouraged to do woodworking, for example, to make furniture. All that seems perfectly reasonable. But once this goal has been achieved and the mountaineer is thus transformed into a superefficient worker—what if he does not become adapted to doing this work within the setting of his own valley? What if he says to himself: "Here I am, living a factory worker's life. But I receive none of the advantages offered by the city, by life in the city. So, good-by, Valley!" A matter of psychology. Peasant psychology. Another world is opened up. And I am not saying that there is not and should not be communication between these two worlds. I am saying that therein lies the problem. Not elsewhere. On the one hand, an economic problem of productivity. And therefore of a comfortable life. On the other hand, a psychological problem. Mountain societies are fragile and threatened; they have long been kept alive as a result of basic economic principles that to us seem quite irrational. If these basic principles are transformed, if they are modified, do we not run the risk of dealing them a death blow? To my mind, it is around *this* question, this agonizing question, that our research should be oriented. Of course objective studies have their place. But studies dealing with vital questions are no less important. The two points of view are not incompatible, and the *Annales* will deal with them in the future.

Once again, man, man above all else! Man, the chief being involved. Man, the subject and object of our preoccupations and our research. Man, who alone can and must give life to our research, who constitutes its sole and true focus, and who permits us to relate to him what we call natural, geographic, and economic phenomena—but which in the end are human phenomena, for man has cast his spirit over them all, has touched them with his hands, and has left his mark upon them.

2

A Manifesto: The Defense and Illustration of Local History

Paul Leuilliot

A preface is always embarrassing to the preface writer, especially when he is asked to write virtually the same preface twice. Having already said all the appropriate good things about the author in my preface to *Georges Dufaud et les débuts du grand capitalisme en Nivernais au* XIXe *siècle* (1959), I do not have to start out by repeating the same compliments. I suspect that Guy Thuillier will not hold it against me if I begin with a *defense* of the local history of which he is so fond. He personally has contributed to its *illustration.** I hope he will pardon me for stressing the illustration rather than the defense, for his text, its appendix, and the published documents are very thought-provoking. The approaches used in his preliminary research have already contributed to the defense; and his work promises to be a true guide to research in local history.

I

L'avenir tel que le concevait un homme du passé fait partie importante de notre histoire.

—Paul Valéry, *Cahiers*

Guy Thuillier proposes that we attempt to establish a few principles concerning local history. Indeed, such principles ought to be and deserve to be part of a clearly defined theoretical framework. While the works of local

Annales, E.S.C. 22 (January–February 1967): 154–77. Translated by Patricia M. Ranum. This article served as the preface to Guy Thuillier's *Aspects de l'èconomie nivernaise au XIXe siècle,* Publication of the Centre d'études économiques (Paris: Armand Colin, 1966).

*Leuilliot is referring to Joachim du Bellay's *La défense et illustration de la langue française* (1549), a manifesto proclaiming the literary doctrines of the school of the Pléiade. This manifesto defends the French language by maintaining that it is the equal of all other languages and a

scholars have become more numerous, such scholars are unable to formulate a method, much less develop a policy, for their local history. Once again referring to historians, Paul Valéry wrote that "their own doings"[1] get away from them. Marc Bloch was one of the few historians who was concerned about "doing" history[2]—in this case local history—and by implication, about "doing" research itself. He was concerned with the pursuit of research strategies, a pursuit that "has scarcely made any noteworthy progress despite the fact that logic has been applied to the organization of knowledge for centuries. . . . As a science, [research procedures] are still in the baby-talk stage," as Le Lionnais recently remarked.[3]

On the matter of what principles to follow when doing local history, I should like at the outset to venture one observation: the principles in question are autonomous and as a result run contrary to those applicable to general history as it is studied in schools and universities. Naturally, general history should not neglect or be disdainful of the work of local historians, who are not overly fond of manipulating partial curves, who do not even like to deal with series of statistics, and who are less interested in cycles than in micro-details, village "events," or the daily life of their town. Those "contemptuous pedants," as Bloch called them, are only interested in European or world or quantitative history. To this, local historians might reply as Auguste Jal did a century ago in his preface to the *Dictionnaire critique de biographie et d'histoire* (1864): "I confess, in all humility, that I am one of those people who enjoys probing into *those wretched matters,* as our brilliant minds have called them. I am short-sighted, and minute details are just right for my eyes—I mean my myopic mind. I am interested in a mass of microscopic facts that arouse pity in those historians and critics who are said—and who proudly make the same claims about themselves—to have the wings and eyes of an eagle. *De minimis curo,* as compared with the praetor, ancestor of those fortunate and clairvoyant individuals. . . ." So the struggle to do local history is not new. Let me add, in passing, that local historiography has yet to be done, that the names of local scholars are quickly—too quickly—forgotten, even when, as sometimes happens, their works are purloined. For local history is very important, quantitatively; it even represents the major part of the historical bibliography of France.[4] In view of its undisputed importance, local his-

---

suitable vehicle for the noblest themes. It also recommends the *illustration*—that is, the rendering illustrious—of French by the invention of new words or the recovery of ancient ones and by the assimilation of literary models provided by classical authors. Hence, in this article Leuilliot's aim is to defend local history as a valid historical discipline and to indicate ways in which it can be improved.—Trans.

[1]Paul Valéry, *Cahiers,* vol. 21, p. 424.

[2]Marc Bloch, *Apologie pour l'histoire, ou métier d'historien,* Cahiers des Annales 3, 5th ed. (Paris, 1964). English translation by Peter Putnam, *The Historian's Craft* (New York, 1964).

[3]F. Le Lionnais, "Science et politique nationale," *Revue politique et parlementaire,* July-August 1965.

[4]I am happy to quote the homage paid the late J. Joachim, of Delle, long the "dean of Alsatian historians," in the recent dissertation by Jean Suratteau, *"Le département du Mont-Terrible sous le régime du Directoire"* (1965): "During my frequent visits to [Joachim] I would always come out

tory has a right to claim autonomy. In this manifesto expounding the doctrine of local history, several principles seem of prime importance.

First principle.   Local economic history of the nineteenth century leads into the present; it is related to our contemporary problems, our present-day preoccupations.

First of all, local economic history permits us to discern a number of constants, a number of fundamental characteristics of the present situation, such as the repeated economic failure of certain businesses. The economic development of France necessarily requires this historical perspective; tomorrow's problems must be seen in terms of the century. One must take into account traditional aptitudes, available manpower, certain activities that often have long been carried on in a specific region, different types of regional growth, a locality's tendency to be thrifty and to store things up or to favor (or reject) a Malthusian spirit of enterprise. All these "current events" have repercussions upon the future.[5]

Regional economics—a new discipline[6]—must rely heavily upon local history, which provides not only documentation but also methods of approach, just as earlier in this century geographers in the French school of regional geography, such as Albert Demangeon and Jules Sion, had to rely upon history in their studies of the provinces.[7]

Therefore, it is appropriate and essential to begin at once studying the

---

equipped with a mass of precious and irreplaceable information..." (introduction). A "local historian" of the department of Pas-de-Calais recently wrote me: "A certain number of these village scholars have acquired world renown, among them my poor Edmont, who died penniless after having teamed with Gilliéron to create linguistic geography...."

[5]Thus, Guy Thuillier contrasts the routine apathy and technical stagnation of the faïence workers of Nevers with the spirit of enterprise shown by the ironmasters of Nivernais. His chapter on the paper mills of Corvol-l'Orgueilleux is equally revealing. On the Vespa works of the A.C.M.A. (1950–63), see below. Likewise, for the distant antecedents (chiefly during the Second Empire) of the Alsatian textile crisis, especially in the Vosges mountains, see my "Action syndicale dans le textile du Haut-Rhin," *Revue de l'action populaire,* February 1965, pp. 171–80.

[6]The Institut de Science Economique Appliquée has published the debates of the Association de Science régionale de langue française. For example, *Structure et croissance régionale,* Colloquia of 1961–62, Cahiers of the I.S.E.A., *Economie régionale,* Suppl. 130, October 1962. See also J. Martens, *Bibliographie de Science économique régionale,* Cahiers of the I.S.E.A., no. 125 (Paris, 1962); and René Gendarme, *La région du Nord* (Paris, 1954).

[7]Jean Chardonnet (*Géographie industrielle* [Paris, 1965], vol. 2) includes history in his study of the conditions of industrial work. Conversely, geography can provide certain working hypotheses for the historian. Another example of having recourse to history is the work of sociologist Placide Rambaud, *Les transformations d'une société rurale, la Maurienne (1561–1962)* (Paris, 1965), and her earlier *Economie et sociologie de la Montagne: Albiez-le-Vieux-en-Maurienne* (Paris, 1962), for which I wrote the preface. In the introduction to her latest book, Rambaud writes: "A historical event, a land register, a statistic are above all important because they are a condensation of social forces, the secret crystallization of a complex network of decisions, of daily life that would be even more difficult to grasp without them. They are the stabilized replies made to countless efforts. To ask questions of a statistic amounts to asking questions of a man.... Their value gives them a formal identity, and the identity of these statistics is not the same in different epochs, nor do they all have the same value for social investigation..." (p. 13).

regional history of the past century—say, 1880–1985[8]—so that it may be used in government plans for the future that are now being drawn up. The predictions of economic planners are also an inseparable part of history, for Marc Bloch referred to history's role as a predictor in *The Historian's Craft* at a time when the techniques of economic planning had not yet been created. Indeed, this "century-long" history can be of great value in indicating future actions. Thus, Thuillier's history of the decline of the faïence industry might lead to a suggestion that this artistic craft be revived by establishing a trade or technical school or by giving grants to artisans. Made prudent by history, the government administrator will find himself on firmer ground. In the end, politics is inseparable from economics,[9] which is in turn influenced by history when it comes to making forecasts for the next twenty years. Urbanism is a perfect example of this—pardon me for not going into obvious details—for urban growth remains linked to historical constraints. Moreover, doing the history of the period 1880–1985, for example, would require that background work be done at the local level, in view of the vast amount of printed and archival materials to be consulted.

But local history is not solely concerned with immediacy. Its methodology is *régressive,* or "retrogressive," in the sense in which Bloch used the word.[10] Thus the local historian, by definition rooted in a very specific bit of territory, moves from the present back to the past. This is also true for agrarian history, for financial history, and for the history of technology.[11] Thuillier provides fine examples of this in his work dealing with the *"lèpre de l'embouche"* [the conversion of wheatfields into pastures for fattening livestock]; the history of banking and insurance; and the development of metallurgical skills in the Nivernais region of which he is so fond, a region that has long been known for its metallurgy. The local historian is able to use his observations, and at times even his professional knowledge, about the present when interpreting documents of the past. Such is the case with the notary studying his minutes or the inspector of public records (two cases specifically mentioned in Thuillier's study of communities). It is obviously preferable to

[8]See *Réflexions pour 1985* presented to the Guillaumat Commission. Indeed, the mimeographed reports of Ducros and Fraisse on the regionalization of the French economy in 1985 are of great significance, as is Professor Bernard's *L'homme en 1985: Aspects physiologiques et médicaux.* Guy Thuillier is also interested in social and medical problems of the past in Nivernais.

[9]This was pointed out in the *Journées d'études,* a study of political forces in eastern France (Strasbourg, 1964). See my "Réflexions d'un historien à propos de l'Alsace," *Bulletin de la Société industrielle de Mulhouse* 4 (1964): 13–20, and especially my *Recherches sur les forces politiques,* Cahiers de l'Association Interuniversitaire de l'Est (Paris, 1966).

[10]Bloch, *Historian's Craft,* pp. 45–47.

[11]A. Birembault has written a very thought-provoking study, "Quel bénéfice le technicien peut-il retirer de l'histoire?" *Revue de Synthèse,* no. 37–39, 1965, pp. 181–268. The technician answers the question of what he can learn from history by using both history and his own professional recollections. For him, "the detailed history of a technical skill and its diffusion requires the previous completion of regional studies" (p. 213).

know all about the functioning of today's banks before beginning a study of
the history of banking. Thus, a continuous circulation, an interpenetration that
eventually bears fruit, is established between analyses of the present and those
of the past. Now, "this faculty of understanding the living is, in very truth,
the master quality of the historian."[12] This contact with the here and now
gives local history its characteristic stamp, explains its vigor, and makes it
important to people today.[13]

Second principle.   Local history is qualitative, not quantitative; whether
we like it or not, it cannot be conveyed by statistics.

This is true in part because figures lose their meaning on the local scale. If
great care is not taken, figures are all too often incorrectly interpreted. In most
cases statistics have intentionally been distorted at the local level. This is true
in Nivernals for vineyards; for faïence, through the collusion of the manufacturers; and for forges. Production figures are also distorted by cheating on the
part of the workers (a memorandum dated 1795 tells of the "customary
abuses" committed by forge workers), as well as by distrust on the part of the
owners, who fear being taxed on the basis of the products included in their
lists. The complicity of some and the indifference of others—indeed, a general indifference—make these recorded figures very dubious. For example,
the average prices of bread were often calculated in different ways; in like
manner, neither the average prices of wheat for the various departments of
France nor the average market prices are very reliable figures.

As far as agriculture is concerned, it is especially difficult to obtain good
statistics, even today. Hence, agricultural statistics can only be used with
great caution. Local history should strive to be critical of statistics rather than
use them as the basis of overly assertive conclusions. It should try to perceive
the discrepancies in order to interpret general curves; should try, for example,
to note the discrepancy between the market price and the actual price received
by any individual farmer. Let me add that in the case of long-term
phenomena, during the period in question transformations may have occurred
in structures that are understood to varying degrees and that are all too often
poorly understood.

A recent article by Désert bears this out as far as sown fields, the price of
meat or butter, and agricultural wages are concerned.[14] "The prefect [the head
of a French department] acts upon the principle that the subprefects have
undervalued or overvalued certain parcels of land, and he makes corrections

---

[12]Bloch, *Historian's Craft,* p. 13.

[13]In one sense, the local historian is a person trying to "do the history" of his profession or
trade: the physician does the history of his hospital; the insurance broker studies the development
of insurance in his city or region; the manufacturer studies the history of his business. Behind this
research lies a sense of ownership that calls to mind Saint-Phlin in Maurice Barrès's *Appel au
soldat.*

[14]G. Désert, "Les sources statistiques de l'histoire de France (Basse-Normandie, xixᵉ siècle)",
Annales de Normandie, March 1965, pp. 22–52.

(based on what criteria?). The subprefects have exactly the same attitude toward information sent to them by municipal governments. The result is an increasingly inflated total as one moves up the administrative hierarchy. . . . It is essential that these statistics not be viewed as true economic records. The peasants in the Calvados region of Normandy continually lied to the government all through the century, or else they refused to cooperate at all. Fear of increased taxes; fierce individualism; or simply the inability to answer questionnaires, or at least certain questions included in them owing to the unfamiliar vocabulary used—I am specifically thinking of agricultural units of measure—are among the possible explanations of their attitude. We have evidence of this open or hidden hostility throughout the nineteenth century."[15] And further on in the same article: "Let's say you can easily obtain the price of meats from market quotations or from hospital archives. Does that price accurately reflect the price of cattle on the hoof? I don't think so." We must also distrust price records for markets in the chief towns of the various arrondissements. "How can one really believe that, with the exception of the month of June 1839, the cost of a kilogram of butter purchased at Falaise never varied between January 1838 and December 1849!" The same extreme caution must be applied to data gathered about wages; for indeed, since very little data are available about agricultural wages, "the ideal would be to discover accounts of farms. But how many farmers in that day did regular bookkeeping?"[16] Désert has expressed the problem in a nutshell.

Moreover, local history must work with qualitative information, with unreliable statistics that are only useful as corroborating evidence. In the case of demography, birth and death rates are undoubtedly less important than an examination of the causes of mortality—malnutrition, poor hygiene, poor housing, occupational illnesses, and the "intermittent fevers" caused by the many marshes of Nivernais that had not yet been drained.[17]

In like manner, it seems less important to work out for a twenty-year period the "average price" of a product such as iron or coal than to evaluate the different components of this average. The average price for coal might be influenced by the prices of coal of poor or uneven quality.[18] The variations in the production of the different qualities of iron can partially explain variations in the curve as a whole. Likewise, in regard to wages, one must take into account wage variations according to occupational categories (as can be seen in the rural mine at La Machine) and the method of payment, particularly what part of the wages went for such workers' expenses as candles or repair of equipment (in the same coal mine).[19] The manner in which wages were paid is

[15]Examples cited for 1818, 1837, 1855, 1873, and 1888; ibid., p. 51, n. 22.
[16]Ibid., pp. 28, 34, 37, 44, 51.
[17]See the recent study by Pierre Pierrard, *La vie ouvrière à Lille sous le Second Empire* (Paris, 1965), which seems to indicate a favorable trend. Thuillier discusses both typical diet and medical and social problems in this book.
[18]Accounts of 1859 for the coal mines at La Machine.
[19]For similar deductions (for light, motor, etc.) see Pierrard, *La vie ouvrière*, p. 201.

also important, for the employer might pay in copper coins,[20] or he might withhold one liard per franc,[21] and so forth.

In short, when working on the local scale the historian writing a monograph about a business or a region must reconstitute an economic mechanism as precisely as possible, rather than measure statistical variations. Besides, we know that prosperity-depression cycles do not mean the same thing from one region to another or from one business to another. Statistics cannot indicate these differences, which in part result from the extremely variable influence of a specific sector of the economy and, in the case of businesses, from the unequal volume of investments.

The best example in support of giving local history a qualitative orientation might be bread. For certain historians the prime concern has been to measure the price curve of wheat as revealed in rapidly changing market prices; yet a history of bread would show that it is more important to learn what really went on by ascertaining, among other things, the amount kept by the miller (either in money or in kind), how honest the miller was about the quantity, how he affected the quality by mixing flours, or how much bran was included—all ways of cheating that increased whenever there was an economic crisis. Other important factors were the cost of the bakers' supplies, which could not fail to influence the cost of bread, and fraud by bakers when they cheated on the weight of a loaf of bread or on the quality of the bread, which declined markedly during periods of economic crisis. To this must be added sales on credit; the way selling was conducted and how sales were affected by the *taille* and by coins made of billon; technical difficulties involved in establishing the bread tax, which all too frequently was done in a rather approximate fashion; and the role played by private ovens, a role that varied from region to region and even from town to town according to the price of wood.

These are among the factors that should be included in a detailed study, which in turn should permit a more judicious interpretation of general curves. Such research and interpretation can only be significant on the strictly local scale. Indeed, on the national scale it is almost impossible to make anything but generalizations. The existence of "growth poles," of "dynamic" industries, and the variable importance of "innovative investments" in spurring regional growth explain the frequent discrepancy between regional and "general" economic conditions.[22]

Third principle. Local history requires a certain flexibility, for it is a loosely knit history compared with the often quite rigid sort of history found in

---

[20]See Guy Thuillier, "Pour une histoire monétaire de la France: le rôle des monnaies de cuivre et de billon," *Annales, E.S.C.* 14 (January–March 1959): 65–90, and the second part of this preface.

[21]Pierrard, *La vie ouvrière*, p. 201.

[22]The relationships between the "cycle" and investments are still not very clear. For the effects of such factors, see François Perroux, *Les techniques quantitatives de planification* (Paris, 1965), which offers a fair number of working hypotheses for the historian (especially on the role of innovation).

doctoral dissertations. The dissertation must deal with a very specific period and cannot overlap the past and go back to the "origins"; it especially cannot overlap the future in order to "follow" the development of a given sector that is the subject of the research in question. In the end, in order to adhere to the outline of this "masterpiece" that gains him entry into the profession, the author of the dissertation must also exclude certain other complementary sectors from his purview.[23]

The same is true for dates and for the way in which the subject is planned. As far as dates are concerned, it is hardly possible to do anything but look back from the nineteenth to the eighteenth century when going back to the "origins" and to "follow" developments up to the present. Despite the title of his book, I do not criticize Thuillier for having called to mind the origins of major industries in his chapter on Louis Le Vau's unfortunate speculations at Baumont-la-Ferrière [in the 1660s], nor for having included a memorandum on forests [in 1735] or on the state of forges in Nivernais circa 1770.

Dissertations dealing with regional studies rarely follow the thread up to the present. Nor are they free to delve at will into especially interesting sectors, which, although relatively small on their own, would unbalance the dissertation as a whole.[24]

Now, we should not hide the fact that such dissertations have a great influence upon local history, for in a way they impose a model that local historians feel obliged to imitate. Some lose heart when confronted with such an undertaking. It goes without saying that this influence should be neither abusive nor exclusive. I believe that local history requires a high degree of flexibility in approach and execution; it is the history of the individual—meaning by "individual" both the company and the municipality or, strictly speaking, the region. Depending upon the characteristics of this small region, the sector being studied and the period being considered will of necessity be different, and the chronological limits of the setting will be blurred if not altogether out of focus. As a result, local history cannot build carefully planned edifices; it must in a sense be modulated to conform to the imperatives of its subject. Thus, we are obliged to accept this flexibility: this would avoid the very evident wasted efforts of those local scholars who are either virtually wearing themselves out trying to imitate these "models" or else falling back, perhaps in despair, upon subjects that are too fragmentary. Recognizing the autonomy of local history means at the same time giving it the freedom of movement it needs.

Fourth principle.   Thus conceived, local history becomes the history of a sector and, consequently, the history of structures viewed in terms of sectors

[23]For example, the remarkable dissertation of Pierrard, *La vie ouvrière*, scarcely went beyond 1870 and not much before that date either. On the other hand, one of the great merits of Maurice Lévy-Leboyer's *Les banques européennes et l'industrialisation internationale dans la première moitié du XIXe siècle* (Paris, 1965), lies in its having gone back to the period 1750–70.

[24]The history of insurance is often omitted from financial histories, as is the history of food from social histories, especially as far as workers are concerned.

(and products). After—but only after—this indispensable analytical groundwork has been laid does synthesis become possible.

The specific problems of a given sector should be studied in depth—for themselves, in a way; then certain constants or permanent elements can be discerned on the basis of certain given products. For example, technical and commercial problems relating to vineyards can be studied in order to reveal certain permanent elements, of yesterday and of today; and in all probability the unchanging element will be the vinedresser's propensity for preferring quantity to quality in his vineyard, as Robert Laurent has shown.[25]

Such a study of problems according to sectors would undoubtedly permit us to break with our preconceptions and eliminate the traditional prejudices of history in order to grasp instead psychological mechanisms and,[26] at the same time, to discern the variable and basic mutations that permit us to go beyond the local situation and make undisputed generalizations: for example, that the very slow spread of the bank note until 1914 resulted in the development of credit. The same is true for agrarian history and for the history of technical knowledge.[27]

Such a study of sectors offers more than one advantage over general history: it is easier to comprehend a sector, and doubtlessly to comprehend it better as well. Sometimes, for lack of a "model," the local historian must invent a method of approach for a particular problem; for local history this method, based on selective elimination, may differ from the method appropriate to general history, for the simple reason that a history of a sector must develop its own original hypotheses for discovery and inquiry. Obliged to work from life, the local historian cannot deduce his history a priori on the basis of a few general ideas; he must *invent* his subject in the strictest sense of the term. Such is quite commonly the case for those fields that have until very recently been scorned by university-based research.[28]

I can only deplore the dearth of autobiographies and memoirs by local historians that could reveal their methodology and, in most cases, their professional knowledge of a subject as well. We must return to the historian's craft as revealed by Marc Bloch, whose position is very similar to that of Paul Valéry, and to my own position in this manifesto.

Fifth principle. Local history must become increasingly concrete and must become related to daily life and to actual procedures involving technical

---

[25]Robert Laurent, *Les vignerons de la Côte-d'Or au XIX*[e] *siècle* (Dijon, 1957).

[26]Such is the case for the psychology of the metallurgical worker; see J. Vial, "L'ouvrier métallurgiste français," *Droit Social*, 1950, pp. 58–68.

[27]J. Coutin, *Transformations de l'économie et de la vie dans une commune rurale de la Limagne, Saulzet depuis 1914*, which deals with the shift from sickle to scythe; see also by Coutin, "L'invention en métallurgie (et ses conditions)" *Revue d'Histoire économique et sociale*, 1949, pp. 233–73. Coutin is completing a dissertation on French metallurgy from 1814 to 1864. I must also cite André Thuillier, *Emile Martin (1794–1871)*, a publication of the Chamber of Commerce and Industry of Nevers and of Nièvre, 1964.

[28]Simply think of the notarial archives. See P. Massé, "A travers un dépôt de minutes notariales," *Annales historiques de la Révolution française*, 1953, pp. 297–315.

skills and credit, the history of material life (food, shelter, and hygiene), and medical and social history, as well. Let me quote Bloch again: "Who believes that electrical companies have no archives, no records of power consumption, no charts of the enlargement of their networks?"[29] The history of the spread of electrification has yet to be done.

But in addition to being concrete and material history, local history is the history of the invisible aspects of daily life, of things that cannot be seen, such as contraceptive practices; it is the history of things that are given, that do not have to be talked about—though so much the better if they are—such as money and its less visible confrere, thrift (we have only to remember how the new French five-franc pieces became scarce shortly after their recent minting);[30] and it is the history of the durable, of things that last over the years, of age-old traditions, or folklore, if you prefer to call it that. Here local history overflows into the history of mentalities, of attitudes toward life, death, money, and innovation.[31]

That sort of history can hardly be done in Paris or in any other very large city, for it requires an intimate knowledge of a locality and of its people, the personal experience of local and provincial life that outsiders only rarely possess. Let me also emphasize that this sort of history attracts a local clientele composed of local notables. Thus, the history of medicine is of interest to physicians, and the history of technical skills attracts engineers, to the degree that these histories deal with a town or a small region and are buttressed by a solid and durable local patriotism that still shows a spark of life.

My definition of the principles of this concrete history has undoubtedly not been defined sufficiently or thoroughly enough, and the methodology to be used may still seem vague. Moreover, local history as I have portrayed it is surely a privileged branch of history. It is not isolated, as if it were made up of erudite speculations, of pure abstractions; instead, it is involved with the present and thus facilitates our understanding of the profound mutations that have occurred since the nineteenth century. It is significant that among such "witnesses for the common people" as Nadaud, Sand, and Guillaumin, Fourastié includes Le Play's two monographs that deal with the miner in the argentiferous lead mines of Pontgibaud and with the agricultural laborer of the Morvan region. "His monographs are of greater importance than his opinions. Indeed, they describe the real situation of European families so carefully and precisely *that some of them should be included in the course work of our high schools.*"[32]

As evidenced by the authors I have mentioned, this is the true vocation of

---

[29]Bloch, *Historian's Craft,* pp. 66–67.

[30]Y. Gaillard and G. Thuillier, "Sur la thésaurisation," *Revue économique,* September 1965.

[31]See Robert Mandrou, *Introduction à la France moderne. Essai de psychologie historique (1500–1640)* (Paris, 1961); English translation, *Introduction to Modern France: An Essay in Historical Psychology* (New York, 1976); and Mandrou, *De la culture populaire aux XVIIe et XVIIIe siècles* (Paris, 1964).

[32]See especially Françoise Fourastié and Jean Fourastié, *Les écrivains témoins du peuple* (Paris, 1964), pp. 343–66. Le Play described refining in Nivernais in 1843.

local history, which cannot be isolated in a sort of ghetto, for it is a part of life. Most historical works are conceived on a national scale, and few if any are specifically local studies. If carried out on the basis of the principles of this manifesto, the local history I envisage will become involved with the history of the material and technical structures of daily life; for example, the history of problems involving water in both city and countryside, or the history of bread that I have already mentioned.

Sixth principle. Local history is differential history. It must therefore attempt to measure the discrepancy between developments as a whole and developments within a particular locality, and also to measure the differences in the rhythms of these changes. As a result, it will be able to provide specific information about the level of economic development or about the banking organization within a region, and also to discern the level of any given "regional" technical skill—for example, metallurgy or textiles.[33] This permits us to verify, appraise, and even measure how slowly technical knowledge spread and the degree of psychological resistance it encountered.

This differential history is of course particularly difficult, especially since the levels of development in other regions and the general evolutionary pattern are still relatively unknown. But such an analysis of differences will surely bear fruit; such differences in growth rates depend to a considerable, if not a major, degree upon nonmeasurable psychological or sociological factors stemming from daily, undiscernible history—such as population decline resulting from birth control, a very new subject of research and still poorly understood.[34] It is no less difficult to perceive a weakening in the spirit of enterprise, for example, as a result of tensions that might arise in a manufactory. The study of the causes of growth or of decline would surely be of major interest to the economist.

There are certainly other principles applicable to local history. Local economic history, written by local scholars, can briefly—and provisionally—be defined as a history that is concerned with the present, a history that is qualitative, a history with a "flexible" time scale, a history of sectors that studies daily life, a history that is essentially differential. This doubtlessly is how we should interpret Lucien Febvre's remarks about the knowledge of our provinces and minor cities during the Restoration. "It would be extremely interesting for us to know the situation of each of our provinces during the very interesting period 1820–30, a period when they still retained most of the traits of their distinct and traditional personalities on the eve of the great

---

[33]See, on this subject Pierre Léon, *Les techniques métallurgiques dauphinoises au XVIIIe siècle* (Paris, 1961).

[34]See Y. Hilaire, "Les missions intérieures face à la déchristianisation pendant la seconde moitié du XIXe siècle," *Revue du Nord*, January–March 1964, pp. 51–68.

inventions that would change the appearance of the old world by overturning the whole established system of relationships."[35]

Although for various reasons the fact often goes unnoticed, local or regional history necessarily has a different orientation from that of "general" or national history; its concerns and methodology are also quite different. Its ambitions are a priori limited, for one of its basic tenets is a temporary refusal to make syntheses at a time when too few valid studies exist. It claims to be work that is being carried on while waiting for future regional or general works. This is the real basis for the work of local scholars, whose raison d'être lies in willingly and humbly doing the needed background research, working, in the words of Lucien Febvre, as good craftsmen who make possible *grande histoire* [that is, general as contrasted with local history].

University research—more prestigious, more centralized (a good part of it centered in Paris, despite an increasing number of dissertations being defended in provincial universities), based upon the doctoral dissertation written in accordance with the "principles" and directions of a mentor, and well funded—cannot, figuratively speaking, crush local research. Yet in many ways it influences local history by proposing, if not imposing, its "models" and the accompanying methodology, as well as its "fashions."[36] Think how hard it is for a provincial to consult documents in Parisian collections, even though the National Archives in Paris will lend its documents to departmental archives. How can a local scholar thinking of working in the National Library in Paris manage to thread his way through the maze of manuscripts, given the inadequate collection of manuscript catalogs? The local scholar has usually had no formal historical training and absolutely no opportunities to learn critical methodology. Often doing his history after business hours, he frequently receives the very disheartening impression that he is writing marginal history that will be looked down upon since it is being done far from the centers of innovating trends. He generally works alone, often without the help of the usual traditional associations—*a fortiori* the university—and owing to these circumstances and to his isolation, he does not keep abreast of the most recent work, since he is far from good libraries. But that is another problem.

Years ago Charles Morazé stressed this separation: "A minor historian has a larger public than the major specialists of the same period. Who is at fault? The public? The writer? The discipline? I will answer that question without the slightest hesitation: the discipline. The breath of life has not yet been breathed into it, so it has done nothing to take advantage of the public's taste

---

[35]Lucien Febvre, *La Franche-Comté,* Les régions de la France (Paris, 1905), p. 64. I used this passage as a motto for my *L'Alsace au début du XIXe siècle* (Paris, 1959), vol. 2.

[36]For example, no detailed catalog has been made of the Joly de Fleury collection, which is, however, of great importance for the history of the French provinces. I should like to refer the reader to my article, "Problèmes de la recherche, II. Catalogues et bibliographie de l'histoire de France," in *Annales, E.S.C.* 19 (November-December 1964): 1147–56.

and to make use of these efforts, which are often disinterested and which are always useful.''[37] These are indeed major obstacles; yet the local historian today plays a very important role. As Morazé's judicious remarks indicate, the scientific, university-based sort of history is cutting itself off from its public and shutting itself up in its ivory tower, so the public is trying to satisfy its craving for history in a different manner.[38] It is significant that reviews of historical works in the press are scarce and that historical journals are read almost exclusively by "professionals."[39] A dangerous and very regrettable separation and divorce. Is local history perhaps to play the desirable role of mediator?

First of all, in such an event local history would indeed assume the primordial function of diffusing knowledge, while maintaining in the provinces the taste, and the feeling, for history. Here we are touching upon a much debated problem, recently brought up among the learned societies,[40] some of which are unquestionably much less active than others.[41] Yet these societies have led some individuals to choose the historian's craft. We must also deplore the failure to stress local history in our school curricula, official policy notwithstanding. The successful efforts of the educational services of the departmental archives, now active in about forty French departments, should be implemented throughout France, and these services should be granted

[37]Charles Morazé, *Trois essais sur histoire et culture* (Cahiers des Annales 2, 1948).

[38]On the current state of affairs in the world of history, I should like to cite the study by R. Kaes, "Les ouvriers français et la culture (enquête 1958–61)," 1962, mimeographed, Editions Dalloz; in the chapter "Curiosity about the Past: History" (pp. 203–12), we find that 61 percent of workers show some interest in history, 53 percent of non-trade-union workers are interested, as is 70 percent of the managerial staff. A sociological study of familiarity with history by social group would probably reveal unusual regional differences.

[39]See the maps in J. Hassenforder, *La diffusion du périodique français (histoire et géographie),* a publication of the Centre d'études économiques (1957).

[40]See my article "Problèmes de la recherche, III. Pour une politique des Sociétés Savantes," in *Annales, E.S.C.* 20 (March-April 1965): 315–26. Among the letters received on this subject, I should like to quote a passage dealing with learned societies: "Their members have a terrible failing: independence. They believe neither in prejudices, orders, nor intrigues; they have neither supple backbones nor weak characters. Too bad! But they do have knowledge and experience; they are not seeking personal advancement; and the sacred fire burns within them. Our universities can mass-produce archivists and holders of advanced degrees; once they receive their sheepskins they delve into facts, monuments, texts, and seek data from: *us*. We must be indulgent with them; we will help them save time, twenty years of patient, unpublicized, accumulated labor, accessible to all comers. . . ." At the same time this correspondent noted the existence of nine or ten learned societies within the department of Pas-de-Calais alone. I also wish to point out the *Actes* of the first two colloquia of the presidents of learned societies, held at Lyon in 1964 and Nice in 1965, and published by the Comité des travaux historiques et scientifiques (1965–66).

[41]The Société d'agriculture, sciences, et arts de la Sarthe publishes both memoranda and a monthly bulletin. The Amis du Vieil Annecy have just published an issue of *Annesci* (vol. 11, 1964) devoted to R. Blanchard's account of changes occurring in their city (1954–62). The *Revue du Bas-Poitou et des Provinces de l'Ouest,* March-April 1965, which is also concerned with current events, published Y. Chataigneau's "L'avenir de la France et la région de demain"; and as early as 1961 it published J. P. Soisson's "Difficultés et espoirs de l'action régionale. Deux ans d'expansion dans les Deux-Sèvres (1958–60)."

adequate funds. More good textbooks on local history should be published (and kept by the pupils).[42]

Second, local research deserves to attract more attention, since it is breaking ground in barely cultivated and even virgin fields. The local historian, who has so much freedom of movement in his research, is freed from university "fashions." As a result, the innovative role of local history should not be neglected. Take as an example the works on the agrarian history of Poitou by Paul Raveau, supplemented by those of Dr. Louis Merle.[43]

Third, the local historian, rooted in his very concrete and precise territory, often ends up comparing general history and its long-term theories with his own strictly local problems. A certain number of local histories of the French Revolution probably resulted from a desire to compare the actual situation in a specific area with political or economic theories, that is, from a desire to verify the Revolution on a local scale. Sometimes it turns out that nothing at all happened, or virtually nothing.[44] In my own case, I recently asked myself, "What exactly was a Jacobin? or a man from Colmar?"—citing Georges Pariset, who observed that "one of the characteristics of the Revolution is that local life is infinitely diverse and that the histories of even the smallest cities and regions are never identical."[45]

In a sense, this is experimental history. Local history, defined as a science of the individual and the particular, seems to serve the authentic and definite function of restructuring history by creating at the outset a critical distrust of tenets, of theories that are always more or less inaccurate for lack of local monographs.[46]

[42]See Baudot's report to the *Archives* group of the national government's Fifth Plan. We also need handbooks in local history for adults. Paperbacks have been performing such functions in Germany and England but have not yet had much effect in France. I should, however, like to cite G.-B. Cabourdin and J.-A. Lesourd, *La Lorraine (histoire et géographie)* (1960), published by the Société Lorraine des études locales dans l'enseignement public, and the *Bulletin* of that society, which began a new publication series in 1956; A.-G. Manry, R. Seve, and M. Chaulanges, *L'histoire vue de l'Auvergne* (1951–59), a three-volume publication of the educational services of the Departmental Archives of Puy-de-Dôme; and H. Forestier, *L'Yonne au XIXe siècle (1800–1848)* (1959–63), a three-volume work published by the Departmental Archives of Yonne, with an introduction by J. P. Rocher.

[43]Paul Raveau, *L'agriculture et les classes paysannes dans le Haut-Poitou au XVIe siècle* (Paris, 1926), and *Essai sur la situation économique et l'état social en Poitou au XVIe siècle* (1931). Dr. Louis Merle, *La métairie et l'évolution agraire de la Gâtine poitevine de la fin du Moyen Age à la Révolution,* which fortunately has become a part of the collection *Terre et hommes* (Paris, 1958).

[44]Such was the case in a village of the Morvan. See the conclusions drawn by A. Thuillier, "Semelay de 1793 à 1795," *Actes du 87e Congrès National des Sociétés Savantes, Poitiers, 1962* (1963), pp. 233–68.

[45]Paul Leuilliot, "Si j'avais à récrire les Jacobins de Colmar . . . ," *Saisons d'Alsace,* no. 9 (Winter 1965).

[46]Pierrard (*La vie ouvrière,* p. 8), when discussing G. Duveau's pioneering dissertation, "La vie ouvrière en France sous le Second Empire" (1946), noted that "this classic work, which has been criticized for being based on too few sources and sources of debatable reliability, is especially ignorant of matters in Lille."

In short, the moving spirit behind such monographs seems less systematic and more "liberal" than similar work done within the university system. Devotion to detail, which has so often been denounced and criticized, is not necessarily synonymous with narrow-mindedness. Perhaps not enough heed is paid to the working hypotheses, methods, and intentions of local scholars, or to their publications, which are not circulated very far afield. Yet Marc Bloch used to pay very close attention to local and provincial journals, and Lucien Febvre reprinted in his *Annales, E.S.C.*, an article that had caught his eye in a journal dealing with the region of Montbéliard.

I shall conclude this "defense" by briefly suggesting a few ways to strengthen local history, which is too often misunderstood and whose concerns are, in my opinion, quite different from those of general history.

First of all, we must give it pedagogical help. In most cases, the local historian has trained himself on the job, so to speak, and has learned history as he went along. He needs a research manual that can supply adequate methodological "instructions" about research and writing and about the numerous catalogs of such national archives as the National Library in Paris. He also needs guides to the departmental archives—which archivists have fortunately begun to provide—not to mention a general record of all archives.[47] In addition he must be provided with regional bibliographies, bibliographies specializing in the different "sectors," and publications of various documents of general interest.[48]

Next, meetings or colloquia must be organized. The annual National Congress of Learned Societies could with profit be expanded to include sessions devoted to methodology. In addition, professors holding chairs of local history in provincial universities should be provided with sufficient funds to make sure they can effectively fulfill their advisory functions. Above all, financial help must be given to the various learned societies. The fact that financial reasons prevent local historians from publishing their work has had a marked effect upon the amount of research being done in certain provinces. If these societies no longer had to beg for funds, they could once again earn the respect due their renewed activity.

Lastly, it should be possible to organize certain activities involving the diffusion of information and the coordination of projects for the field as a whole. There is no question that local studies should be encouraged; but they should also be made available through discussions on radio and television, and reviews in the local press. This information must be as widely diffused as

---

[47]This is the goal of the *Archives* group of the Commission de l'Equipement culturel du Ve Plan. See also the reports of J. Richard and J. Vidalenc on archival catalogs. The reports of this group, for which Guy Thuillier was the general secretary, will soon be published.

[48]I am thinking of the reports of the Procureurs généraux, which provide rich documentation on many questions. The Commission d'Histoire économique et sociale de la Révolution française has published in its bulletins various studies by M. Reinhard on the population during the Revolution and the Empire (1959–60), and by M. Bouloiseau on emigration (1961).

possible, for local history can provide documentation for a host of individuals: geographers, sociologists, and economists, for example. This diffusion should be carried out either by centers for the history of a sector—such as the Iron Museum at Nancy, the museum of printed fabrics at Mulhouse, or the Museum of Banking and Books at Lyon—or by the university-based centers of regional history, which, as I have mentioned, are inadequately funded, if they exist at all. As far as coordination is concerned, the improvement of basic research procedures would lead to joint activities in certain sectors. Learned societies already exist and could act as coordinators. The creation of regional commissions for technical archives has been suggested along the lines of the departmental committees for the economic history of the French Revolution. Thus, a certain amount of help could be given to local history, and there is little doubt that university-based research, which reaps many of the rewards stemming from the efforts of local historians, would as a result be greatly helped.[49] It is not enough to try to make a clear definition of method; an attempt must be made to help, direct, motivate, and launch a veritable policy for local history. At the end of this "defense," if I were to anticipate history and make predictions, I would ask, "What should—and what will—be the place of local history and the role of local historians in 1985?"

II

Ce monde, si ignoré, et pourtant si proche de nous, qu'est le xixe siècle.

—G. Désert

Among the documents included in the "illustrations" in the appendix of *Aspects de l'économie nivernaise au XIXe siècle*, Guy Thuillier had the excellent idea to include Prefect Fiévée's "Confidential Note" about Nièvre at the beginning of the second Restoration, before the "revolution of the forges."[50] This serves to place the subject in its setting as clearly as a map would do. Indeed, "the province of Nivernais is part of the kingdoms of Lyon and of Paris," equidistant from the two cities and crossed by one single major road running north-south.[51] Of course, Nivernais was, and still is, more strongly attracted by the magnet that is Paris. It is a region of woods—"immense woods"—and of marshes. Prefect Fiévée stressed the importance of small *métairies* [sharecropping farms], the absence of large tenant farms, and the

---

[49]Need I say that with the exception of the "Que sais-je?" collection (which has some very fine books), no collection dealing with provincial history has been planned since the war? Good guidebooks to local history intended for the layman are very scarce. But the need exists, and I believe that such books would find numerous buyers. In fact, histories of Bordeaux, Besançon, and Lille are now in press.

[50]Guy Thuillier, "Crédit et économie sous l'Empire: les 'Notes sur la Banque' de Fiévée (1806)," *Revue d'Histoire économique et sociale*, 1963, pp. 56–68.

[51]A later road ran from east to west, from Clamecy to Nevers. Indeed, little work was done to improve the network of highways, except during the reign of Louis Philippe. See R. Baron, "Histoire d'une route, la Nationale 77," *Nivernais-Morvan*, May 1959–May 1960.

relatively few villages; but he also pointed out the extensive livestock trade. For the Morvan region he noted "the skimpy food of the inhabitants." According to him, the chief occupation of the nobles and bourgeois was to "supervise their *métayers* [sharecroppers] and keep up on market prices." Thus, more grain was grown than was needed for food and seed, and more wine was produced than could be consumed.

So, there were livestock and breeding, but also wood (which was expensive) and many iron mines and metallurgical works. Although the peasant remained calm within the isolation of his *métairie* ("while the rest of France was becoming aroused"), the workers in the foundry of Nevers and in the forges of Guérigny and Cosne—three royal establishments—were "of a turbulent nature," to say nothing of the workers in the river port at Nevers and the boatmen of the Loire.

But Nevers was not a centrally located capital. Indeed, the department of Nièvre, as created in 1790, reveals this quite clearly. At that time the provinces of Nivernais and Auxerrois [the region around Auxerre] felt no common bonds, and the city of Clamecy felt more a part of Auxerrois and even of the region of Orléans. Geographical social barriers separated lumber merchants—shipments of wood to Paris provided the livelihood of three-quarters of Clamecy's inhabitants[52]—workers involved in floating timber, and boatmen on the Yonne River from legal officials, the local nobility, and the bourgeoisie.[53]

These subtle contrasts, from the Morvan region, to Clamecy, and on to Nevers, were clearly perceived by Vidal de la Blache: "The region, which has remained one of the most thickly forested of France, reproduces in its population of woodcutters, miners, cattle breeders, and vineyard workers, all the contrasting elements of its heterogeneous soil. Situated between the provinces of Burgundy and Berry, it remains distinct. It poses an obstacle that interrupts the continuity of the natural relationships among the regions along the outskirts of the Paris basin."

Guy Thuillier has not failed to add literary evidence to his geographical and historical data: first Stendhal and Balzac, whose *Peasants* is set in a sub-prefecture that could well be Clamecy; and later authors, such as the pamphleteer Claude Tillier and Romain Rolland, whose *Colas Breugnon* was in part inspired by the notebooks of H. Bachelin, one of his uncles.

But Thuillier's book is above all a quantitative history, in the form of a succession of monographs. As Thuillier observes at the outset, up to this point no demographic history, no history of communications, and especially no social history has been done, so the necessary background work and basic research are lacking. As far as the population is concerned, to cite only total

[52]See another article by R. Baron, "Une famille nivernaise de marchands de bois: les Tournouer," *Bulletin de la Société scientifique et artistique de Clamecy,* 1957.

[53]A. Mirot and L. Mirot, "La réunion de Clamecy au département de la Nièvre," *Bulletin de la Société scientifique et artistique de Clamecy,* 1946.

figures: there were 230,000 inhabitants in 1800; 326,000 in 1856; 347,000 in 1886; 240,000 in 1956; and 242,000 in 1962. I shall return later to the exodus from rural areas to the newest industries.

Situated between the Yonne and the Loire rivers, the province of Nivernais became a crossroads of canals: the Berry canal, the lateral canal to the Loire; and the Nivernais canal, which was built in the late eighteenth century for the purpose of floating wood and supplying Paris, a new section being added in the first half of the nineteenth century to permit the shipment of coal from Decize.[54]

Lastly, Thuillier wishes a monograph existed about the bourgeoisie of Nivernais, about the "notables" of the *Monarchie censitaire*, [in which suffrage was limited by property qualifications]. Let us hope that one day soon this precious contribution to social history will be written in answer to his wish.[55] But we already have some revealing biographic information. Take Bonneau-Lestang, the brilliant faïence maker, that "curious personage of Nevers," son of a lumberyard owner, brother of an ironmaster, himself a banker (as was his son-in-law, Desveaux, future mayor of Nevers), and an ardent proponent of "free trade." Or take a banker such as Manuel, who was a deputy under Louis Philippe, a backer of Claude Tillier's newspaper, and finally a senator during the Second Empire. Or Frébault, who directed the Comptoir d'Escompte [a lending bank] at Nevers from 1848 until its bankruptcy in 1867, and who also was mayor of Nevers and president of the Chamber of Commerce as well.[56]

Thuillier first considers the evolution of economic structures, then the rise of big business—after all, he wrote the history of the ironworks at Fourchambault and the biography of Georges Dufaud—and lastly the "revolution of the forges."

In this evolution of structures, he has focused upon agricultural transformation and the expansion of cattle raising, which he shows to have been carried on and directed by big landowners, who represented half the lands included in

[54]In 1832 Decize had to keep six kilometers of road in repair in order to transport its coal as far as the Loire River. The coal mines were constructed near railroads: seven kilometers, inaugurated in 1843, linked them to the Nivernais canal; see Lévy-Leboyer, *Les banques européennes*, p. 314 and n. 13.

[55]André-Jean Tudesq, *Les grands notables en France (1840–1849)* (Paris, 1964); See "Nièvre" in his index of place names. See also Adéline Daumard, *La bourgeoisie parisienne de 1815 à 1848* (Paris, 1963); Daumard was authorized to consult notarial minutes only on condition that no proper names be used. Thus, "Narcisse L." stands for Narcisse Lafond, who in a note on p. 314 is unmasked as "deputy from Nièvre."

[56]It is not completely accurate to say that the fortune of the Dupins was built upon forges and wood. See R. Baron, "La bourgeoisie de Varzy au xviie siècle," *Annales de Bourgogne*, 1964, pp. 161–208. In Tudesq's *Les grands notables en France*, everyone was expecting some daring revelations about the Dupins, at least about Dupin the Elder, "the powerful monarch of Clamecy," as Claude Tillier called this true-to-type, if not creative, personage of the July Monarchy.

the land registries. However, this evolution chiefly involved that portion of Nivernais around the city of Nevers. Before we can make any generalizations, we must reconsider the entire history of land ownership and the consequences of the sale of national property, in all probability initially purchased by bourgeois but subsequently sold; the shift from sharecropping *métairies* to direct management by a tenant farmer, a development whose economic and social importance Prefect Fiévée stressed in 1815; and perhaps the effects of the Civil Code. As early as the Consulate and the Empire, and especially under the Restoration, small landowners persisted amidst large landowners and the great domains of the Ancien Régime, many of which were probably reconstructed. Let me point out that between 1822 and 1840 everyone strove to acquire more land through a whole network of local agents—notaries, who at that time were accumulating great amounts of property, but also bourgeois. Take, for example, the bourgeois of Corbigny who could live off his investments and bonds.[57] Another important event was the creation of artificial pastures—what Bonneau-Lestang called *la lèpre dévorante de l'embouche* [the devouring leprosy of livestock fattening, that is, the pernicious spread of cattle raising in open pastures at the expense of wheat growing].[58] More must be learned about when and how communal property was shared among the local inhabitants, a process that occurred quite slowly. The *communautés* [jointly held property] of *laboureurs* [wealthier peasants],—which attracted the attention of Claude Tillier and the jurisconsults Guy Coquille and Dupin in their comments upon the Customary Law of Nivernais—had in any event been censured on the eve of the Revolution as barbarous servitude.[59]

Next come two excellent chapters on the forest and the vineyard. The latter study, which is relevant for the entire period prior to the phylloxera disaster [of the 1860s], supplements Dion's and Laurent's general books on this subject. The especially revealing documents dealing with the forests and the floating of lumber downstream are precious, for in general the forests of Nivernais, and those in the Yonne basin, constituted a whole economic and social way of life. More precise information must still be obtained about who had the right to cut communal firewood, how forests were divided into sec-

[57]See also Philippe Vigier, *Essai sur la répartition de la propriété foncière dans la région alpine, son évolution des origines du cadastre à la fin du Second Empire* (Paris, 1963), which uses the agriculture report of 1866 as a basis for the conclusion that "a frenzy of buying occurred before 1848" and that a "frenzy of land fragmentation and selling occurred during the Second Empire."

[58]See Gabriel Debien, *Avant la révolution agricole: Les prairies artificielles dans le sud du Haut-Poitou (XVIᵉ–XIXᵉ siècle)*, published by the history section of the Faculty of Letters and Social Sciences (Dakar, 1964).

[59]See Pierre de Saint-Jacob, *Documents relatifs à la communauté villageoise en Bourgogne du milieu du XVIIᵉ siècle à la Révolution* (Paris, 1962); and, for comparison, A. Bigay, "Les communautés paysannes dans la région de Thiers," *Actes du 88ᵉ Congrès National des Sociétés Savantes, Clermont-Ferrand, 1963* (1964), pp. 843–59; and H. Dussourd, "La dissolution des communautés familiales agricoles dans le Centre de la France," *Actes du 89ᵉ Congrès National des Sociétés Savantes, Lyon, 1964* (1964), vol. 1, pp. 309–19.

tions, and the criteria for grading lumber.[60] But Thuillier has presented a very clear picture of the relationships between the economy of the forests and the economy of the forges.

Two other chapters are especially innovative: the chapter dealing with the prevailing diet, about which there is even less documentation than usual, and the chapter about social and medical problems. In this "region that forms the frontier between butter and lard," only a limited amount of meat seems to have been eaten before World War I. The documents selected for publication here provide interesting data about the effects of the decree of 1863 that suppressed government control of bakeries, the restablishment by certain mayors of controlled bread prices in order to keep prices down after the poor harvest of 1866, and the ephemeral existence of cooperatives.[61]

The social policies of the Ancien Régime, so heartless toward the weak and the poor, also continued until 1914. Medical and social transformations only began during the 1850s, for physicians were not appointed for each canton until 1853,[62] as a result of the food crisis of 1846–47.[63] It was a matter of "social laissez faire," along the lines of economic laissez faire. "You have to be rich and have influence in order to get into a hospital." Over a long period beggars were a major problem in the countryside. Thuillier deals with the problem of dechristianization,[64] as reflected in abandoned old people and children.[65] The inquiry of 1848, a constantly used yet apparently inexhaustible source of information, reveals the inequities in living conditions within a single department, often within a single canton, and reveals how precarious life could be for the peasantry, as in the case of the worker-peasants of Nivernais.

Thuillier provides a judicious discussion of banks, money, and insurance, and he frequently draws parallels with the current situation, shedding light upon the past by means of his observations and thoughts about our own day.[66] Nivernais banks were land oriented, with a clientele composed of farmers and

[60]See the work of Michel Devèze, *La vie de la forêt française au XVIe siècle* (Paris, 1961); *Histoire des forêts,* Collection "Que sais-je?" (Paris, 1965); and Devèze's comments on research in the field in the *Bulletin de la Section d'Histoire moderne et contemporaine du Comité des travaux historiques et scientifiques,* 1962, pp. 49–58.

[61]On rural food and shelter, see Jean Drouillet, *Folklore du Nivernais et du Morvan* (La Charité-sur-Loire, 1959), which is thought-provoking, although vague, about dates and localities. Changes are, of course, difficult to date, as Guy Thuillier has observed.

[62]How different from Alsace! See Leuilliot, *L'Alsace au début du XIXe siècle,* vol. 2, p. 18 (physicians were established in Bas-Rhin as early as 1810, and in Haut-Rhin in 1825).

[63]See André Thuillier. "La crise des subsistances dans la Nièvre (1846–47)," *Actes du 90e Congrès National des Sociétés Savantes, Nice, 1965* (1966), which stresses the psychology of the population. The economic crisis created a new awareness about certain agricultural problems.

[64]On dechristianization, see *Colloque d'histoire religieuse* (Lyon, October 1963), pp. 123–54; *Cahiers d'histoire* 1 (1964): 89–119; and the thought-provoking book of Christianne Marcilhacy, *Le diocèse d'Orléans au milieu du XIXe siècle* (Paris, 1964).

[65]See M.-C. Martin, "Les abandons d'enfants à Bourg et dans le département de l'Ain à la fin du XVIIIe siècle et dans la première moitié du XIXe," *Cahiers d'histoire* 2 (1965): 135–66.

[66]With an equal concern for "sources" and "statistical obstacles," Guy Thuillier studied "La formation du revenu dans le département de l'Hérault," *Revue économique,* 1961, pp. 956–99.

persons seeking funds to expand their pastures for livestock fattening. While the Boigues family of Fourchambault had been working closely with the Seillière Bank ever since the First Empire, the Bank of France only opened an office at Nevers in 1854 (although the board of directors of the bank had requested that agencies be set up in that department as early as the economic crisis of 1812). Thus, the question is whether banks played a passive or a decisive role in economic development, a question that was the subject of Maurice Lévy-Leboyer's recent doctoral dissertation.[67]

In like manner, complaints in the past about the scarcity of money are strangely similar to those of present-day industrialists who complain about a lack of capital and about centralized credit. What used to be called a "scarcity of money" would today be termed a "lack of liquidity" in the economy. I wish to emphasize this, as did Marc Bloch, for whom "among those phenomena upon which the historian focuses his attention, monetary phenomena are the most deserving of our attention, the most revealing, and the most vital. . . ."[68] In his book, Thuillier discusses the monetary difficulties at Nevers (which were already evident during the First Empire, between 1806 and 1810) and speculation based upon scarcity of specie. Indeed, gold was virtually unknown in this region between 1830 and 1850, and silver was hoarded; so gold and bank notes were not fully used until the 1850s. The importance of widespread usury is also discussed.

The Restoration was a period of bank organization, and everyone "sold insurance" at that time as well. The increased wealth of the countryside favored the development of insurance during the 1830s, but rural people remained hesitant, even as late as the 1880s. More than half those suffering losses from fire between 1875 and 1885 were uninsured. Insurance remained a form of speculation, and for a long while capitalists preferred to invest their money in mortgage loans.

Two monographs, which can serve as models for other scholars, deal with the faïence of Nevers and the paper mills of Corvol-l'Orgueilleux. The faïence works had gone into a rapid decline at an early date, as early as the second half of the eighteenth century,[69] when they were unable to make the technological innovations necessary to compete with imitations and English competitors. Still, a joint salesroom was organized by the various faïence works in 1818;

[67]See P. Bleton, "Les banquiers français font-ils un bon usage de l'argent?" in *Le Monde*, 22, 23, 24, 27, and 28 April 1965; and S. Comte, "Les banques sont-elles assez sévères à l'égard de leurs clients?" in *Le Monde*, 18 July 1965.

[68]In addition to Guy Thuillier's "Pour une histoire monétaire," see his "Troubles monétaires à Bordeaux en 1810," *Annales du Midi*, 1961, pp. 403–8; "Spéculations sur l'or et l'argent en 1857," *Annales, E.S.C.* 17 (July–August 1962): 722–31; and "La crise monétaire de l'automne 1810," *Revue historique*, 1967, pp. 51–84.

[69]For the period before 1789, an exhibit, "Faïences de la Renaissance à la Révolution," was held in 1965 at the Musée des Arts décoratifs in Paris. The Second Empire saw a rebirth in high quality faïence. In the papers of the chemist Hellot at the Library of Caen is a memorandum on faïence that can be traced back to Réaumur. See J. M. Janot, *Recherches sur les faïences d'Epinal* (1960).

but it was declared illegal by the court of appeals, the first such decree in the history of French jurisprudence.

"In the very curious buildings of an old forge,"[70] the paper works of Corvol are still to be found. Theirs is a history of technological innovation that involved the importation in 1821 of the first English continuous paper-making machine. In addition to his notes on the lives of a number of bourgeois, Thuillier includes the story of a certain Thomas-Varennes, the owner of vast forests who also possessed two lumberyards in Paris and a town house on that city's prestigious chaussée d'Antin. Encountering the opposition of both the wood merchants and the men who floated wood down the river to Paris, as well as that of the ironmasters, he fell victim to a series of shady intrigues and perhaps to the commercial crisis of 1830–33 as well.

Last but not least, metallurgy occupies many pages in this fat volume. The metallurgical tradition of the Nivernais proudly boasts of Pierre Babaud de la Chaussade at Guérigny and of Georges Dufaud at Fourchambault.[71] Thuillier has explored and analyzed in detail the whole metallurgical sector, from north to south, from Cosne (where Madame de Sévigné saw the very vision of "Vulcan's forge") to Decize, following a path through La Charité, Guérigny (where the offices of the directors are located in the eighteenth-century structures), Fourchambault, Nevers, and Imphy—not forgetting the coal mines of La Machine, whose vicissitudes call to mind those of Ronchamps in the Vosges, which has already been closed down. He begins with the origins of this major business venture and with Louis Le Vau's unsuccessful speculations; he describes the establishment of metallurgy at Fourchambault in 1828, after the first experiments using coal to refine iron conducted by a prefect-ironmaster, J. J. Sabatier, aided by Georges Dufaud, whose "Metallurgical Memos" appear in the appendix. The documents are meaningful: a memorandum by Berthier, a mining engineer, dated 1813, deals with the anarchic way in which a mine that had been turned over to peasants was being worked. This memo also discusses the waste of the ore itself after the law of 1810, which was still too recent and still considered "prejudicial to liberty and worthy of Tiberius, Nero, and Domitian." This comparison comes to mind when one thinks of the coal mines near Liège during the same period.

The importance of the legal setting is not insignificant, so we are carried back to the beginning of joint-stock companies in 1828, when the town of Imphy had to seek governmental authorization for such a move. And the unfortunate consequences of such an ill-conceived investment are not negligible either, for, again at Imphy, an error in anticipating the output of the factory coincided with a price collapse in 1856 and the years that followed.

---

[70]Bernard de Gaulejac, *Nivernais, Morvan, Puisaye* (1958), p. 54.

[71]The church at Ouagne contains a neo-Gothic high altar of cast iron given by the Rambourg family; without doubt it came from the foundry of Fourchambault (ibid., p. 57). The "Château-Vert" built during the nineteenth century in the vicinity of Clamecy by the Rambourgs has become a summer camp for the city of Saint-Maur.

The mining industry was also beset by difficulties caused by modernization during the Second Empire, as can be seen at the mines of the Aubois basin.

Resistance to technological innovation must also be taken into account; a special chapter, which reinforces the others, is even devoted to this development. The Chevalier de Grignon's prophecy did not come true overnight: "Coal from the mines, a gift of the gods, will bring about a revolution in metallurgy." The advent of the steam engine did not immediately do away with water wheels, nor did coal eliminate wood as a fuel for metal works. Workers had to become accustomed to new techniques; new managerial personnel had to be trained and had to gain experience in analytical accounting based upon profits, thus avoiding investment errors.[72]

The creation of Fourchambault in 1822 had brought about protests by ironmasters throughout Nivernais. Probably influenced by one of them, Berthier de Bizy, mayor of Guerigny, opposed the new factory that threatened to snatch up raw materials—wood and pig iron. He denounced the factory's goal of gaining control of the market through its inferior products, expressed his fear of inevitable unemployment, and above all attempted to show that it was impossible to transform the old forges. "Clever arguments that keep cropping up in almost those identical words in all the debates raised by the introduction of a new technique involving mass production."

The progressive decline, and even the destruction of small, marginal coal mines inevitably followed. These same problems continue today in the French coal industry. In Nivernais, the mines at La Machine are scheduled to close in 1970.[73] Forest-based metallurgy has already disappeared, so industrial use is currently represented by two charcoal works at Clamecy and Prémery.

Until 1870 the miners at La Machine lived as part of a rural world with peasant reactions, mores, and traditions. After 1885 the sons of the men who had entered the mines in the 1860s left and emigrated to Paris. The woodcutters for the mines of the Aubois basin, men of a revolutionary turn of mind, were almost the only ones to become stirred up in 1848. Such was not, however, the case for the wood-floaters of the Yonne River.[74] Emile Martin's

---

[72]Lévy-Leboyer, *Les banques européennes,* gives a general but very detailed picture of metallurgy, "the second technological stage" of industrialization during the first half of the nineteenth century; he also discusses investments. A specific example of such investments can be found in André Thuillier, "La fonderie de Fourchambault (1825–1835)," *Actes du 88e Congrès National des Sociétés Savantes, Clermont-Ferrand, 1963* (1964), pp. 475, 477, 483. In 1830 Emile Martin was contemplating new workshops in which to construct boilers for steam engines; in 1830 he also seems to have contemplated building a locomotive factory; by 1838 he had created research offices in Paris.

[73]See Paul Leuilliot, "Le bilan d'un colloque international: Charbon et Sciences Humaines," *Annales, E.S.C.* 19 (January–February 1964): 55–79. See also the *Actes* of this meeting published in 1966. And cf. R. Ratel, "L'industrie métallurgique du fer en Côte-d'Or au xixe siècle," *A travers notre Folklore et nos dialectes,* published by the Association bourguignonne des Sociétés Savantes (Dijon, 1966), vol. 2, pp. 96–158.

[74]See P. Cornu, "Les grèves des flotteurs de l'Yonne aux xviiie et xixe siècles," *Les cahiers du Centre,* January 1911, and "Clamecy et le Coup d'Etat de 1851," special issue of the *Bulletin de la Société scientifique et artistique de Clamecy,* 1951. On the "turbulence" of the woodcutters

paternalistic program at Fourchambault reveals management's social policy; he developed mutual aid and benefit funds during the Second Empire.[75] If the strike of 1837 was motivated by jealousy toward English workers, that of 1870 was of a more political nature, with workers parading on 12 April through the streets of Nevers singing the "Marseillaise" and crying "Long live the Republic!" Records of the telegrams sent by the public authorities are like snapshots of the demonstration and at the same time reveal the divergent reactions of those in power.

The final chapter, a sort of diptych, is called "Traditions and Resurgences." I am referring to the history of the factory created at Fourchambault in 1950 to manufacture Vespa motor scooters. Having tried unsuccessfully to replace the Vespa by a small car, the factory had to close down in 1963 "under the double pressure exerted by the international market and by new technology, following the very same path taken by the big Boigues ironworks, located at Fourchambault, which had had to close down in the early nineteenth century." Indeed, thoughts about the present recur often throughout these successive chapters dealing with nineteenth-century Nivernais—and with the region in the eighteenth or twentieth centuries.

The Nevers portion of Nivernais remained oriented about the Loire River. Today this department [Nièvre] is handicapped by its proximity to Paris and by the depopulation of its rural areas, a sizable number of unemployed women, and a lack of trained workers. Despite its metallurgical traditions, there is no industrial specialization. In addition to Clamecy (with Varzy and Coroigny), its "poles" are Cosne, Nevers (with La Charité, Prémery, Guérigny, Fourchambault, and Imphy), and Decize (with Cercy-la-Tour and its refrigerator factory, the "factory in the fields," as it has been so aptly christened).[76] But it is clearly in the old urban and industrialized centers of population that recently installed industries seem to have been the most beneficial, by recruiting on some occasions an already trained work force, as at Cosne, or on other occasions by recruiting among farm workers in some fifty neighboring communities, as at Clamecy.

Fiévée was already aware that the department of Nièvre lost about a thousand young people a year to Lyon or Paris—in a great many cases it was to Paris—as part of a century-old exodus. But this proximity to the "corona" formed by the 200-kilometer-wide belt about Paris can also be a favorable

---

of the Gâtinais and of the "navy" of Gien, see Marcilhacy, *Le diocèse d'Orléans;* and F. Pelloile, "Le procès des Mariannes du département du Cher (1851–1852)," *Mémoires de l'Union des Sociétés Savantes de Bourges,* 1959–60, pp. 123–58.

[75]See also André Thuillier, "Aux origines de l'acier Martin," *Actes du 86e Congrès National des Sociétés Savantes, Montpellier, 1961* (1962), pp. 341–81, previously unpublished fragments from the author's notebooks. Cf. D. Herrendschmidt, "Les caisses de secours entre ouvriers à Mulhouse de 1800 à 1870," *Bulletin du Musée historique de Mulhouse,* 1958, pp. 89–113.

[76]I am citing here J. F. Lorit, "La décentralisation industrielle dans le département de la Nièvre" (research paper for the Ecole nationale d'administration, class of 1964). These research papers constitute a sizable body of documentary studies for historians dealing with the period 1946–65.

factor. The city of Nevers thus can be seen as playing a double urban role: as a satellite of Paris and its suburbs, and as a distribution center for the triangle formed by Paris, Lyon (along the Saône and Rhone valleys via Autun and Chalon-sur-Saône), and Clermont-Ferrand (along the same National Highway 7 mentioned by Thuillier's prefect of yesteryear, and along the modern railroad system).

I saw *Aspects de l' économie nivernaise au XIXe siècle* gradually take shape in the form of the various articles included in it, articles that it is both convenient and useful to have within a single binding. The book also includes new chapters and an appendix and numerous documents of the period that complement the various chapters and articles. Each document merits discussion in its own right. Trained at the National Administrative School, Thuillier has remained a faithful historian, first of Fourchambault and now the whole of Nivernais. He has just contributed an excellent "illustration" to the "defense" of local history. His first contribution to the history of French metallurgy analyzed the respective relationships between technical innovation, financing, and the general economic situation that constantly interfered with the individual efforts of the heads of various enterprises. These themes all reappear in this volume but are developed and amplified far beyond the realm of metallurgy. Indeed, I should like to conclude by quoting Lucien Febvre: "I, for one, have always known, and still know, only one way in which to understand *grande histoire* and to place it in its setting: that way lies in knowing the history of a region or of a province from top to bottom, in every aspect of its development. . . !"[77]

---

[77]Lucien Febvre, *Autour d'une bibliothèque, Pages offertes à M. Charles Oursel* (Dijon, 1942).

3

The Place of the Revolution in the Agrarian History of France

Georges Lefebvre

I

It hardly seems necessary to labor the point that problems related to the peasantry are important to the history of the French Revolution. France was, after all, an essentially rural country in 1789; how can we imagine that the peasants did not make their voices heard at such a crucial moment of social change? The new regime could not have lasted very long if the peasants had had no stake in it.

What, then, were the measures of the revolutionary assemblies that particularly concerned the peasants? Everyone will immediately distinguish two kinds: the abolition of privileges, especially in the area of taxation, and the abolition of the tithe and of feudal rights, both of which were decided—at least in principle—during the night of 4 August 1789; and the sale of national property. These measures have attracted the attention of those historians who in the last thirty years have devoted their efforts to the study of the social and economic history of the French Revolution. Although their work is not yet very far advanced, the facts already uncovered are beginning to shed new light on certain problems. In the past, those who wanted to write the history of the French Revolution usually went to sit, as it were, in the revolutionary assemblies or their administrative bodies; they analyzed the laws, described the efforts of the authorities to implement them, and to a lesser degree, tried to gauge their effectiveness. These historians always stressed the point that, in the final analysis, the changes wrought by the Revolution fully satisfied the

Annales d'Histoire économique et sociale 1(1929): 506–23. Translated by Elborg Forster.

wishes of the peasants. Some historians condemned the Revolution as entirely too radical; others, who were in favor of it, could not even conceive of the idea that at least some of the peasants might have wanted the Revolution to go further.

And yet the history of the abolition of feudal rights clearly makes us question the assumption that the peasants were satisfied. The Constituent Assembly was forced to take this step in the wake of the rural revolts of July 1789, for the peasants were almost unanimously opposed to the seigneur. But while the revolutionary bourgeoisie was perfectly willing to proclaim civil equality and the abolition of the tithe, it was very hesitant when it came to feudal rights, which were considered to be private property and, moreover, often belonged to the bourgeois themselves. The Constituent Assembly tried to resolve this quandary by submitting this kind of property to legal scrutiny. Legal scholars made a distinction between, on the one hand, "wrongly acquired" rights—a term that was applied to rights that were either contrary to natural law, such as mortmain; usurped from public power, such as the right of justice; or imposed, they said, by force, such as the *banalités* or seigneurial monopolies of mills, ovens, wine presses, etc.—and, on the other hand, those obligations that were part of the concession of a leasehold. The first were abolished without compensation; the second were declared "redeemable" or purchasable. However, the peasants refused to accept this distinction. They rarely redeemed or purchased feudal rights, and they also refused to pay them, or only did so under duress. In 1792 and 1793, after the fall of Louis XVI and especially after his execution, when foreign armies invaded France and when the country was torn apart by royalist and Girondist insurrections, the Legislative Assembly and the Convention needed the support of the peasants and therefore decided to drop the redemption payments of feudal rights, among other measures. Finally, the law of 17 July 1793 permanently abolished all feudal rights without providing for any compensation whatsoever. Thus, it is perfectly clear that the measures of the Constituent Assembly had not satisfied the wishes of the peasants; it was only the Convention, which voted the unconditional abolition of feudal rights, that brought them satisfaction.

Once this fact has been established, it seems appropriate to ask similar questions with respect to the sale of national property.

We know that for financial reasons the Constituent Assembly declared that Church property belonged to the nation and decreed its sale. Later it included the royal domains in this decree, and eventually the Convention also decided to sell the property of schools, charitable institutions, convicted prisoners, exiled priests, and especially émigrés. The needs of the treasury determined the conditions of these sales, which explains why the national properties were sold at auction to the highest bidder. The adoption of this method of sale determined the distribution of this property among the different classes of the nation, for it naturally fell into the hands of the richest or, if one prefers, the least poor among the citizens. It is true that under the Directory the law of 28 ventôse, Year IV, was to do away with sale by auction, replacing it with sale by officially estimated price; but it is no secret that this made it even easier for wealthy buyers and speculators to keep out the poor. By contrast, the Montagnard* Convention of 1793 adopted laws that endeavored to favor modest and even indigent buyers. But it upheld sale by auction, and although this legislation was moderately effective, it is no less true that the Convention sacrificed its social convictions to the need for maintaining the value of the *assignat.†* In short, the national property was offered to the wealthiest buyers throughout the Revolution. In this respect the policies of the otherwise radical Convention were not very different from those of the Constituent Assembly, unlike, as we have seen, its policies with respect to rents of seigneurial origin.

Does this mean that the peasants were fully and unanimously satisfied with the manner in which the national properties were sold? Does it mean that we must consider the legislation of the Montagnard Convention, mild as it was, as mere demagogical window dressing, as laws that the rural masses had not demanded, and of which they did not take advantage because they were not interested in acquiring land? And, if this was not the case, why did the peasants not put pressure on the revolutionary assemblies to modify their legislation, as they had been able to do with respect to the feudal rights? This may well be one of the most far-reaching questions in the entire agrarian history of France.

II

Selling the national properties to the highest bidder could only have satisfied all French peasants if there had been no agrarian crisis, that is, if every peasant had owned enough land to live independently. Had that been true, we can be quite certain that the peasants would have considered it worth their while to take over their share of the nationalized properties, along with the bourgeoisie and the wealthiest of the rural inhabitants. But, of course, the situation was different.

It must be said at the outset that in comparing France with England or the countries of Eastern Europe, one immediately realizes that the French peasant was much better off. In general he was free, as was the English peasant, and in those cases where he was still a serf or was subject to mortmain, his burdens were not even comparable to those of the German *Untertan* or the serf of Eastern Europe. Such things as *Gesindedienst*, arbitrary labor service, were unknown in France. Furthermore, the French peasant often owned some land, subject, to be sure, to the payment of seigneurial dues. By contrast, the vast majority of English peasants were reduced to the status of day laborer, while

---

*The most radical members of the revolutionary assembly, led by Maximilien Robespierre, were seated in the top rows of the amphitheater and therefore called Montagnards, or "the Mountain."—Trans.

†The revolutionary paper money guaranteed by the national property.—Trans.

those peasants of Eastern Europe who cultivated a plot of rented land usually held it under more or less precarious terms. What proportion of the land was owned by the French peasants? This varied greatly from one region to another, even in adjoining territories; indeed, it varied from village to village. Peasant ownership was considerable in certain parts of Flanders, Alsace, and Aquitaine, rather small in areas of marshes, forests, and heath [*landes*], and minimal in the vicinity of Versailles. The mean value of all the local variations will probably turn out to be something like 30 or 40 percent, once the question has been studied more closely.

Nor is this all. Calling it a country of small landowners does not sufficiently emphasize the most important feature of France's rural physiognomy, the one characteristic whose underlying influence may well have had the most profound consequences for the history of the French Revolution. The English aristocracy, which had created extensive farms by the enclosure movement, rented these properties to a small number of usually well-to-do, well-educated tenants; in eastern Germany, the *Gutsherr* managed his vast domain himself by means of the labor services his peasants owed him. But in France, priests, nobles, and bourgeois almost never managed their properties directly; their domains were extremely fragmented and rented out as middle-sized farms, even as individual fields. Almost all the property of priests, parishes, or charitable foundations were cultivated in this manner. A very large number of French peasants thus cultivated land they did not own. Some were tenants on large farms, most were small sharecroppers; even day laborers were often able to rent a small piece of meadow or a garden plot. Not all those who rented land were necessarily owners as well. The tenants on large properties often did not own any land; on the other hand, small owners frequently rounded out their farms by cultivating adjoining land under the terms of a lease. Thus, in France, almost all of the arable land was already directly cultivated by the peasants, who were individually responsible for the losses and profits of their operations.

The condition of the peasants varied considerably not only from region to region, depending on how much land was owned by the aristocracy and the bourgeoisie, but also from family to family. In other words, the mass of the peasantry was already markedly differentiated. Solidarity against the seigneur, their common enemy, remained strong; but in every other respect the large tenant, the sharecropper, and the day laborer did not share the same interests. Actually, this process of differentiation would have been even more marked if ownership by the family, which was still very common, had not continued to prevail; it did prevail, not, as is often claimed today, because of the constraint of inheritance laws—for peasant property was not subject to primogeniture, and testamentary freedom had already been considerably curtailed—but because the general economic situation did not encourage the awakening of an individualist attitude among humble people.

III

Nonetheless, despite the foregoing statements, a more careful investigation reveals that there was indeed an agrarian crisis.

First of all, by stressing the fact that France was a country of small landowners, one is apt to forget that not all peasants were landowners. The proportion of heads of families who owned no land at all, not even a cottage, was also very variable; indeed, the regions where such a condition prevailed were in the majority. The heads of families who were landless accounted for 75 percent in the coastal plain of Flanders, 70 percent in certain villages in the vicinity of Versailles, 30 to 40 percent in Lower Normandy. Holding land under perpetual leaseholds sharply reduced this figure in Flanders, attenuated it somewhat in Lower Normandy, but never reduced it to zero. Thus there was in France, as in England, a veritable rural proletariat. While this proletariat was very unevenly distributed, it was always anxious to acquire or rent a little property, if only a small garden and a miserable cottage. Throughout the eighteenth century we hear complaints about encroachments on communal land, especially near the edge of forests, by poor wretches looking for a place to live.

Secondly, the vast majority of small peasants did not have enough land to live independently. In the future department of Nord, south of the River Lys, three-fourths of the farmers worked less than one hectare. That is why encroachments on communal land were not perpetrated exclusively by the indigent; it is also why the *cahiers** called for the sale of royal and sometimes Church property. Since the peasants were unable to make a living from their land alone, they were always trying to earn supplementary wages, especially by working for well-to-do farmers at the time of the grain or wine harvest or by practicing a craft, usually on commission from a merchant in the neighboring town. But not all of them were able to make ends meet, and many were reduced to begging. In bad years the number of roaming beggars could easily assume threatening proportions.

This situation was steadily worsening during the last years of the Ancien Régime because the population of France was increasing rather rapidly, while the price of food was continually rising.

IV

The crisis clearly had demographic causes, and to that extent there was no cure for it. The only way it could be dealt with was to engage the surplus of peasants in manufacturing or tell them to emigrate. But the crisis also had economic and social causes, and in this respect two solutions could have been

*"Notebooks" of grievances submitted to the Estates General of 1789.—Trans.

adopted: either agricultural techniques could have been improved sufficiently
to enable more and more peasants to subsist on smaller and smaller holdings,
or land could have been made available to those who did not have it, either by
dividing up large farms or by expropriating nonresident owners.

In eighteenth-century France the progress of agriculture was hindered not
only by the routine ways of the illiterate peasantry but also by the interests of
the rural masses, which historians are wont to dismiss rather too casually.
Except in Flanders, where fallow fields had almost entirely disappeared,
arable land was generally divided into three parts: one-third was planted
in wheat, one-third in spring grain, and one-third was left fallow. The
fallow fields, as well as the cultivated fields after the harvest, were common
land and subject to communal rights of free pasture; that is, all peasants had
the right to pasture their livestock on them. This was also true for meadows
after the second haying, frequently even after the first. It should be added that
fields often lay fallow for much more than one year; in western France and in
the mountains the land was cultivated only after very long periods of rest.
Moreover, in many regions the communal lands, wasteland, heath, marshes,
and forest were very extensive. Also, the rights of usage in privately owned
and royal forests, such as the pasturing of livestock and the taking of free
wood for firewood and construction, subsisted for a long time and were
difficult to eradicate. Nor should we neglect gleaning and the right to the
stubble, which was very high since the grain was cut by the sickle.

For all these reasons the landowner was far from exercising over his property the absolute right that was his under the Roman law. Even if the customary law did not always oblige him, as it did in Alsace, eastern, and even
northern France, to adhere to the triennial crop rotation of the village community, the right of free pasture made it a practical necessity to conform to the
usage of neighboring owners. As far as rural opinion was concerned, even
enclosure did not necessarily permit an owner to keep out other people's
livestock. Under these circumstances agricultural improvement was difficult
to achieve, especially with respect to the use of natural meadows and the
development of artificial ones. For their part, the rural masses considered
these collective rights as a property that was as sacred as any; and if they were
not founded on written titles, they were based on the prescriptions of customary law. And it is a fact that the very existence of most peasants depended on
them. Those who worked only a small plot of land, and even those who did
not have any land, were able to raise a cow, a pig, or a few sheep thanks to the
communal pastures. Once they lost this resource, they had nothing. Thus
progress in agricultural techniques could only be achieved at the expense of
the poor.

Exactly the same thing was true for the rise in the price of foodstuffs, which
in part depended on freedom of trade for grain and other agricultural produce.
A day laborer had to buy at least enough grain to feed his family; many small
owners had to sell theirs in order to raise the money for taxes, thus running

short by the end of the summer; sharecroppers were even more likely to find themselves in that situation. Those who profited from the rising prices were the large tenant farmers, the large landowners, the owners of tithes, and the seigneurs who collected produce rents and dues. For this reason the over-whelming majority of peasants was as much in favor of regulating the grain trade and controlling the price of bread as were the townspeople.

However, the policies of the royal government at the end of the Ancien Régime were diametrically opposed to the customs and the interests of the peasantry. The government was anxious to put an end to the shortages that inevitably led to disturbances in the countryside and to increase the production of food needed to increase the population, which would in turn increase the tax base. Impressed by the urgent pleading of the economists and the example of England and also under pressure from large landowners interested in aug-menting their revenues, the government handed down edicts permitting land-owners in some provinces to enclose their fields, thus putting an end to the right of communal pasturing. It also handed down the so-called edicts of *triage,* which permitted village seigneurs to take over one-third of the com-munal land in their parishes; encouraged clearing and drainage, which further reduced the areas available for communal pasturing; favored the rise in the price of grain and other produce by building roads and canals, by concluding a commercial treaty with England in 1787, and above all, by permitting free trade in grain which, under the edict of 1787, could even be exported abroad. In short, the government encouraged the agricultural producer to produce for the market and for profit, like the English tenant farmer and the Prussian Junker. But these efforts were only partly successful and provoked increasing irritation.

For one thing, it was often difficult to enclose in the English sense unless an entire property was regrouped, but this was a step that was never considered. The royal government could not possibly endorse it, for it would have meant uprooting the peasants, jeopardizing the collection of taxes, and increasing the floating population. Even the seigneurs themselves do not seem to have con-sidered it seriously, the reasons being that the produce rents, which were an essential element of their revenue, were attached to the existing leaseholds and that it would have been impossible in practice, as well as risky in every respect, to reorganize both their landed property and their feudal rights. Some of the largest landowners made a few minor adjustments by merging the small farms within their direct domain into one or more large ones. Moreover, a number of administrators and agronomists continued to favor small-scale agriculture for political as well as economic reasons.

Secondly, the new economic ideas were designed for the profit of large-scale tenants and large-scale landowners. They alone were able to benefit from the rise in the price of agricultural produce and from enclosures; and the *triage* edicts clearly favored the seigneurs. The rural masses protested vigorously and sometimes engaged in open resistance. More than once, the local authorities took their side. Not only did the shrinking of the communal pastures increase the poverty of the people, it also made tax collection more difficult. In addition, it affected the towns, where meat, milk, butter, and cheese became progressively more expensive owing to the reduction in the quantity of livestock raised.

An increase in production, however, would not have been the solution to the agrarian crisis, since production could not in any case have kept pace with the increase in population. Nor was this the ambition of the royal government, which seems to have felt that, aside from charity, the best way to help the poor peasant was to encourage the development of rural industry. This development was therefore given free rein in the last years of the Ancien Régime and reached a remarkable stage in certain areas, such as the present department of Nord, Picardy and Normandy. But even there it was never more than an insufficient palliative, and many other regions, such as Limousin, had not yet derived any benefits from it by 1789.

Yet the policy of the Ancien Régime was not really ill conceived and could have contributed to maintaining order and strengthening the authority and prestige of the monarchy, had it not been for two factors. On the one hand, the largest possible number of peasants should have been given a chance to benefit from these policies through a reduction in their financial obligations; this could have been achieved by taxing the privileged and by abolishing tithes and feudal rights or at least by converting these obligations into monetary payments. On the other hand, the impression that the king's intervention in agricultural affairs was designed to favor the aristocracy should have been avoided at all costs; but as it happened, the edicts of *triage* openly favored the aristocracy. It can therefore be said that the very reforms of the Ancien Régime hastened its downfall by arousing the wrath of the peasants. In the course of the rural disturbances that began in the spring of 1789 and degenerated into a general uprising by the end of July, the protesters did not limit themselves to attacking the seigneurs and refusing to pay tithes and seigneurial dues. It is not often understood that the peasants availed themselves of this opportunity to regain possession of the communal rights that had been taken from them; everywhere they demolished enclosures and reasserted their right of free pasture, restored to the communal lands the third that had been taken by the seigneurs, and invaded the forests. Furthermore, they also stopped the transport of grain and demanded price control, a demand that was also voiced by townspeople. As far as we can see, the great majority of rural people wished to uphold the traditional agriculture and the time-honored regulations which, in effect, curtailed individual property rights.

V

Under these circumstances, it can be said that the peasant saw only one way to deal with the agrarian crisis; namely, to limit by law the size of farms in order to create a greater number of holdings or at least to prevent the decrease in the number of existing farms, and also to distribute to the peasants as much land as possible.

Actually, the Ancien Régime did not fail to take these measures into consideration. But a law sanctioning the fragmentation of farms was so contrary to its agricultural policies that it could not be adopted. Nonetheless, the government would have been glad to increase the number of small property owners. By favoring the clearing of wasteland, it indirectly encouraged the peasant takeover of communal land; and it is quite obvious that on more than one occasion the peasants viewed the royal declarations of 1764 and 1766 as implicit authorization to take possession of such land. Later the edicts of *triage* permitted or indeed ordered the distribution of the two-thirds of the communal land that had been left to the parish and not been taken by the seigneur. But the rural inhabitants wanted more. Their *cahiers* often demanded the sale of the royal domains and sometimes also alluded to Church property. The division of communal property was a much less satisfactory solution. Since common land had always been most useful to those who owned the most livestock, the poor peasants felt that, on balance, its division would probably be helpful; but, on the other hand, the reduced area of pasturage certainly caused misgivings.

When the Constituent Assembly placed the lands of the Royal Domain and of the Catholic Church on sale, the peasants of the regions where these properties were very extensive, especially Picardy and the region of Versailles, hoped to be able to buy them cheaply or to gain possession of at least some of them under long-term mortgages [*arrentement*] that would provide each head of a household with one arpent of land upon payment of an annual installment. When these hopes were dashed, there were outbursts of anger. In June 1793 the Convention was obliged to calm the unrest around Versailles by according one arpent to each indigent peasant, to be paid for under a long-term mortgage. Throughout the years 1791 and 1792 the peasants of Picardy violently disrupted the auctions of national properties and forced the authorities to sell the public land in their villages to them at officially appraised prices. It has been said that the Montagnards tried to pacify the peasants by distributing the communal lands and by dividing up such land before selling it. But since the land was still sold to the highest bidder, the protests continued, as we clearly see from the petitions of 1793 and 1794, most of which are still unpublished. We also know that *sans-culotte* administrators frequently complained to the revolutionary government that the conditions of sale still did not permit the poor to compete. The petitions also stressed, again and again, that the large farms should be broken up and that sharecropping leases should be regulated, given the fact that in many communities the amount of land for sale was rather small and that, furthermore, the properties in question were often sold as a unit. It is possible that the pressure brought by the peasants explains the frequent demands by the *Enragés* and the *Héber-*

tistes for the confiscation of the property of all suspects. It is also possible—
and this is the opinion of M. Mathiez—that the Robespierrists used the
decrees of ventôse, Year II, promising the distribution of national property to
the indigent, to attach the poor to the cause of the Montagnard revolution.
Furthermore, this pressure may be one of the reasons for Babeuf's eventual
adoption of agrarian communism, for he came from Picardy and had lived
among peasants who, more than the peasants elsewhere, had made a concerted effort to lay their hands on the nationalized property.

VI

The fact is, however, that the demands of the poor peasants—continuation
of traditional agricultural practices and regulation, and at least partial distribution of nationalized property—met with quasi-unanimous hostility on the part
of the members of the revolutionary assemblies, whatever their opinions and
policies in other respects. Peasants were scarce among their ranks, and those
who were members necessarily belonged to the more affluent class of the
peasantry. The other deputies did undoubtedly have some contact with the
countryside, but their relations were with the peasant bourgeoisie. The rural
code of the Constituent Assembly, which was left completely intact by the
Convention, gave the landowner an entirely free hand in the management of
his land: it permitted him to enclose his land, thereby eliminating communal
pasturing on his property; it allowed him to cultivate his land as he saw fit and
thus implicitly took away any legal power the regulations of the old rural
community may have possessed. The Convention, like the Constituent Assembly, remained deaf to the petitions demanding the breaking up of large
farms and the regulation of sharecropping. Free trade in grain and agricultural
produce became one of the principles of the new regime. It would be mislead-
ing to cite the law of the maximum here, for the Montagnard deputies reluc-
tantly adopted it only under severe pressure from the sans-culottes of the
towns; and while the deputies subsequently realized that price control, as well
as requisitioning, was a useful expedient in the conduct of the war, they were
never prepared to make it a permanent institution of the republic. As for the
national property, the deputies never lost sight of the fact that its purpose was
above all to guarantee the value of the assignat. Even the Montagnards upheld
the practice of selling these lands to the highest bidder, and there is no
indication that any of them objected to the law of 24 April 1793, which
prohibited peasants from forming associations for the purpose of buying the
nationalized communal lands. Having given the poor the possibility of buying
one arpent under a mortgage plan on 3 May 1793, the Montagnard Convention in September of the same year reversed itself and returned to sales by
auction; and it was only at the end of the Year II (1794), at the time the
left-wing Thermidorians felt increasingly threatened by reaction, that some of
them protested the accumulation of national properties by the rich. There is

even reason to believe with M. Mathiez that the Robespierrists hastened their own downfall by pressing for the confiscation of the properties of all suspects and the distribution of these properties to the indigent, since their colleagues were unwilling to go as far as that. Moreover, it is clear that such an operation would not have solved the problem. In any case, putting an end to the agrarian crisis was never a priority of the revolutionaries. In his report on the rural disturbances in the region of Versailles that eventually led to the decree of 3 May 1793, Delacroix declared flatly that the poor of the countryside must turn to industry and that, furthermore, giving them land would mean depriving the manufacturer and merchant of needed labor.

The agrarian evolution of France thus continued in the direction it had already taken in the eighteenth century. In this respect as in many others, the Revolution promptly and energetically undertook, almost without realizing it, the implementation of measures the monarchy had timidly outlined. French agriculture was not transformed by the Revolution—fallow fields and communal rights of pasture persisted long after it. What was broken were the legal obstacles to individual initiative. And while it did not condemn large-scale farming, the Revolution—like the monarchy before it—was rather sympathetic to the small property owner and to small-scale farming, since the sale of national property and the division of communal land necessarily increased the number of both to a certain extent. An economist may find these two goals of revolutionary policy somewhat contradictory, for small-scale farming and the fragmentation of the land were definitely not conducive to a rapid transformation of agriculture. But from a social point of view this economic contradiction was conducive to harmony. The agricultural revolution was bound to harm the peasant who had no land, or very little land. Its unfortunate consequences could only be mitigated if agricultural change progressed slowly. Precisely because the agricultural revolution was delayed, a greater number of peasants benefited from it.

VII

One cannot help wondering why the same peasants who so vigorously attacked the aristocracy and who mounted a concerted effort to pressure the revolutionary assemblies into the unqualified abolition of feudal rights did not remain united when it came to strenghtening the regulation of sharecropping, upholding collective rights, and distributing to the rural population all or part of the nationalized land.

The first reason is that the peasants were united only against the seigneur. As I have shown, the mass of the peasantry was already too differentiated to have the same opinions regarding other agrarian problems. The large tenant farmer could only improve his position by remaining the master of his farm and freely selling his grain; he was not displeased to see the sale of national property to the highest bidder because he was rich enough to buy some of it.

We know that he wielded considerable influence in the village because he provided work, ploughed the land of peasants who lacked draft animals, and sold grain to those who needed it. The peasants who already owned some land might have more or less pronounced reservations about auction of national property, depending on their wealth. Many of them would undoubtedly have been happy to see a more democratic method of sale, but since they were accustomed to buying land as individuals and with the means acquired by their personal effort, they simply could not pass up such an opportunity. Once they had taken advantage of such a sale, or even begun to hope for it, their cause was morally no longer that of the village proletarians. It was only a matter of time before they would adapt completely to the new liberal economy.

Nor could there be the same solidarity with respect to the agrarian crisis as there had been with respect to feudal rights in the different regions of France, or even from one village to the next. The question of collective rights did not have the same implications throughout France. The amount of Church property was extremely variable; western and southern France, for example, had very little of it. This situation was even more pronounced for émigré property. In many villages, none was for sale, for all the nobles did not leave their homes, and those who stayed were not all guillotined, contrary to what is often believed abroad and even in France. In the villages where there was little national property, the peasants had no one to despoil.

As can be seen in our own day, the countries of Eastern Europe are more or less solving their agrarian crises, not only at the expense of mortmain property or the property of "Enemies of the State," for they have expropriated all of the great domains. In the same manner the French peasants could have demanded that the Republic buy up, if necessary with devalued assignats, enough land to make a general distribution. As far as we know, this idea did not occur to them; this can be explained by what we have emphasized as the most characteristic feature of the agrarian physiognomy of France. The land that the Republic would have expropriated was already in the hands of the peasants, who worked it as sharecroppers or tenant farmers; and these peasants were numerous and often very humble. While it is true that each one of them would have come to own a small plot of land outright, he would also, by the same token, have lost a much larger farm that provided his livelihood or completed the property he already owned. The importance of this consideration becomes clear when one observes the alarm that seized the countryside at the end of 1790 when it looked as if the Constituent Assembly would permit the buyers of national property to cancel the existing leases. This is an indication that the turn of events during the Revolution was in part determined by the agrarian history of the old France.

In addition, however, some of these developments must be laid to the policies of the revolutionary assemblies. The members of the Constituent Assembly decreed that the different lots of the same property should be auctioned off separately, and that bids for individual lots should be given preference over bids for the entire property as long as the individual bid brought the same result for the National Treasury. As we have seen, the Montagnards went even further, ordering all properties to be divided and sold separately. Both bodies accorded very long delays of payment. In addition,the Convention permitted the division of communal property and, in those communities that had no communal land, authorized the poor to buy 500 livres worth of national property, payable over twenty years. As to the question of how much land the peasants were able to buy, there is no doubt that many were able to round out their properties and that quite a few became owners for the first time. It is also certain that, since many farms were broken up, a greater number of peasants were able to rent land. Circumstances, incidentally, also played a role and helped the law, for many nobles and bourgeois were ruined by the misfortunes of the times and by bankruptcy, and when they had to sell their land, the peasants benefited. There is no question that the number of proletarians was reduced in this manner.

I do not mean to charge the members of the revolutionary assemblies with a kind of class-oriented Machiavellianism, and there is no reason to accuse them of having acted like greedy and shrewd bourgeois who, in their desire to obtain the lion's share, attempted to divide their adversaries. Like many administrators and agronomists of the Ancien Régime before them, a number of the Constituents sincerely believed that in the interest of agriculture, law and order, and the general progress of society, it was necessary to increase the number of small property owners. As for the Montagnards, they felt that a political democracy was not viable in a country where differences in wealth were excessive; their ideal was a society of small property owners and craftsmen. It cannot be said, of course, that calculation was totally absent from their behavior; after all, the more people who bought national property, the more support the new regime would have. But this was a political calculation, a kind of defense strategy. Whatever the motives, the results are clear enough. It is as if the revolutionary assemblies had been willing to make a small sacrifice in order to forestall concerted action by the rural proletariat and assure the continued practice of selling the national property to the highest bidder, which eventually brought most of that property into the hands of the bourgeoisie and the well-to-do peasantry. In any case, the generosity or the skill of the revolutionary assemblies alone could not have brought about this result; their measures may have channeled a tide they would have been unable to stem if it had ever reached its full height. The weakness of its impact can only be explained by the agrarian conditions of the Ancien Régime.

VIII

To conclude this brief essay, it should be stressed once again that the Revolution vigorously resumed the task begun by the monarchy. By creating the legal framework for a modern, progressive, commercial, and capitalist agriculture, it put the finishing touches to an evolution that had begun long before. By increasing the scope of small property and small-scale farming, it probably slowed down the innovations it had legally authorized; but by the same token it also accentuated the characteristic feature of the agrarian physiognomy of France, created a better climate for social equilibrium, and saved some of the people from the suffering that technological progress brings to the poor.

In addition, it should be pointed out that the Revolution was much more moderate than it might have been. If the majority of the peasants had had their way, they would have done away altogether with large-scale ownership and large-scale farming. Whether this would have been a bad thing is a question that cannot be dealt with here. Suffice it to note that the revolutionaries would have been unable to prevent it by their will alone and that France was preserved from it by her history. We must therefore acknowledge the rather modest dimensions of that great agrarian transformation, which did not open an unbridgeable gap between the old France and the new.

Bibliographical Note

I. For the agriculture and the peasants at the end of the Ancien Régime and during the Revolution, the only general bibliography is in the work by P. Boissonnade, published twenty-five years ago: "Les études relatives à l'histoire économique de la Révolution française (1789–1804)," *Revue de Synthèse historique* 10 (1905): 57–74, 194–232, 343–68; ibid. 11 (1905): 94–111, 205–42, 339–67. Offprint, 168 pp. (Paris, 1906). Other bibliographical indications are to be found in Henri Sée's works on the economic history of France: *La vie économique et les classes sociales en France au XVIIIe siècle* (Paris, 1925); *La France économique et sociale au XVIIIe siècle* (Paris: Collection Armand Colin, 1925); *Esquisse d'une histoire économique et sociale de la France depuis les origines jusqu'à la guerre mondiale* (Paris, 1929). Complementary information is contained in the monographs cited below as well as in purely bibliographical publications.

Preliminary reading should include the short exposition in the works of Henri Sée and, concerning the questions treated in the present article, N. Kareiev's *Les paysans et la question paysanne en France dans le dernier quart du XVIIIe siècle,* trans. Woyharowska, 2 vols. (Paris, 1899). Detailed descriptions appear in Arthur Young's *Travels in France* (Dublin, 1793). Those who desire a general outline of the problem will be disappointed by M. Kovalewsky's *La France économique et sociale à la veille de la Révolution,* 2 vols. (Paris, 1909–11), and even by F. Wolters's *Studien über Agrarzustände und Agrarprobleme in Frankreich von 1700 bis 1790* (Leipzig, 1905) (Staats- und sozialwissenschaftliche Forschungen, herausgegeben von G. Schmoller, vol. 22, no. 5)—although the latter may be useful in certain other respects, as I shall point out later.

While there are not many general works, we do possess a considerable number of monographs. See, for example, Théron de Montaugé, *L'agriculture et la vie rurale dans le pays toulousain depuis le milieu du XVIIIe siècle* (Paris, 1869), for the region of Toulouse; A. de Calonne, "La vie agricole sous l'ancien régime dans le Nord de la France" (Paris, 1883) (3d ed. in *Mémoires de la Société des antiquaires de Picardie* 39 [1920]: 1–593) for the region of the department of Nord, particularly Artois and Picardy; M. Marion, *Etat des classes rurales dans la généralité de Bordeaux* (Paris, 1902), on Guyenne; H. Sée, *Les classes rurales en Bretagne du XVIe siècle à la Révolution* (Paris, 1906), on Brittany; Ch. Hoffman, *L'Alsace au XVIIIe siècle,* 2 vols. (Colmar, 1906) and *Bibliothèque de la Revue d'Alsace,* vols. 9 and 10, on Alsace. To these should be added the works by geographers, especially A. Demangeon, *La Picardie.* Thèse de lettres (Paris, 1906) on Picardy; J. Sion, *Les paysans de la Normandie orientale.* Thèse de lettres (Paris, 1909), on Upper Normandy; and R. Musset, *Le Bas-Maine.* Thèse de lettres (Paris, 1917), on Lower Maine.

Unfortunately, these monographs almost never contain statistical information, at least for the period with which we are concerned here. Moreover, they approach the study of peasant life from the standpoint of the liberal economy, as Arthur Young had already done in his day. These authors are interested in France's evolution toward the modern economy and in the progress achieved by large tenants and wealthy farmers. At least they rarely see the old economy as a complete entity, as a way of life in which the poor peasant enjoyed resources that have since been taken from him, resources— and this may be the most important fact—that he looked on as a right to be defended, as the birthright of the poor. Like the landowners and jurists of the eighteenth century, most of our contemporaries see this attitude only as leading to abuses, to encroachments on private property that had to be combated in the public interest by overcoming the resistence of ignorance and routine. We must begin to see these matters in a broader perspective. It should also be noted that these works ignored the demographic factor.

The peasant problem has been studied more broadly for the province of Artois by V. Laude, *Les classes rurales en Artois à la fin de l'ancien régime* (Lille, 1914). I myself have tried to treat this problem within the limits of the department of Nord in *Les paysans du Nord pendant la Révolution française.* Thèse de lettres (Paris, 1924).

II. Here are some indications as to the main problems that should be investigated.

The first of these that naturally comes to mind is the distribution of landownership and size of farms. For the present state of our knowledge on that subject and for the documents to be used as well as the problems they present, I refer the reader to my article "Les études relatives à la répartition de la propriété et de l'exploitation foncières à la fin de l'ancien régime," *Revue d'Histoire moderne,* 1928, pp. 103–30. Some useful information can be gathered from the *cahiers de doléances,* which are virtually the only source used by Kareiev and Wolters. But there is no hope for progress in this kind of study without statistical research. Such research must also be applied to farming techniques; but at the moment a study of this kind exists only for the department of Nord.

The study of the fragmentation of property has not even been begun. Sion's work on Normandy is the only one to furnish some indications; at least it states the problems and suggests a way to study them. First of all, the study of the fragmentation of property is a necessary corollary to studying its distribution. It also permits us to measure the obstacles to the implementation of the enclosure acts. Finally, it may sometimes make it possible to understand the old agrarian economy of the village; for instance, it may reveal the existence of a system of crop rotation and tell us whether it was compulsory. Fragmentation can be studied by means of surveyors' maps and the list of owners attached to the seigneurial *terriers.* For these documents, see Marc Bloch's study "Les plans parcellaires," *Annales d'Histoire économique et sociale,* 1929, pp. 60–70, 390–98. For the information to be derived from them, see, for example, A. Meitzen's *Siedlungen und Agrarwesen der Westgermanen und Ostgermanen* (Berlin, 1895), and especially G. Des Marez's "Le problème de la colonisation franque et du régime agraire en Belgique," *Mémoires de l'Académie de Belgique,* 2d ser. 9, no. 4 (1926).

There is no general work on the collective rights, such as the right of free passage, free pasture, pasturing on harvested fields [*regain*], and gleaning. The most important of these is the right of free pasture, of which the *regain* is one variety. The history of these rights in the eighteenth century is closely related to the efforts by the royal government to stimulate the progress of agriculture, a question that will be considered presently. See Marc Bloch, "Les édits sur les clôtures et les enquêtes agraires au xviiie siècle," *Bulletin de la Société d'histoire moderne,* 1926, pp. 213–16; Henri Sée, "Une enquête sur la vaine pâture et le droit de parcours à la fin du règne de Louis XV," *Revue du Dix-huitième siècle* 1(1913): 265–78; Henri Sée, "La question de la vaine pâture en France à la fin de l'ancien régime," *Revue d'Histoire économique et sociale* 7 (1914): 3–25. The last article was incorporated into a book, *La vie économique et les classes sociales en France au XVIIIe siècle,* cited above.

A vast variety of documents (reports, official complaints by peasants, conflicts, disturbances) can be found in the *cahiers de doléances,* preserved in the National Archives (series H, subseries DXIV). Some of these have been published by P. Sagnac and P. Caron: *Les Comités des droits féodaux et de législation et l'abolition du régime seigneurial,* published by the Comité d'histoire économique de la Révolution (Paris, 1907). Others are kept in series F^{10}, for which a detailed inventory has been established by G. Bourgin in *Les papiers des Assemblées de la Révolution aux Archives Nationales; Inventaire de la sous-serie F^{10} (agriculture),* published by the Société de l'histoire de la Révolution française (Paris, 1918), and also in the Departmental Archives (series C). The judicial archives (series B of the Departmental Archives) should also be consulted.

For the communal lands, see Henri Sée, "Le partage des bien communaux à la fin de l'ancien régime," *Nouvelle Revue historique du droit français et étranger* 47 (1923): 47–81. (This study, like the article on free pasture, was incorporated into *La vie économique,* cited above.) See also the local studies by C. Trapenard, *Le pâturage communal en Haut-Auvergne (XVIIIe siècle).* Thèse de droit (Paris, 1904), and P. P. Lefeuvre, *Les communes en Bretagne à la fin de l'ancien régime.* Thèse de droit (Rennes, 1907).

The *cahiers* and the archival series cited are also useful for the study of the communal lands. The documents of subseries F^{10} of the National Archives have been partially published by G. Bourgin, *Le partage des biens communaux. Documents sur la préparation de la loi du 10 juin 1793* (Collection de documents publiés par la Commission d'histoire économique de la Révolution) (Paris, 1908). Communal Archives should also be consulted for this subject.

For the development of rural industry, see the studies by E. Levasseur, *Histoire des classes ouvrières et de l'industrie en France avant 1789,* 2d ed., 2 vols. (Paris, 1901); E. Tarlé, *L'industrie dans les campagnes à la fin de l'ancien régime* (Paris, 1910); and C. Ballot, *L'introduction du machinisme dans l'industrie française* (posthumous ed. by A. Gevel, Paris, 1923) (Comité des travaux historiques, section d'histoire moderne et contemporaine, publication no. 9). These studies only furnish general indications. Their sources are very dispersed. For studies on this subject, the use of series H of the National Archives and series C of the Departmental Archives will be most fruitful. Frequently, however, documents of the revolutionary period and of the Empire must be used to complete these data or even to obtain any information at all. (See subseries F^{11} and F^{12} of the National Archives, for which there are detailed inventories; series L of the Departmental Archives; statistics of the prefects of the Consulate and the Empire, for which A. de Saint-Léger has established a bibliography: "Les mémoires statistiques des départements pendant le Directoire, le Consulat, et l'Empire," *Le Bibliographe moderne* 19 (1918–19): 5–43.

For the rise in population, information can be found in Moheau's *Recherches et considérations sur la population de la France* (1778), ed. R. Gonnard (Paris, 1912), and in Messance's *Recherches sur la population des généralités d' Auvergne, de Lyon, de Rouen et de quelques provinces et villes du royaume* (Paris, 1766), both of which were written in the eighteenth century. In certain cases it is possible to use the population figures established by the intendants' offices at the end of the Ancien Régime and the census figures of the revolutionary period. It would be particularly important to obtain statistical data from the parish registers, as Messance has done for a few *généralités* [areas under the administration of an intendant].

For the problem of begging, see C. Bloch, *Procès-verbaux et rapports du Comité de mendicité de la Constituante,* published by the Comité d'histoire économique de la Révolution (Paris, 1911). Other important sources are the reports on the number of beggars drawn up in 1790 by order of that committee, often found in series L of the Departmental Archives.

Agricultural production and methods, the agricultural policies of the royal government, and theories of agriculture have been treated in a number of publications. Aside from the work by H. Pigeonneau and A. de Foville, *L'administration de l'agriculture au Contrôle général des finances (1785–87), procès-verbaux et rapports* (Paris, 1882), one should first consult the regional monographs cited above, as well as those on the various intendants. On the economists and their influence see, for example, G. Weulersse, *Le mouvement physiocratique en France de 1756 à 1770.* Thèse de lettres (Paris, 1910), and M. Augé-Laribe, *Grande ou petite proprièté? Histoire des doctrines en France sur la répartition du sol et la transformation industrielle de l'agriculture.* Thèse de droit (Montpellier, 1902). The already cited work by Wolters is mainly devoted to these questions. See also H. Sée, "Les sociétés d'agriculture; leur rôle à la fin de l'ancien régime," *Annales Révolutionnaires* 15 (1923): 1–16; "La mise en valeur des terres incultes à la fin de l'ancien régime," *Revue d'Historie économique et sociale* 11 (1923): 62–81. For the grain trade see Afanassiev, *Le commerce des céréales en France au XVIIIe siècle* (Paris, 1894), and the excellent monograph by J. Letaconnoux, *Les subsistances et le commerce des grains en Bretagne au* XVIIIe *siècle* (Rennes, 1909). For the department of Nord, see G. Lefebvre, Les *paysans du Nord* (cited above), pp. 243–57, and the Introduction to *Documents relatifs à l'histoire des subsistances dans le district de Bergues,* 2 vols. (Lille, 1914, 1921), published by the Comité d'histoire économique de la Révolution.

Documentaion for the state of French agriculture is very dispersed. See series H and subseries F¹⁰ of the National Archives and series C and L of the Departmental Archives.

For the study of the end of the Ancien Régime, the revolutionary series of both the National and Departmental Archives furnish many retrospective indications. Many studies concerning the peasants are inadequate because their authors have neglected these sources. The questions raised in the present article must be studied in their entire context, rather than in a fragmentary manner; and it is a mistake to separate the Ancien Régime from the Revolution.

III. For the revolutionary period and for the sale of national property, the reader is referred to G. Lefebvre, "Les recherches relatives à la vente des biens nationaux," *Revue d'Histoire moderne* (1928): 188–219.

There is no general study of the communal lands, nor even a monograph studying this question for an area larger than a present-day department. Lefebvre's *Les paysans du Nord* (see above) is a monograph for that department and cites the extremely varied sources on which it is based.

For the ventôse decrees of the Year II, see A. Mathiez, "La Terreur, instrument de la politique sociale des Robespierristes. Les décrets de ventôse sur le séquestre des biens des suspects et leur application," *Annales historiques de la Révolution française* 5 (1928): 193–219.

The present article has not dealt with the matter of the seigneurial obligations to which the peasants were subject or with the abolition of the feudal system. For an approach to these problems, see M. Marion, *Histoire financière de la France depuis 1715,* vol. 1 (Paris, 1914); P. Gagnol, *La dîme ecclésiastique en France au XVIIIe siècle.* Thèse de lettres (Paris, 1911); H. Marion, *La dîme eccelésiastique en France au* XVIIIe *siècle et sa suppression.* Thèse de droit (Bordeaux, 1912); P. Sagnac and P. Caron, *Les Comités des droits féodaux* (cited above); P. Sagnac, *La législation civile de la Révolution.* Thèse de lettres (Paris, 1899); A. Aulard, *La Révolution et le régime féodal* (Paris, 1919); J. de la Monneraye, *Le régime féodal et les classes rurales dans le Maine au XVIIIe siècle* (Paris, 1922); A. Giffard, *Les justices seigneuriales en Bretagne aux XVIIe et XVIIIe siècles.* Thèse de droit (Paris, 1903); Soulgé, *Le régime féodal et la propriété féodale en Forez* (Paris, 1923); A. Ferradou, *Le rachat des droits féodaux dans la Gironde* (Paris, 1928).

4
Persistence of "Feudalism" in the Rural Society of Nineteenth-Century France

Albert Soboul

In light of the recent debate among historians concerning the nature of society under the Ancien Régime—was it a society of orders or a society of classes?—and hence the fundamental significance of the French Revolution, it may be helpful to consider the problem of the persistence of feudalism in the rural society of nineteenth-century France.

Even though feudalism was abolished once and for all by the decree of the Convention of 17 July 1793, certain aspects of feudalism persisted throughout the first half of the nineteenth century and sometimes until the very dawn of the twentieth. Essentially, these aspects affected the regions where small-scale farming and sharecropping were prevalent, that is, western and south-western France, where the "agricultural revolution" had scarcely penetrated. These feudal aspects survived in the economic and social reality that was determined by the complexity of agricultural life under the Ancien Régime, by the imperfection and the half-heartedness of the revolutionary legislation, and by the reactionary atmosphere under the Empire and the Restoration. But, as Ernest Labrousse has written, "social change lags behind economic change, and change in attitudes lags behind social change." In the collective consciousness of the French peasantry the memory of feudalism and seigneurial exploitation lingered on, giving proof—if indeed proof is needed—that they were hard to eradicate and that the burden was heavy. The peasants' hatred remained as vivid as ever, producing storms of anger at the slightest provocation, and it was only toward the end of the nineteenth century that its waves gradually subsided.

Annales, E.S.C. 23 (September–October 1968): 965–86. Translated by Elborg Forster.

I

The persistence of the economic aspects of feudalism (which certainly must not be exaggerated) had its legal foundation in the timidity and the legalistic finessing of the revolutionary legislation concerning the abolition of the tithe and of feudal rights; in practice it resulted from the efforts of landowners to turn this legislation to their own advantage.[1]

The tithe was abolished in principle by the decree of 4–11 August 1789.[2] The decree of 14–22 April 1790 stated that the tithe would no longer be collected after 1 January 1791.[3] But—and this was an important restriction— the decree of 1–10 December 1790 stipulated: "Tenant farmers and share-croppers on lands whose harvests were heretofore subject to ecclesiastic or feudal tithes will be obliged to pay to their proprietors, beginning with the harvest of the year 1791, the value of the tithe they have paid in the past."[4] Thus, only the peasant who owned his land was freed; those who rented land, that is, tenant farmers and sharecroppers, remained subject to these levies.

This legislation, as Pierre Massé has pointed out,[5] fits neatly into the traditional mentality of the leasor-leasee relationship. Since the price of the lease made allowance for the payment of the tithe, that charge had to be paid regularly by the leasee, as before. All that changed was the receiving party: payment was no longer made to the owner of the tithe [*décimateur*] but to the landlord; but the obligation itself remained unchanged. This aspect of agrarian mentality obtained in regions of money leaseholds as well as in sharecropping regions.[6]

The brief decree of 1–10 December 1791 was completed by that of 11 March–10 April 1791: "The value of the tithe included in each lease having been established by mutual agreement or by the word of experts, the tenant farmer will pay that amount to the owner every year until the expiration of his lease; he will pay it in cash, at the same time and in the same proportion to the price of his lease" (article 1).[7] The traditional deduction of a certain amount

---

[1]For the details of this legislation, see *Bulletin d'Histoire économique de la Révolution. Années 1920–21* (Paris, 1924), p. 19: "Recueil des textes législatifs et administratifs concernant la suppression des droits féodaux," presented by P. Caron. The article "Propriété féodale" in Dalloz's *Répertoire méthodique et alphabétique de législation, de doctrine, et de jurisprudence en matière de droit civil* (Paris, 1846–52) contains a complete outline of the problem, including its repercussions in lawsuits and jurisprudence until the middle of the nineteenth century.

[2]Article 5 states: "Tithes of any kind and such dues as have taken their place, under whatever name they are known or collected, even those that are farmed out by secular and regular religious communities . . . shall be abolished" (p. 20).

[3]Article 3: "The collection of tithes of all kinds abolished by article 5 of the decree of 4 August last and the following days . . . shall cease, without exception, after 1 January 1791" (ibid., p. 33).

[4]Ibid., p. 83.

[5]Pierre Massé, "Survivances de la dîme dans la région de Bonneuil-Matours aux xviiie et xixe siècles (1790–1834)," *Annales historiques de la Révolution française*, 1958, p. 1.

[6]See Georges Lefebvre, *Les paysans du Nord pendant la Révolution française* (Lille, 1924), chap. 1 of the second part, "La fin de l'ancien régime agraire."

[7]Dalloz, *Répertoire*, p. 101.

of produce [*prélèvement*] was thus replaced by a payment in money, which was more advantageous to the landlord, until the end of the lease term, but this obligation applied only to leases signed before the decree of 14–22 April 1790. Article 6 stated that "proprietors who have signed leases after the promulgation of the decree of 14 April last will not be able to demand the value of the tithe from their tenants, subtenants, sharecroppers, or *colons*." However, a major restriction in this article served to legitimize the continued levy of the tithe, "*unless it is the object of a special clause in the lease.*" In practice the situation remained unchanged for the tenant and the sharecropper.

This mentality and these kinds of procedures also explain the persistence of feudal rights. Since the sharecroppers had already been accustomed to paying these charges under the Ancien Régime,[8] the abolition of these charges turned out to be to the landlord's advantage. Article 5 of the decree of 25 August 1792 abolished "all seigneurial rights, whether feudal or *censuels*, whether perpetual or declared redeemable by earlier laws." No indemnity was foreseen in this decree, "unless these rights can be shown to be based on the original concession of the land," which would have to be proven by the "original act of infeudation or the contract by which the quitrents [*cens*] attached to a property were verified or leased."[9] But article 14 extended the clauses concerning the tithes contained in the decree of 10 April 1791 to the very feudal rights that had just been abolished. *Champarts* and *terrages* [both produce rents], as well as all similar rights that had formerly been borne by the leasee, would henceforth be paid in money to the proprietor "in addition to the price of the lease."[10] The burden to tenant and sharecropper remained the same.

"I leased my land to you in January 1789, when it was subject to various

[8]See Pierre Massé, "Survivance des droits féodaux dans l'Ouest (1793–1902)," *Annales historiques de la Révolution française*, 1965, p. 270. According to the examples cited, it seems entirely clear that the leasee was obliged to pay the noble dues out of his share of the produce. According to Georges Lefebvre, who, however, dealt with a region where money rents were prevalent, "when it came to paying dues, [the tithe and other obligations] affected the tenant less than the owner" (*Les paysans du Nord*, p. 160). The same assertion is made by Paul Bois: "It is the owner who must sign the *aveu;* it is he who must make the payment" (*Les paysans de l'Ouest* [Le Mans, 1960], p. 388). Yet we should find out, by analyzing the clauses of the leases more closely, whether the owner did not pass on this charge to the leasee. On the same page (n. 1) Bois adds: "To this, it could be objected that leasehold contracts always charged the leasee with any quitrents and dues that might be owed to the seigneur of the fief, but this precaution precisely serves to underline the fact that the owner passed on this obligation more or less legally to the tenant." What interests us here is not so much the legal aspect of this question as its social and economic reality; the burden of these rights was, in fact, borne by the tenant farmer or the sharecropper.

[9]Dalloz, *Répertoire*, p. 180.

[10]Article 14: "The dispositions of the law of 10 April 1791, regulating the manner in which tenants and owners will decide between them how to deal with the abolished tithe, which the tenants were heretofore obliged by custom or *under the clauses of their lease* to pay in addition to the price of their lease, will be binding on both the tenants and the owners of land subject to various feudal and *cens* rights, such as the *champarts, terriers, tasques* [produce rents], and others that were also paid by the said tenants in addition to the price of their lease, all of which are abolished without indemnity by the present decree" (ibid, p. 181).

strictly enforced seigneurial rights," a landowner in the present department of Indre wrote to his tenant farmer. "If I had not charged you with these payments in kind, the price of your lease would have been considerably higher. So now I, the owner, rather than you, the tenant, must be the one to profit from the abolition of these feudal rights."[11] Obviously, the leasees, especially the sharecroppers, did not see it this way. They considered themselves partners of the owners, entitled to half the fruits of the land, and therefore felt that the expenses of the land should be borne half and half (the practice of subtracting the tithe before the harvest was divided seems to be derived from this idea). Hence, between 1791 and 1793, there was trouble in sharecropping areas in the West and Southwest, particularly in the departments of Charente, Landes, and Gers. In their protests the sharecroppers claimed that since they continued to pay the tithes and the feudal rights to their landlords, they had not gained anything from the Revolution.

The legislation abolishing feudal rights was once again debated following the report of Merlin de Douai. In the preamble of its decree of the first day of the second month of Year II (22 October 1793), the Convention censured the abuses to which the laws of 11 March 1791 and 25 August 1792 had given rise, "with respect to the practice of owners who demand from their tenants, sharecroppers, and *colons* compensation for the tithes, feudal rights, and seigneurial dues that have been abolished since the beginning of their tenure; *colons* and sharecroppers who are not bound by a lease continue to be subject to charges that are hateful to every friend of liberty."[12] Consequently, article 1 of the decree forbade landowners whose tenants or sharecroppers worked the land "without a lease or under the terms of leases signed after the promulgation of decrees providing for abolition" to demand, "either in kind or monetary equivalent, any rights, whether tithes, *agriers* [produce rents], seigneurial *rentes*, or dues of any kind, whether ecclesiastic, feudal or *censuelles*, in the form of produce, food, or money, whatever name might be given to such dues, and *regardless of any previous stipulations, which shall be null and void,* since they encourage the revival of a regime that is justly held in horror by every Frenchman."

Yet here again, one article provides a loophole: "The present decree does not invalidate the option of proprietors and tenants, *colons,* and sharecroppers to establish by mutual consent *any agreements they deem appropriate* concerning the division of the harvest or the payment of taxes, provided that such agreements are not in any way, either in name or in effect, related to the rights mentioned in article 1 of the present decree (article 4)."

Tithes and *champarts* [payments in kind] thus disappeared, since the Convention prohibited the use of these hateful words, but from the vocabulary

---

[11]Cited by Pierre Massé, "Survivance des droits féodaux," p. 286. The information is based on Archives Nationales, D III, 112 (hereafter cited as A.N.).

[12]Dalloz, *Répertoire,* p. 201.

only. But the economic and social reality remained unchanged for those farmers whose leases predated the "decrees providing for abolition." Compensation demanded by proprietors for the loss of the tithe and of seigneurial rights was expressly prohibited only with respect to farmers who worked a proprietor's land without a lease (for example, the *bordiers* of western France and the *grangiers* of Burgundy, who usually rented their small plots under a verbal agreement and who were normally kept on from year to year under the same terms) and farmers whose leases were signed after the "decrees providing for abolition." Moreover, article 4 left a loophole for landlords: wielding the power of eviction, they might well be tempted to impose "agreements" of their own choosing, thus continuing to pocket the dues in question—provided only that the old "names" were banished from the vocabulary of the countryside.

These clauses were strictly upheld by the decree of 26 prairial, Year II (14 June 1794). When the tribunal of the district of La Châtre (department of Indre) formally demanded to know whether the proprietor was "authorized to make his tenant pay the tithes and dues that were attached to his land before their abolition, or whether the abolition, being general and absolute, should benefit both the tenant and the proprietor," the Convention, upon the recommendation of its legislative committee, cited the law of 1 brumaire of the previous year (22 October 1793) as well as the restrictive clauses of the laws of 10 April 1791 and 25 August 1792 (both of these laws had granted the proprietor "the right to make the tenant or *colon* pay such abolished dues as he had agreed to pay in his lease," provided the lease had been "signed before the abolition"). The Convention also ruled that these clauses were not subject to debate.[13] This goes to show that the Montagnard—but bourgeois—Convention felt very strongly about the sacrosanct nature of the contract, about the unbreakable tabu of the "primordial concession" and the "original title." "The abolition of the tithe and of feudal rights attached to the land, which were after all the most important, did nothing for tenants, sharecroppers, and all who owned no land," wrote Georges Lefebvre.[14]

Not satisfied with upholding this class-oriented legislation, the Directory even strengthened it by reaffirming the stipulation of the decree of 11 March–10 April 1791, which had subsequently been applied to feudal rights in the decree of 25 August 1792. "The tithe and feudal rights," the framers of the law of 27 brumaire, Year V (17 November 1796), noted, "which appeared to be a burden to the tenant, were in reality borne by the owners because the price of the lease made allowances for produce deducted from the total harvest in order to pay these dues." "In order to reestablish a just balance," the Constituent Assembly had ordered in its decree of 1–10 December 1790, "that tenants . . . pay the owners the equivalent of the produce

---

[13]Ibid., p. 216.
[14]*Questions agraires au temps de la terreur,* 2d ed. (Paris, 1954), p. 132.

remaining in their hands following the abolition of the tithe and feudal rights."[15] The decrees of 11 March and 10 April 1791 and of 25 August 1792 had furnished precise regulations as to the dates on which these stipulations became effective; and even stricter regulations were laid down in the decree of 1 brumaire, Year II. "At that point the abolition of feudal rights ceased to benefit the landowners, and the tenant farmers took the place of the former collectors of the tithe and the seigneurs." This statement is obviously exaggerated. Still, the time had come to consolidate the position of the landowners, not only in terms of political power but also in terms of social preeminence.

This is why the clauses of the decrees of 11 March–10 April 1791 and of 25 August 1792 were reinstituted and why article 1 of the decree of 1 brumaire, Year II, was annulled. "Owners who, in compliance with the decrees of 11 March 1791 and 25 August 1792 and before the decree of 1 brumaire, Year II, had stipulated in their leases that they were to be paid, in addition to the price of the lease, a sum amounting to the equivalent of the tithe and other abolished rights, have the right to demand the payment of this sum, albeit without interest, notwithstanding the stipulations of article 1 of the decree of 1 brumaire, Year II, which do not apply to *leases and mutual agreements concluded before its promulgation.*"[16]

This decree has been called the birth certificate of the "bourgeois tithe" or "neo-tithe." Despite the law abolishing the payment of feudal rights on 17 July 1793, their survival in the economic life of tenants and sharecroppers was assured once the backlash of the Year V (1797) upheld the rights granted to landowners by the decrees of 11 March 1791 and 25 August 1792. The offensive words, to be sure, were banished; but the economic burden and the social reality remained.[17]

Once their legality was safeguarded, thanks to the finessing of the revolutionary legislation, these remnants of the feudal system immediately contributed to the climate of social and religious reaction that settled over France

[15]In fact, feudal rights were not mentioned in the decree of 1–10 December 1790, which dealt exclusively with the tithe. It was only the decree of 25 August 1792 that extended the dispositions previously adopted for the tithe to feudal rights.

[16]Dalloz, *Répertoire*, p. 220. Recall that the decree of 1 brumaire, Year II (22 October 1793), invalidated *all stipulations* contrary "to the decrees providing for the abolition of rights" that had been included in leases signed after the promulgation of these decrees. The cut-off date before which these stipulations were permitted was thus changed to 1 brumaire, Year II.

[17]This is not the place to examine the matter of *rentes nobles arroturées,* which continued to be levied in certain cases. Pierre Massé has dealt with this subject ("Survivance des droits féodaux," p. 272), but I do not feel that it is exactly germane to the subject under discussion here. *Rente noble arroturée* should be taken to mean a noble rent, such as a *champart* [produce rent] on the arable land that is sold to a third party, even though the seigneur keeps the *cens* [seigneurial quitrents] on the domain proper for himself. Separated in this fashion from the *cens* and all the seigneurial obligations that go with it, the *terrage* [produce rent] became a simple *rente foncière* [ground rent]. The "noble rent" became a "common rent." As such, the law of 17 July 1793 decreeing the abolition of feudalism did not apply to it; it was simply a ground rent that could not

with the Consulate, reached its high point at the time of the Concordat, and maintained its hold well into the Restoration. The peasants were uneasy in the face of the legal precautions taken by the landowners and the aspirations of some of the clergy, whose claims were growing apace.

The atmosphere in the countryside of western France has been described from this point of view by Pierre Massé, who has made a careful study of the notarial minutes of the region.[18] Certain landowners had not given up hope of recapturing their former rights, even though these had been abolished. Various formulas designed to take advantage of future developments made their appearance in leases and contracts of sale, especially after the religious reaction had set in. "In case the payment of the various dues and payments in kind abolished by law should be demanded in the future . . ." (14 January 1803); "In the case that following the Revolution (sic) payment of the tithe should be reestablished . . ." (22 September 1807). One lease, signed on 9 June 1797 and renewed on 5 January 1805, contained a new kind of clause: "That, if in the course of the new lease, the government should reestablish and reinstate either tithes or other land-charges" (read "feudal rights"), these tithes and rights would have to be paid by the leasee. Similarly, on 29 August 1805, the Marquise de l'Isle included the following significant clause in the lease for the rental of her domain of Saint-Remy-en-Plaine (department of Deux-Sèvres): "In case the leasor should recover the dues and *terrages* [payments in kind] that were formerly attached to the said domain," the present lease would be null and void and new conditions would be drawn up. Such half-disguised hopes on the part of the landowners prompted the peasants to take precautions as well. On the occasion of the sale of a small *borderie* at Chenevelles (department of Vienne) on 14 January 1803, a hitherto unknown formula appears in the contract of sale: "The two parties agree that if payment of the various dues and payments in kind abolished by law were to be enforced at any time in the future, they will have to be borne by the buyer, and none of these sums can be charged to the seller." And finally, there was the overriding concern of public administrators. On 7 June 1805 the mayor of Bonneuil-Matours made an official statement concerning the municipal fairgrounds and its buildings, "in order to forestall the collection of certain feudal rights" that had been "abolished by a wise legislation."

The First Restoration increased the concern of the peasants, who were further aroused by the unwarranted oratory of certain overzealous preachers. Napoleon took advantage of this fear felt by the peasantry; recall the statement he made to the mayor of Autun on his return from Elba: "You have been

---

be amortized. If such a rent had not been repurchased with devalued paper money by the Year III or IV, it survived. But occasionally those who had to pay the "common rent" were aware of its feudal origins and used this argument in court to free themselves of this charge; hence the numerous lawcases that constitute such an important aspect of rural life under the Empire and the Restoration. Massé gives some examples of the more or less prolonged survival of the *rente noble arrourée*, one being a *terrage* that was collected at Savigné (department of Vienne) as late as the Third Republic.

[18]"Survivance des droits féodaux," p. 279.

manipulated by the priests and the nobles who wanted their tithes and feudal rights.'' François-Yves Bernard, in his *Souvenirs d'un nonagénaire*,[19] has described at some length the manner in which the rural clergy of western France pressed its claims. ''At that time most of the new village priests of this area made no secret of their opinions concerning the imminent restoration of Church property. . . . As for the tithes, they made it a moral obligation for their parishioners to pay them, just as they were paid by most of the inhabitants of the Vendée, who paid willingly.'' Hence the general enthusiasm in the canton (Bernard is speaking of the community of Rasley in the department of Vienne) when Napoleon returned from Elba. ''The reason for this enthusiasm was fear that the tithe might be reinstated and that the sale of national property might be revoked—both possibilities being openly hoped for by priests and nobles.''[20]

The Second Restoration rekindled these fears, which appeared to be founded both on the claims of the clergy and on the debates concerning the revival of the tithe.

The claims of the clergy were denounced by [Abbé] Grégoire in a widely read brochure published in 1822 under the title *Des catechismes qui recommandent et préscrivent le rétablissement de la dîme, l'obéissance et le respect aux seigneurs des paroisses, etc., etc., et de leur réimpression sous l'empire de la Charte*.[21] ''The tithe has been abolished by law. How is it, then, that ever since 1814 French bishops have not been prevented from including more and more of such articles in the catechisms?'' Grégoire denounces ''the pretention with which grand vicars and bishops work for the return of the feudal regime in their catechisms by inculcating obedience *to the seigneurs of parishes,* as if there still were such a thing. . . .'' ''Thus, prelates who are in revolt against the basic law of the state want to reestablish, in the name of Heaven, the feudal regime that may well bring in its wake perpetual quitrents, mutation fees, dues, titles, mortmain, utility fees, labor service, rights to jettisoned cargo, produce rents, etc.'' Grégoire concludes: ''A peer of France, M. Ferrand, in his *Vie de Madame Elisabeth*,[22] has predicted that France will one day wish to recover her ancient property. No doubt the feudal system and the tithe are included in this prophecy.''

An informal sampling of the many catechisms published during the first years of the Restoration confirms Grégoire's assertions.

The obligation to recognize the authority of *the seigneurs, the temporal*

---

[19]Published in 2 vols. by Célestin Port (Paris, 1880).

[20]Ibid., 2: 264.

[21]M.G., a.e.d.b. [pseud.] *On the catechisms recommending and prescribing the revival of the tithe, obedience and respect for the seigneurs of parishes, etc., etc., and on the reprinting of these catechisms in the light of the Charter* (Paris, 1882) in 8°, 12 pp. (Bibliothèque Nationale, Paris, hereafter cited as B.N., 8° Lb 48, 2253). This brochure was first published in 1820 in the *Chronique religieuse*, vol. 4, p. 533; vol. 5, p. 1; vol. 6, pp. 89, 455. On the same subject, see *Le Constitutionnel*, 20 February 1821; *Le Courrier français*, 18 February 1822; *La Quotidienne*, 1822, no. 39.

[22]A. Ferrand, *Eloge historique de Mme Elisabeth de France, suivi de plusieurs lettres de cette princesse* (Paris, 1814).

seigneur, or *the seigneur of the parish* is included among the Ten Commandments, namely under the Fourth in a number of catechisms in geographically dispersed dioceses. Here, for example, is the catechism for the dioceses of the province of Avignon (1815): "*Q:* What other persons are included in the expression *Father and Mother? A:* Our relatives in proportion to their age and authority, and all those who are our superiors, such as the Pope, our Bishop, our Priest, the King, the Seigneurs.''[23] The same or very similar formulations can be found in the catechisms for the dioceses of Auch, Montauban, and Oléron (1814), Vienne (1817), Saint-Malo (1818), Châlons, Langres, Reims (1819), and Arles (1820). The obligation to pay the tithe is included in the Seventh Commandment, usually couched in the following formula:

Hors de temps noces ne fera
Payant la dîme justement.

[Do not marry out of season and
Pay your tithe as you should.]

In the catechism of the diocese of Tarbes (1814), this commandment is explained by the following questions and answers: "*Q:* What is the tithe? *A:* It is a part of the produce of the land and of the herds that the faithful must pay for the upkeep of the Ministers of the Church. *Q:* To whom must the tithe be paid? *A:* It must be paid (1) to the Bishops who are the head shepherds, (2) to the Priests who have charge of the people's souls, (3) to Churchmen, monks and nuns, according to their rights and the usage of each parish. *Q:* Is it a sin to refuse arbitrarily to pay the tithe? *A:* Yes, it is a sin, (1) because it is a refusal to obey the Church, which orders it, and (2) because it is always a sin to keep that which belongs to others.''[24] Broadly speaking, the tithe is mentioned in connection with the Seventh Commandment in the catechisms of the dioceses of southern and southwestern France, regions in which sharecropping was prevalent. These are the catechisms of Marseilles, Béziers, Le Puy, Montauban, and Oléron, all of which were printed in 1814;[25] those of Montpellier (1815) and Tarbes (1818), as well as the catechism for the "dioceses of the province of Avignon"; and that adopted by the archbishop of Arles in 1820.

Further data will be needed to show at what exact date obedience to the

[23]*Catéchisme imprimé par l' ordre du dernier concile provincial d'Avignon, pour être seul enseigné dans les diocèses de la province* (Avignon, 1815), 208 pp. (B.N., D14311).

[24]*Catéchisme ou agrégé de la foi et des vérités chrétiennes . . . pour être seul enseigné dans l'ancien diocèse de Tarbes* (Tarbes, 1814), 144 pp. (B.N., D29010).

[25]The catechism for the diocese of Auch (n.d., but "undoubtedly written after 1814," according to Grégoire) brands "those who pay only part of the tithe, give their worst produce, or refuse to pay at the traditional rate, as violators of Church law" (p. 79). This is an indication that the traditional peasant mentality was still very much alive. The catechism for the diocese of Oléron (1814) was translated into the Gascon dialect and into Basque, "the better to impress the doctrine of feudalism on the rural inhabitants," according to Grégoire.

seigneur ceased to be included in the Fourth Commandment and payment of the tithe in the Seventh. The tithe was no longer mentioned in the catechism of Le Puy in 1815 or in that of Montpellier in 1819.

Bills for the reestablishment of the tithe sought to implement these clearly expressed aspirations of the clergy. They ran counter to article 7 of the Charter of 1814, which specifically charged the National Treasury with providing for the needs of the *Christian* religion.[26] The reinstatement of the tithe seems to have been seriously considered in a certain number of Church circles, and the problem was brought to the attention of the ministry in charge of religious matters by letters and memoranda of varying importance. Nonetheless, the ministry was not prepared to face the technical difficulties of such an action or the trouble that this step was bound to cause in the countryside. The administrator's reply to a memorandum from a priest of Cambrai (the date is probably 1825) advanced the argument that the tithes had been abolished "not as the result of an orgy of petulance," but because they represented a combination of privileges for the clergy, servitude for [small] owners, and feudalism for the seigneurs." It was therefore impossible to retain them "once privilege and feudalism had been abolished." Furthermore, reinstatement was "out of the question, because the abolition of the tithe was at the time demanded everywhere in France, because its abolition ha[d] been in force for twenty-five years, because it ha[d] been upheld by all successive regimes, because it always tend[ed] to be burdensome and to lower property values . . . and because any attempt to reinstate it . . . in opposition to freedoms enjoyed for so long would mean to provoke resistance and perhaps plunge France into an abyss of disorder again."[27] Not even an "Ultra"-government* could afford to take such a chance.

Bills for the formal reinstatement of the tithe during the Restoration, then, came to nothing, but the tithe itself (and, to a lesser degree, the other feudal rights) remained a factor to be reckoned with in the economic reality of the regions where sharecropping was prevalent. There it was protected, as it were, by the moral climate of the time and stubbornly defended by the landowners. Feudal rights, and especially the tithe, were to persist for various lengths of time.[28]

The continued practice of exacting feudal rights under various guises gen-

[26]"Only the ministers of the Catholic, apostolic, and Roman religion, as well as those of the other Christian faiths, are to receive salaries from the royal treasury."

[27]Jean Vidalenc, "Le problème du rétablissement de la dîme sous la Restauration. Rapport du 30 mars 1825 (?)," *Annales historiques de la Révolution française,* 1961, p. 515. This theme should be investigated systematically on the basis of subseries F 19 (*Cultes*) of the National Archives.

*The "Ultras" were the arch-conservatives who were hoping to "undo" the Revolution during the Restoration.—Trans.

[28]I am not concerned here with reactionary activities in the narrowest sense, such as the case of a *ci-devant* seigneur who went to court in order to recover his church pew. This case is reported in the *Gazette des tribunaux* of 25 September 1829.

erally did not last long. When stipulated in sharecropping contracts, these rights were sometimes still collected in their traditional heterogeneous form even under the Directory; the sharecropper paid in money as well as in kind, in measures of grain, in capons, hemp, honey, and so forth. However, this situation was usually short-lived, since it was too patently reminiscent of the "feudal" past. Rather more frequently, dues in kind were replaced with more convenient dues in money, and stipulated as such in the lease. Even more frequently, and for the same reasons of convenience, these dues were included in the "gross price" of the contract and absorbed into it. As soon as this happened, they could no longer be traced or measured.[29] Once part of the lease and indistinguishable from the "gross price," feudal rights disappeared almost completely under the First Empire. On the other hand, this period also witnessed a steady rise in the price of all money leaseholds and sharecropping contracts.[30] Those feudal rights that still subsisted were bound to disappear rapidly for the very reason that they were so exceptional.

As for the tithe, by now legalized as "neo-tithe" or "bourgeois tithe," it continued to show vitality, at least in western and southwestern France, where it was most often paid as a compensation to the landlord, who was henceforth responsible for paying the taxes on his land.

Yet the tithe did not survive for long, at least in western France as a whole. Pierre Massé has drawn attention to the case of the region of Bonneuil-Matours, department of Vienne,[31] where a tithe of one-tenth or one-eleventh of the harvest was still being levied under the July Monarchy. Included in the price of the lease, they could be collected without difficulty. But, beginning with the First Empire, the tithe had begun a slow evolution, one that went hand in hand with the change in the condition of the sharecroppers. It gradually came to be nothing more than a compensation for the landlord who, beginning with the Consulate, had to pay the taxes on the land, a cost that had theretofore been borne by the sharecropper. It then gradually disappeared from the contracts, which tended to become less onerous for the sharecropper. At Prinçay (department of Vienne) for example, a tithe of the eleventh sheaf was stipulated for the last time in the sharecropping contract for the lease of the farm of Beauvais in 1834. At that date the disappearance of the tithe reflected the general transformation of the French agricultural system. The regrouping of farms under the impact of demographic pressure, changes in land use and greater emphasis on direct management, and also the adoption of new cultivating techniques finally dealt the death blow to the tithe, which was no longer suited to the new system of agriculture. What the revolutionary legislation had been unable to achieve was finally accomplished under the impact of a new system of production.

[29]On all these aspects, see Massé, "Survivance des droits féodaux," pp. 292–93.

[30]See A. Chabert, *Essai sur les mouvements des revenus et l'activité économique en France de 1789 à 1820* (Paris, 1949). Between 1789 and 1802 and 1817 and 1820 the price of leaseholds rose by about 50 percent.

[31]Massé, "Survivance de la dîme."

By contrast, the tithe often survived until a late date in southwestern France. In 1791 and 1792 its persistence—under the terms of the decrees of 11 March and 10 April 1791—had already caused disturbances in the department of Landes, and in 1793 there were disturbances in the department of Gers.[32] In the nineteenth century the stipulation that the sharecropper pay the tithe in addition to his rent seems to have been the rule in the contracts of Haut-Armagnac; frequent in those of Bas-Armagnac, where it amounted to one-eleventh of the harvest; and rare in western France, although the tithe was levied on wine throughout the Southwest. It gradually disappeared only after 1850. But certain contracts still mention the landlord's right to the tithe at the beginning of the twentieth century; a sharecropping contract at Lectoure (department of Gers) includes this obligation in 1909.[33] In the region of Marsan (department of Landes) certain sharecroppers seem to have paid the tithe until World War I, which shows that such usages die hard. (Furthermore, tradition links this "neo-tithe" to the Revolution, and rightly so).[34]

Pierre Massé has used the expression "teratology of the law" in connection with this more or less prolonged survival of the tithe and of feudal rights. This is certainly true, from a narrow legal point of view. But this survival also sheds a great deal of light on the social structure and the mentality of old rural France. The continued practice of deducting feudal dues in regions where small-scale agriculture was prevalent appears to be intimately connected with the old agricultural system as a whole, not only in its economic aspects but also with respect to its social configuration and its psychological consequences. The "agricultural revolution" put an end to this long career and dealt the death blow to the "bourgeois tithe"; but this simple statement cannot hope to convey an idea of the slowness with which this phenomenon took shape or of the varying pace it assumed in the different regions of France.

II

In the light of history, the persistent memory of feudal exploitation in the collective consciousness of the rural masses of nineteenth-century France appears to carry greater weight than the persistence of feudal elements in the economic sphere. "Why is it that feudal rights have kindled such hatred in the hearts of the people of France that this hatred has outlived its very object and appears to be well-nigh inextinguishable?" These lines were written by Tocqueville in 1856.[35] This inextinguishable hatred had spawned peasant violence

---

[32]See especially Antoine Richard, "Les troubles agraires des Landes en 1791 et 1792," *Annales historiques de la Révolution française*, 1927, p. 564.

[33]Pierre Féral, *Le problème de la dîme, de la coussure et de la glane au* xviii*e et au* xix*e siècles dans le Lectourois* (Auch, 1950), reprinted in *Approches. Essais d'histoire économique et sociale de la Gascogne* (Auch, 1957).

[34]See André Rebsomen, *La crise agraire dans les Landes* (Bordeaux, 1922), p. 142.

[35]*L'Ancien Régime et la Révolution*, ed. J. P. Meyer (Paris, 1952), p. 105. Chap. 1 of book 2: "Pourquoi les droits féodaux étaient devenus plus odieux au peuple de France que partout ailleurs."

long before the nineteenth century. Many episodes of violence—crimes against property, burning of châteaux, outbreaks of fear, panics and defensive reactions, punitive actions and violent behavior of all kinds—in the French countryside, usually occuring in regions of small-scale agriculture, appear to be related to the deep-rooted memory of the hated times of feudalism and seigneurial exploitation, as well as to the fear that they might be revived. This attitude is clearly visible in the judicial documents found in nineteenth-century archives; in a transposed, but equally suggestive manner, it can also be seen in certain trends of the peasant novel of the nineteenth century. In the absence of an oral investigation for which it is now too late, these indications will have to suffice. Had such an investigation been conducted forty or fifty years ago among peasants born around the middle of the last century, it would undoubtedly have yielded reliable testimony.

With respect to the judicial archives, the most obvious approach would be based on an analysis of judicial statistics. In 1827 appeared the *Compte rendu général de l'administration de la justice criminelle pendant l'année 1825* [*General report on the administration of criminal justice for the year 1825*]. This was the first issue of a series that was to be published regularly by the statistical division of the Ministry of Justice and that included the data of all jurisdictions, from police and assize courts [*cours d'assises*] to the high court of appeals.[36] For the subject under discussion here, a detailed analysis of the statistics of offenses and crimes against persons and property would be invaluable, especially with respect to the statistics of offenses committed in the countryside and brought before the rural correctional tribunals. Another, even richer, source is the ample documentary material deposited in the National Archives by the Ministry of Justice, in particular the general correspondence of the criminal division and of the public prosecutors.[37]

Throughout the nineteenth century, peasant protests with antifeudal overtones in most instances naturally became part of more complex protest movements in which the antifeudal reflex was only one component. But whether the disturbances were a matter of defending communal rights in the fields or in the forests or whether they were subsistence riots or protests against taxes, they almost always elicited the traditional reflexes whose roots were deeply imbedded in the past. "Attitudes," Fernand Braudel has said, "are a long prison term." Who can fail to see that the persistent hostility against the Château of the nineteenth century is related to the memory of seigneurial exploitation of the eighteenth century?

---

[36]A.N., Series AD XIX, J 7 and 8; B.N., Lf 107, 6. See also Bertrand Gille, *Les sources statistiques de l'histoire de France, des enquêtes du* xviiᵉ *siècle à 1870* (Geneva and Paris, 1964), p. 170.
  [37]A.N., BB 18, BB 30. See *Etat sommaire des versements faites aux Archives nationales par les ministères et les administrations qui en dépendent* (Series BB, *Justice*), vol. 4, intro. Georges Bourgin (Paris, 1947), p. 87.

The antifeudal reflex is clearly evident in the pillaging and burning of châteaux that took place in July–August 1830 in the departments of Corrèze and Dordogne, where peasant uprisings [*jacqueries*] were a tradition.[38] The rural disturbances of 1848, although diverse in their motivation and their effects, again elicited this reflex. Among the fears and panics which, in March–April 1848 and even more after the June Days, affected various regions of western France, from Upper Normandy to Deux-Sèvres and the Charente, "plots of nobles and priests" frequently played as important a role as the fear of "reds" and "those who want to divide the land." Often triggered by a trivial incident, fear soon crystallized around the memory of the hated days of the past, turning to anger against the master of the château and descendant of the seigneur. On 19 July 1848 the imagination of a child who claimed to have been attacked by some ruffians aroused alarm in the community of Bernay (department of Charente-Inférieure). The tocsin was sounded and the National Guard mobilized in ten surrounding communities; but no brigands intent on pillage and burning could be found. "Soon the uproar of the moment was attributed to the nobles and the priests," and the suspicion focused on a rich Legitimist landowner. The agitation continued to spread: "Everywhere the peasants have risen," wrote the assistant public prosecutor of Poitiers, to strike down "the plots of nobles and priests," which were, in fact, but a figment of their imagination.[39] Nobles and priests—in other words, tithes and feudal rights. On election day, 27 April 1848, in Tournon (department of Lot-et-Garonne) one sieur Bonnefous, known for his staunchly Legitimist opinions, declared publicly that "tithes and dues would soon be reestablished." This statement resulted in a public uproar the authorities were hard put to quell.[40] In his report on the elections to the General Assembly of May 1840 the public prosecutor of Bordeaux explained the success of the "socialists" of Dordogne in terms of "the overblown fears that tithes and *corvées* might be reestablished by the former nobles and bourgeois."[41] The antifeudal reflex had turned into a political awakening. In this connection it would be interesting to compare a map showing the election results under the Second Republic and one showing rural disturbances based on antifeudal sentiments in the departments situated along the western and southwestern slopes of the Massif Central.

When did this antifeudal reflex cease to play a role in the social behavior of the peasantry? It would be important to find out exactly. We do know that under the Second Empire waves of panic still affected the departments of Charente, Charente-Inférieure, and Dordogne, bringing in their wake a whole raft of disturbances that arose between April and September 1868, "oc-

[38] A.N., BB 18 1186, d.3950 and d.3961.

[39] Ibid, BB 18 1462. See also Albert Soboul, "Les troubles agraires de 1848," in *Paysans, Sans-Culottes, et Jacobins* (Paris, 1964), p. 307.

[40] A.N., BB 18 1463.

[41] A.N., BB 30 359, p. 440.

casioned by rumors spreading throughout the countryside that the tithe and feudal rights were about to be reestablished.'' No doubt the feelings of the peasants ran particularly high at that moment, for there was a food shortage, and due to the poor harvest of 1867 the prospects for the period before the next harvest were not good. Nonetheless, it is significant to note that the collective consciousness was still haunted by the specter of feudalism. Originating in the arrondissement of Jonzac, these fears spread to the regions of Barbézieux and Bordeaux. The initial incident that triggered the panic had occurred at Chevanceaux (department of Charente-Inférieure), where, on 13 April 1868, a gathering of several hundred persons had attempted to sack the parish church to which the marquis de Lestranges had recently donated stained-glass windows bearing the coat of arms of his family. This was a clear sign that the privileges of the nobility were about to return! Roving bands went out to the neighboring communities, demolishing in particular the bouquets of lilies which at that season were used to decorate the churches. On 20 April, for example, they burned these bouquets at Saint-Pierre-du-Palais in a great show of fury, for the lily, or fleur-de-lis, was the emblem of royalty and thus of the Ancien Régime. ''Poor peasants, worn out by a hard year,'' wrote the public prosecutor of Poitiers, ''vent their anger on a lion in a coat of arms or a lily branch carried by a statue of Saint Joseph. They all have decided that every community must protest against the return of the tithe and the Ancien Régime.''[42] In order to fix the moment at which the memory of these hated times faded from the collective consciousness of the peasantry, it would be necessary to study the judicial archives over a longer time span.

The novel of peasant life is another testimony to the prolonged survival of feudalism in the collective mentality of the rural masses. One theme, the literary treatment of peasant uprisings, runs through the literature of the nineteenth century and echoes the persistent belief in an ''aristocratic plot'': the nobles will reestablish feudalism. Research on this subject remains to be carried out. May it suffice here to adduce only one rather late, but all the more significant, example. This example is especially powerful because it is not a cold and laborious historical reconstruction, but a vibrant, deeply felt work of art that reflects the writer's milieu in his native Périgord. In 1890 Jacques Le Roy (1836–1907) published his admirable novel *Jacquou le Croquant*. The action takes place at Rouffignac in the province of Périgord, a region where sharecropping is prevalent and where peasant uprisings [*jacqueries*] are a tradition. It involves the château of l'Herm and the old marquis de Nansac, both symbols of ''feudal oppression'' even under the Restoration. But if the author can denounce ''the criminal violence of the most wicked country squires of past times'' and the ''odious tyranny that takes us back to the saddest days of feudalism'' as passionately and as forcefully as he does

[42]A.N., BB 18 1767, d.8502, and BB 24 721.

through the mouthpiece of Jacquou's lawyer,[43] it must be because at the end of the nineteenth century that memory was still so much alive among the peasants of Périgord that a writer could give expression to it.

III

This investigation of the persistence of feudalism over a long period of time cannot hope to be more than a broadly sketched outline. It will be necessary to fill in the details for other places and also to test the hypotheses suggested here. Yet one point appears to be established already. If, in the nineteenth century, feudalism—despite some remnants in the economic sphere—was nothing more than a myth in the consciousness of the peasants ("Myth is that which does not exist in reality," according to Littré), the persistence of this myth testifies to the reality of the past and to the social burden it represented.[44] With the passing of the law of 17 July 1793, feudalism disappeared for all practical purposes, but hatred of it lived on, and more than a century had to elapse before the memory of that hated institution faded from the collective consciousness. Here we come face to face with the power of a myth that proved most tenacious, as attested by so many outbreaks of fear and anger during the nineteenth century. The harsh social reality had turned into the driving force of an idea. It finally died at the turn of the twentieth century, along with the traditional system of agriculture—a transformation that altogether altered the peasant's existence.

At this point I should like to add a few remarks of a historiographical and methodological nature.

It is undeniable that in the last fifty years studies of feudalism and feudal rights and their importance among the causes of revolutionary peasant activities at the end of the eighteenth century have practically disappeared from the historiography of the French Revolution. Georges Lefebvre did not broach these subjects directly in the seminal articles that attempted a synthesis of the rural problems at the end of the Ancien Régime and during the Revolution. To be sure, he outlined the question very succinctly in "La Révolution française

---

[43]Eugène Le Roy, *Jacquou le Croquant* (Paris, n.d.), p. 366.

[44]I strongly disagree with the brilliant but rather unfounded suggestions of Alfred Cobban, *The Myth of the French Revolution* (London, 1955). See also the review of this book by Georges Lefebvre, "Le mythe de la Révolution française," *Annales historiques de la Révolution française*, 1956, p. 377. Cobban's argument is primarily concerned with "feudalism," whose social and economic reality he denies. The Revolution could not abolish it, he says, because it did not exist; feudalism no longer meant anything by 1789. This is to take the word *feudalism* in its original medieval sense. Its reality was much more complex than that. To the men of the time, peasants as well as revolutionaires, this abstract term, which they liked precisely because it was so general, covered a whole gamut of burdens, from the feudal rights that had by no means disappeared to seigneurial authority and the various payments of seigneurial and domainal origin. This social and economic reality was far from being a myth, as the peasants' struggle to free themselves from it and the long-lasting memory it left behind were to prove.

et les paysans'' when he wrote: ''There was a conflict between the general rise of capitalism and the continued existence of seigneurial rights and the payment of quitrents.''[45] And while he devoted two major articles to his own research and the findings of others concerning the distribution and the management of landed property at the end of the Ancien Régime, and again following the sale of national property,[46] Lefebvre did not see fit to attempt a similar clarification with respect to feudal rights and their abolition. The same silence—or the same oversight—is found in Marc Bloch's classic work, *Les caractères originaux de l'histoire rurale française* (1931).[47]

Yet that whole complex of questions had already been outlined, the problem already placed in its proper context by historians who are sometimes slighted by comparison with their more illustrious successors. In 1898 Philippe Sagnac had devoted his secondary thesis to the increased burden of feudal rights and the entire third part of his main thesis to the abolition of the system of land tenure of the Ancien Régime.[48] Furthermore, in 1919 Alphonse Aulard wrote a small and very suggestive, but now totally forgotten, study entitled *La Révolution française et le régime féodal* (1919).[49] So the problem has been broached, but it would be too much to claim that it has been fully treated.

While it is true that every study dealing with the agrarian history of the eighteenth century must necessarily touch on the problem of feudalism and feudal rights, it is also undeniable that we possess few works concerning the various stages of their abolition between 1789 and 1793 and even fewer studies on their survival in the nineteenth century or on the episodes that attest to the continued existence of their memory in the collective consciousness of the peasant masses until the dawn of the twentieth century. In the immense bibliography of the French Revolution—and in the absence of an appreciable number of published volumes of documents concerning special topics on a local or regional level—there is not one general work that elaborates on Aulard's study and furnishes precise information on the nature of the feudal system in its innumerable local varieties. One would like to know just how great a social and material burden the feudal system represented to the peasants—beyond its purely legal aspects, which are of lesser importance to the subject under consideration here—and to what extent it was a factor in the changing distribution of income. One would also like to know more about the

[45]First published in the *Cahiers de la Révolution française* 1 (1933) and the *Annales historiques de la Révolution française*, 1933, and reprinted in *Etudes sur la Révolution française*, 2d ed. (Paris, 1963), p. 338.
    [46]''Répartition de la propriété et de l'exploitation foncières à la fin de l'Ancien Régime,'' *Revue d'Histoire moderne*, 1928; ''La vente des biens nationaux,'' Ibid. These two articles were also reprinted in *Etudes sur la Révolution française*, pp. 279, 307.
    [47]Published in 1931. English translation by Janet Sondheimer, *French Rural History: An Essay on its Basic Characteristics* (Berkeley, 1966).
    [48]*Quomodo jura domini aucta fuerint regnante Ludovico sexto decimo* (Paris, 1898); *La législation civile de la Révolution française. La propriété et la famille, 1780–1804* (Paris, 1898).
    [49](Paris, 1919).

history of the abolition of the feudal system, not only from the political and legal point of view but also as it was reflected in the many upheavals, rural disturbances, and peasant uprisings that, between 1789 and 1792—indeed, 1793—constituted a background for the events of the French Revolution that is not always fully appreciated.

New research in this area is important, both for the advancement of factual knowledge and also for a more balanced appraisal of the role of the French Revolution in the history of the modern world. For it may be that the French Revolution was primarily and essentially a revolt against the feudal system. This is a statement that I, for one, would like to see confirmed by scholarly research at a time when "the social interpretation" of the French Revolution advanced by French historians for over a half-century has been challenged by some authors,[50] while others are toning down the "original characteristics" of the Revolution by submerging them in an Atlantic or Occidental context that does not concern itself with any social content but expresses a distinct ideological bias.[51]

Turning from historiography to methodology in order to place the problem into proper perspective, one must first of all deal with the matter of vocabulary, which does not merely thresh the empty straw of words but makes us come to grips with the very nature of the French Revolution.

The use of the words *feudalism, feudal system,* and *feudal rights* is controversial when applied to the eighteenth century. Medievalists will have none of it. Robert Boutruche has severely criticized this "abuse of language."[52] In the course of an important international debate on "the transition from feudalism to capitalism," George Lefebvre also rejected the use of this term.[53]

No one will deny that feudalism in the narrow sense of the word had long been a system "suffering from the decreptitude of old age" and that it "had already received extreme unction"—to use Carlyle's metaphor, cited by Boutruche—even though the rights pertaining to the rural seigneury were

---

[50]In addition to Cobban, *The Myth of the French Revolution,* see also Alfred Cobban, *The Social Interpretation of the French Revolution* (Cambridge, 1964). And see Robert R. Palmer, "Polémique américaine sur le rôle de la bourgeoisie dans la Révolution française," *Annales historiques de la Revolution française,* 1967, p. 369.

[51]Robert R. Palmer, "The World Revolution of the West," *Political Science Quarterly,* 1954; Jacques Godechot and Robert R. Palmer, "Le problème de l'Atlantique du xviiie au xxe siècle," *Xo Congresso internazionale di Scienze storiche. Relazioni* (Florence, 1955), 5: 175; Jacques Godechot, *La Grande Nation; L'expansion révolutionnaire de la France dans le monde 1789–1799,* 2 vols. (Paris, 1956); Robert R. Palmer, *The Age of the Democratic Revolution: A Political History of Europe and America, 1760–1800,* vol. 1, *The Challenge* (Princeton, 1959); Jacques Godechot, *Les Révolutions 1770–1799* (Paris, 1963).

[52]Robert Boutruche, *Seigneurie et féodalité: Le premier âge des liens d'hommes à hommes* (Paris, 1959), p. 19.

[53]Georges Lefebvre, "Une discussion historique: Du féodalisme au capitalisme," *La Pensée* 65 (1956). See also, *Transition from Feudalism to Capitalism: A Symposium,* ed. P. M. Sweezy et al. (London, 1954).

vigorously enforced on the eve of the French Revolution. Nor is there any doubt that feudalism was blamed for all the hardships imposed by that seigneurial system. But can we not go beyond the cold definitions of dictionaries of law, of legal treatises that only too often disregard living realities and provide us with a static, fossilized, and narrowly legal view of any given situation? What concerns us here is the social dimension of the word *feudalism* at the end of the Ancien Régime, the sense in which it was used, not by the jurists, but by the peasants. With the decline of the institution, the meaning of the word had naturally changed, and by the seventeenth and eighteenth centuries even notaries used *feudal rights* and *seigneurial rights* interchangeably, either from ignorance or in order to simplify. For the peasants as well as for the men who dealt professionally with matters of land tenure, feudalism meant, in the rather fulsom language of the eighteenth century, *servitude to the land,* land that was weighted down with inalienable dues, perpetual rents, mutation fees, as well as tithes—in short, with the *complexum feudale* of the jurists.

It is in this sense that the word was used throughout the Revolution and far into the nineteenth century. Merlin de Douai, an expert in these matters, made a clear statement to that effect in his report of 4 September 1789 to the committee on feudal rights of the Constituent Assembly:[54]

Even though the words *feudal rights* designate, strictly speaking, only those rights that derive from the grant of a fief and are based on a direct act of infeudation, common usage has extended this meaning to all rights that add up to what Dumoulin has called the *complexum feudale* (*Sur la coutume de Paris,* Title I, Ch. 51, gl. 1, no. 1). Thus, seigneurial rents, rights of *champart* [produce rents], *corvées* [free labor services], *banalités* [seigneurial monopolies of oven, mill, forge, etc.], and any payments in kind that have replaced the old labor services, and so forth, are not, strictly speaking, feudal rights. Nonetheless, they will be considered in this report; indeed, I feel that the failure to do so would thwart the intentions of the National Assembly, by which our committee was established.

The abstract word *feudalism* had the advantage of being very general. But those who used it were well aware of the realities to which it referred: (1) feudal rights in the strict sense, among them the *franc fief,* a very onerous charge that had to be paid when a piece of noble land passed into the hands of a commoner; (2) seigneurial authority, marked by the right of justice that gave the seigneur police power which, in turn, was the prerequisite for the enforcement of the *banalités* [monopolies] (the seigneur was the ''first inhabitant'' of the village, a position he was to maintain for a long time, for after the abolition of feudal rights he was still the *châtelain,* or master of the château); and (3) dues of seigneurial or domanial origin, such as the *cens, rentes,* or *champarts.* This was what the peasants meant by feudalism, and it was a living reality. They saw it as originating in violence and as a vestige of their

---

[54]*Rapport fait au nom du Comité des droits féodaux le 4 septembre 1789, sur l'objet et l'ordre du travail dont il est chargé* . . . (B.N., 8° Le 29, 193, in-8°), 30 pp.

bondage. Nor did the bourgeois of the Constituent Assembly quarrel with this popular concept of feudalism. During the night of 4 August 1789 they abolished mortmain and the fees representing it as contrary to the freedom of persons. They also abolished feudal rights because they had been usurped from the State and imposed by violence. But since they themselves had acquired fiefs and were in a position to grant seigneurial leaseholds, they adopted the fiction that the dues represented the amortization of the original price of the land. The peasants did not go along with this fiction, and the result was a full-fledged revolution. For the peasants, feudalism was not a myth, as some historians have claimed; nor did the peasants experience seigneurial domination as that paternal and benign authority which has sometimes been so fondly described.

The historian cannot ignore this living reality of the word *feudalism* in a precise social and historical setting. But beyond that, he must also conceptualize. Any reflection of the historian calls for a theory, and it is only by means of conceptualization that we can hope to lay bare the anatomy and physiology of a society. There is no reason to reject a key word, as long as it is understood that "words have no meanings, only usages,"[55] that words are defined by the verbal network to which they belong, and that, like all other historical phenomena, words assume their true dimension only within their own social context.

Tocqueville saw this very clearly, and surely this perspicacious observer is an unimpeachable witness. He constantly used the word *feudalism* in *L'Ancien Régime et la Révolution* (1856). For him, the French Revolution was essentially antifeudal. Its only effect was "the abolition of those political institutions that had held full sway among most European peoples over several centuries and that are usually designated by the term *feudal institutions*. The *unique achievement* of the Revolution was the destruction of everything that proceeded from the aristocratic and feudal institutions in the old society . . . everything that was marked by them, however slightly."[56] At the end of the chapter on feudal rights, Tocqueville wrote: "Feudalism had remained the most important of our civil institutions, even though it had ceased to be a political institution. Thus reduced in scope, it aroused even greater hatred, and it has rightly been said that the men who destroyed some of the institutions of the Middle Ages made those that remained a hundred times more hateful."[57]

---

[55]P. Guiraud, *La sémantique* (Paris, 1964), p. 122. It is curious to note that the word *féodalité* does not appear in F. Brunot's *Histoire de la langue française* (Paris, 1937), vol. 9, *La Révolution et l'Empire*. It should also be pointed out that the classic treatises of the feudal experts [*feudistes*] usually do not give any definition of this term. See, for example, Edmé de la Poix de Fréminville, *La pratique universelle pour la rénovation des terriers et des droits seigneuriaux*, 5 vols. (1746–57).

[56]*L'Ancien Régime et la Révolution*, 1952 edition, book 1, chap. 5, pp. 95–96: "Quelle a été l'oeuvre propre de la Révolution française?"

[57]Ibid., book 2, chap. 1: "Pourquoi les droits féodaux étaient devenus plus odieux au peuple en France que partout ailleurs" (p. 99).

And indeed, here too, the attitudes of the collective mentality are at least as important as the legal and economic aspects of the institution. Speaking of the French peasant of the eighteenth century, Tocqueville also wrote: "Imagine the condition, the needs, the character, and the emotions of this man, and try to calculate the stores of hatred and envy that have built up in his heart."[58] Hippolyte Taine, a writer whom no one would suspect of sympathy for the peasants, also treated the theme of hatred for feudalism. In a famous passage, he described the wrath of the peasants when France was invaded in the summer of 1792. "For behind the foreigners, they saw the émigrés"—that is, they saw the reestablishment of feudalism. "The agitation was fierce, especially in the lowest ranks, which had borne the weight of the ancient edifice almost alone."[59] Here, as indeed in every historical investigation, the quantitative data that enable the historian to measure incomes and income distribution must be refined and differentiated by the use of descriptive documents. The specific weight of feudal rights is by no means more important than the mood of the people, their collective mentality, and the mass reactions in which this mentality found expression. These reactions constituted the aftershock, as it were, of a great event, testifying to its importance long after it had taken place.[60]

In the last analysis, I wish to propose that we continue to use the term *feudalism* to designate the type of social and economic organization of the French countryside that was destroyed by the Revolution. This organization was characterized not only by remnants of vasselage and the fragmentation of public power but also by the direct appropriation of the fruits of the peasants' surplus labor by the seigneurs, as exemplified by the rights and dues in money, labor, and kind to which the peasants were subjected. Granted, this gives the word *feudalism* a rather wide range of meaning, since it encompasses the material foundations of the entire regime. But this is how the word was understood at the time—not so much, perhaps, by the jurists, who had a clear understanding of the institutions, or by the *philosophes,* who were especially concerned about the fragmentation of public power, but by the peasants, who bore the brunt of the feudal system, and the revolutionaries, who tore the system down. *Feudalism,* then, is the term I propose; not in the restricted sense of the *feudistes* [eighteenth-century experts in feudal law], but as a concept of economic and social history that is defined primarily as a type of land tenure entailing certain economic obligations and a specific variety of social relations.[61] "You ask," wrote Boncerf in 1776 in his pamphlet *Objec-*

[58]Ibid., p. 106. This is an excellent description of peasant life and of the burden that feudalism imposed on it: "Part of the revenue of his [the peasant's] small property was paid as dues to make an income for [the seigneurs]: and these dues could be neither converted nor repurchased."

[59]Hippolyte Taine, *Les origines de la France contemporaine,* 1911 ed., vol. 1, *La conquête jacobine,* p. 176.

[60]For these problems see the remarks by Marcel Reinhard, "Sur l'histoire de la Révolution française. Travaux récents et perspectives," *Annales, E.S.C.* 14 (1959): 558.

[61]This opinion is shared by Pierre Vilar, *La Catalogne dans l'Espagne moderne* (Paris, 1962). See, in particular, vol. 2, pp. 419 ff. It was the historical mission of the French Revolution to

tions to Feudal Rights, "about the origins of these rights and these barbaric laws; you wish to know why it is that no one can own even the smallest plot of land outright. . . ."[62]

For a long time after the Revolution, hatred of the seigneur and hatred of feudalism, a word that had a very precise meaning for those who were subjected to it, was as alive as it was in its heyday in the consciousness of the French peasantry. No peasant, however attached he may have been to the old order of things, to his refractory priest, or even to the person of his erstwhile seigneur, ever regretted the abolition of the tithe and of feudal rights.

In 1820, the municipal council of Auby (department of Nord)—appointed, it should be noted, by a prefect of the newly restored king and hence an unlikely source of revolutionary sentiments—objected to the claims of two landowners who asserted their right to the *flégards*, the trees growing along the border of their properties. "The council does not know whether seigneurs had this right in the time of feudalism. But the Revolution, having crushed the head of this monster, cannot possibly have permitted the continuation of this abuse spawned by the monster."[63] This is an unimpeachable testimony to the peasants' approval of the work of the Revolution, particularly the dismantling of seigneurial authority and the abolition of feudalism. What more is needed to tell us that behind the legal façade of a society of orders, the Ancien Régime experienced the harsh reality of class?

---

destroy feudalism defined in this sense and thus to open the way for the development of the capitalist society. See Georges Lefebvre, *Etudes sur la Révolution française*, 2d ed. (Paris, 1963), p. 354: "They [feudal rights] were an obstacle to the capitalist mode of production, which demands freedom of the individual and hence the abolition of bondage; economic freedom and hence the abolition of seigneurial monopolies [*banalités*]; unified markets and hence the abolition of seigneurial tolls; availability of capital and hence the end of primogeniture, rights of eminent domain [*retraits*], and entrance fees [*franc-fief*].

[62]*Les inconvenients des droits féodaux ou Réponse d'un avocat au Parlement de Paris, à plusieurs vassaux des seigneuries de* . . . (B. N., LB 39 203 [1776]), 46 pp.

[63]Cited by Lefebvre, *Les paysans du Nord*, p. 887.

5
The Deserted Villages
of France: An Overview[1]

Jean-Marie Pesez
and Emmanuel Le Roy Ladurie

On the English side of the Channel the desertion of villages gave rise, very early, to public outcries, accusatory pamphlets, even vengeful couplets, as well as royal commissions and lawsuits. In Sardinia, where the number of abandoned villages is greater than that of living localities, lists of vanished parishes were drawn up as early as the sixteenth century. None of this happened in France. Fiscal documents provide virtually the only record that a village has been deserted, and, as can be imagined, no words are wasted. As far as we know, the disappearance of villages did not particularly disturb either the sovereign power, or the preacher, or the philosopher. The first thing to be stressed, therefore, is the silence of the texts on this point.

But it has been pointed out, rather astutely, that if the documents hardly ever mentioned these facts, the reason was no doubt that the desertion of villages was considered a normal event by contemporaries, precisely because it was so frequent. Thus the argument *a silentio* can be used to support two theses; and it is best not to pursue this approach.

Are there any other quick ways to gauge the extent of the desertion of villages in France? Is it possible to decide whether this was a general trend without becoming involved in a detailed region-by-region analysis? Were these desertions nothing but accidental occurrences of limited historical importance, or did they constitute a major feature of the rural history of France? The answer to this question was formulated some thirty years ago. The important article by Ferdinand Lot on the population of France at the beginning of the fourteenth century provides testimony for the stability of the patterns of resi-

Annales, E.S.C. 20 (March–April 1965): 257–90. Translated by Elborg Forster.
[1]This picture will be developed at greater length in a volume on deserted villages, to be published by the VIe Section de l'Ecole Pratique des Hautes Etudes. [This volume has since appeared under the title *Villages désertés et histoire économique, XIᵉ–XVIIIᵉ siècles* (Paris, 1965).—Trans.]

dence in the French countryside at that period.[2] Lot's patient calculations show that of the 32,500 parishes in existence in 1328, only 900, or 2.77 percent, had disappeared five centuries later. Regional data confirm this tendency toward permanence.

One typical example is that of a large block of dioceses situated in the Paris region and its immediate vicinity. These are the dioceses of Reims, Soissons, Châlons-sur-Marne, Noyon, Arras, Senlis, Beauvais, Amiens, Thérouanne, Laon, Sens, Auxerre, Troyes, Meaux, and Langres. For these dioceses taken together, comparisons over an extended period can be made by consulting certain documents: the medieval parish-censuses [*pouillés*], usually dating from the fourteenth century, though occasionally from somewhat earlier or later periods,[3] and Expilly's population figures of the eighteenth century.

For the fourteenth century, broadly speaking, and for the fifteen dioceses in question, the medieval parish censuses yield a number of parishes that lies between 5,931 (minimum figure) and 6,694 (maximum figure). By about 1750, the same dioceses counted 6,790 parishes. Thus the pattern of settlement had remained intact; indeed, it is possible that a hundred or several hundred new villages had been added.

Generally speaking, Ferdinand Lot's comparisons between the medieval parish censuses and the figures of Saugrain and d'Expilly almost always reveal stability and even growth. This is true not only for the Paris region but also for the Loire Valley (dioceses of Tours, Orléans, and Angers), the Rhône-Saône region, the region of Le Mans, and Brittany—although the data for this last province are rather questionable. According to Lot, the only exceptions to this rule are found in a number of rather narrowly circumscribed areas where a certain "erosion" seems evident. According to Lot, one of these areas is in the extreme southern portion of the Paris Basin, where the diocese of Nevers, situated on the northern slope of the Massif Central, lost about 10 percent of its parishes between 1370 and 1720 and the diocese of Bourges lost almost as many. Other areas would be in Normandy, where the dioceses of Bayeux and Rouen lost 10 percent, and Avranches 22 percent, of their parishes between 1350 and 1400 and between 1720 and 1750.

However, a closer examination of the documents has made us more cautious. By checking the names of the parishes of the diocese of Avranches, we have come to the conclusion that between the fifteenth and nineteenth centuries *all of the parishes* survived as actual settlements—villages and hamlets—although some disappeared indeed as ecclesiastic units.[4]

Ferdinand Lot's figures (whose essential validity may be inferred from the

---

[2]Ferdinand Lot, "L'état des paroisses et des feux de 1328," *Bibliothèque de l'Ecole des Chartes* 90 (1929).

[3]The medieval figures are not absolutely uniform, since we often have two parish censuses, drawn up in two different decades for the same diocese, showing a slight variation in the total number of parishes.

[4]Only the parish of Bois-Benâtre is no longer found on the map; but it is possible that it was absorbed by the neighboring village (department of Manche, commune of Coulouvray-Boisbenâtre).

impression of overwhelming stability they convey) have taught us one preliminary truth—namely, that the disappearance of a parish is not necessarily the same thing as the disappearance of a village. Beyond that point, however, we need a more precise method, one that is based on place names. The unfortunate aspect of Lot's comparisons is the fact that they deal in aggregates. Truly meaningful research must obviously be based on lists of names, which must be individually verified for different periods. If this is done, one will be able to observe a shifting pattern of blank spaces due to the disappearance of certain names from one period to the next, even if the total number of villages or parishes remains constant or even increases.

For Languedoc, the aggregate statistics of parishes can be confirmed thanks to an extensive sampling of place names. In 1908 Louis J. Thomas published a list of the parishes of the region of Lunel and Nîmes, a list that had been drawn up for fiscal purposes.[5] There were 104 villages named for the year 1295. Ten of these villages subsequently disappeared and were striken from the map of communes and settlements at one time or another during the long period between 1295 and 1911.[6] With one exception, these deserted villages were among the very smallest settlements, often no more than hamlets with fewer than 100 inhabitants in 1295.

For the Paris region, another sampling is available in a study of the towns and villages of the present department of Seine-et-Oise, which were included in the old diocese of Paris.[7] The author has found the names of the towns and villages in an exhaustive tax roll, drawn up in 1360, when it became necessary to collect money for the ransom of King Jean le Bon.[8] The author kept track of name changes or "fictitious disappearances"; and his data indicate that of the 304 villages counted in 1370, twenty-five, or 8 percent, had disappeared by 1750, when Saugrain published the figures that were subsequently used by Expilly. Eight percent of these villages disappeared over three and a half centuries. This rather low rate (which holds for most of France) corroborates a certain stability in the pattern of settlement. On the other hand, it is not a negligible rate. There are other statistics to indicate which category of village—small or large—was most likely to disappear.

---

[5]Louis J. Thomas, "La population du Bas-Languedoc (XIIIᵉ–XVIIIᵉ siècles)," *Annales du Midi* (1908).

[6]Here are the names, with the number of households in 1296 or 1300: Aguzan (12 households, commune of Conqueirac); Saint-Jean-de-Roque (18 households, commune of Quissac); Galbiac (20 households, commune of Quissac); Gaujac (15 households, commune of Boisset); Aleyrac (11 households, commune of Claret); Montels, near Lunel (16 households); Saint-Denis-de-Ginestet (41 households, commune of Saint-Nazaire); Ardezan (4 households, commune of Saint-Come); Polverières (4 households, commune of Nîmes); Obilion (22 households, commune of Lunel).

[7]A. Gravier, "Villes et villages de Seine-et-Oise au Moyen Age," *Revue de l'histoire de Versailles,* 1927.

[8]This list of villages was published in the nineteenth century in L. Dessalles, "Rançon du Roi Jean," *Mélanges de littérature et d'histoire recueillis et publiés par la Société des bibliophiles français* (Paris, 1850), 1:144 ff.

Table 5.1—Desertion of Villages in the Paris Region

Size of Village	Number of Villages Counted in 1332	Number of Villages Lost after 1332	Number of Villages Changed to Outlying Farm or Chateau before 1815	Total Number of Lost Villages
50 households and over	69	2 (before 1815)	0	2(3%)
21–49 households	54	5 (before 1815)	3	8(15%)
5–20 households	54	10 (before 1900)	7	17(17%)
Total	177	17	10	27(17%)

SOURCE: Guy Fourquin, *Les campagnes de la région parisienne à la fin du Moyen Age* (Paris, 1964).

In an article published in 1957,[9] Guy Fourquin has studied the villages and hamlets situated to the northwest of Paris (in the region of Poissy, Pontoise, and Beaumont-sur-Oise) for the fourteenth century. A list of settlements drawn up in 1332 permitted him to make detailed comparisons, place-name by place-name, with present day patterns of settlement.[10]

This study permits us to draw some incontrovertible conclusions. First of all, it shows the striking longevity of villages worthy of that name, that is, of places numbering more than fifty households. Of a total of sixty-nine, only two, that is, 3 percent, disappeared in the course of five centuries. This figure certainly confirms the general tendency toward stability to be inferred from the aggregate statistics of Lot. At the same time, Fourquin's study also indicates that there is a *threshold* of size and population below which a certain percentage of villages is apt to become deserted; and this percentage is not insignificant. Fifteen percent of the small villages (twenty-one to forty-nine households) and 30 percent of the hamlets (five to twenty households) disappeared between the fourteenth century and the present. It is therefore at the level of these small units of settlement that the study of deserted villages becomes meaningful, involving as it does an appreciable historical phenomenon; in particular, it is at this level that we find instances of capitalist or aristocratic regrouping that transformed clusters of settlements and separate plots of land into outlying farms or châteaux.

All our research and all the studies we have used for other regions of France confirm both these relatively small percentages of desertion and, among the existing cases, the overwhelming preponderance of small villages and hamlets. In Artois, for example, the tax rolls for the fiftieth-tax of 1296–99 list the taxable population of three towns, forty villages, and five hamlets.[11] Of

[9]Guy Fourquin, "Villages et hameaux du nord-ouest de la région parisienne en 1332," *Paris et Ile de France* 9 (1957–58): 141 ff.

[10]Table 5.1 gives a resumé of this investigation.

[11]These documents were analyzed by A. Bocquet in *Recherches sur la population de l'Artois et*

these, only the five hamlets cannot be identified, a fact that does not necessarily mean that they have disappeared; but the forty villages still exist. The 1299 *terrier,* or rent-roll, of the domain of Artois mentions thirty-one villages, all of which are on the map to this day.

In the diocese of Lyon the reports of pastoral visits in 1378–79 speak of a certain number of very reduced parishes, which is not too surprising given the unfortunate circumstances at the end of the fourteenth century. Nonetheless, only four parishes seem to have disappeared between that time and the nineteenth century.[12]

In Normandy, the *assiette* [inventory of the lands and revenues] of the *comté* of Beaumont-le-Roger, given as an apanage to Robert d'Artois, shows us the patterns of settlement for a substantial part of Normandy, namely the area between Lisieux and Evreux.[13] Verification of the place-names of three *sergenteries* (Beaumont, Le Neubourg, and Orbec) have not revealed any genuine desertions.

For the region that overlapped Champagne and Burgundy and is today in the department of Yonne, the topographical dictionary of Max Quantin mentions a vast number of places that no longer exist.[14] Once we eliminate old chapels, names of fields or areas within the village territory [*climats*], and outlying farms that probably never constituted a real settlement, even in the humblest sense of the term, we are left with 146 villages that no longer exist. But were these real villages? The entire area had only ten parishes or chapels of ease.* The other localities were hamlets, and ephemeral hamlets at that, or so it seems. Most of them are mentioned only in more recent documents, such as the *Etat général du Bailliage de Troyes* (1553), and especially the description of Burgundy by Courtépée, *Etat général du duché de Bourgogne* (1783), as well as the documents of the public registry of the eighteenth century.

Similarly, the topographical dictionary of the department of Seine-et-Marne published in 1954 gives us the names of eighty-seven localities that no longer exist.[15] Only four of them are identified as parishes or villages; the others were hamlets or even outlying clusters of no more than three or four houses. Most of these appear to have been abandoned rather recently, that is, during

de ses annexes pendant la période bourguignonne (1384–1477) (Lille, 1956). This study was written under the direction of G. Mollat for a Diplôme d'Etudes Supérieures.

[12]Abbé Merle, "Visites pastorales du diocèse de Lyon, 1378–79," *Bulletin de la Diana* 26, no. 3 (1937). The four parishes that must have disappeared as settlements are Pouilly-le-Châtel (department of Rhône, commune of Denicé), where the parish was abolished at the time of the Revolution; Chaussagne (department of Rhône, commune of Saint-Alban-et-Montchat); Malatrait (department of Isère, commune of Janneyrian); and Vacieu (department of Isère?). All the other parishes that have disappeared *as parishes* have in fact become hamlets and appear as such in the postal dictionary of the Empire.

[13]Bibliothèque Nationale, ms. français 8 764. Published by H. de Frondeville in the *Bulletin de la Société des antiquaires de Normandie* 45 (1937).

[14]Paris, 1862.

*These were parishes served by an ambulatory priest, or *desservant*.—Trans.

[15]H. Stein, *Dictionnaire topographique de Seine-et-Marne,* rev. ed. by J. Hubert.

the eighteenth or nineteenth century.[16] Finally, for the departments of Haute-Marne and Aube, the figures derived from historical and topographical dictionaries show fifty-five deserted villages, eleven of which are designated as parishes or chapels of ease, for the Haute-Marne, and seventy-eight deserted localities, fourteen of which are parishes and chapels of ease, for Aube.[17] It is only in the provinces of eastern France, essentially in Alsace, and in the mountainous regions of the Southeast that we encounter the relatively frequent desertion of more substantial parishes and villages.

Speaking of the lost village of Malzey[18] (and this was, once again, a very small settlement), P. Marthelot remarked that "at the end of the Middle Ages and subsequently in the early modern period, a profusion of new settlements sprung up, somewhat helter-skelter, within the normal pattern of settlement; but these settlements were extremely vulnerable to every crisis that arose, such as wars and economic, and especially demographic, crises."[19] Our own findings to date generally confirm this opinion. It should be added that this does not make it any less interesting to study the deserted villages of France. But perhaps such research should encompass the entire history of settlement, for in France the lost villages appear to be no more than the fallout of a complex evolution that favored some population centers at the expense of others, leading to progressive concentration in some places and accentuated dispersal in others.

It is not easy to perceive the causes for the desertion of a village. On this point the documents are usually silent. Popular traditions, which are frequently adopted by local scholars, are generally more eloquent, but not always very reliable. But both the tradition and the documents always mention the same facts as leading to desertion: violent destruction by natural causes or by the hand of man, that is, floods, silting, fire, epidemics, or especially, war.

Destruction by natural catastrophe, while sometimes real enough and authentically documented,[20] was too rare to deserve the historian's attention. We can put it aside here. War and epidemics, on the other hand, contributed greatly to desertion. But to attribute the definitive desertion of villages to these factors does not tell the whole story. For what are we to make of the fact

[16]Three of the four "real" villages seem to have disappeared early, before the end of the thirteenth century, and the documents seem to indicate that the eighteen hamlets were in ruins by the end of the fourteenth or the beginning of the fifteenth century.

[17]Essentially T. Boutiot and E. Socard, *Dictionnaire topographique du département de l'Aube* (Paris, 1874); A. Roserot, *Dictionnaire historique de la Champagne méridionale* (Langres, 1942–48); E. Jolibois, *La Haute-Marne ancienne et moderne* (Chaumont, 1858); J. Abraham, "Anciens villages ou hameaux détruits sur le territoire du départment de la Haute-Marne," *Bulletin de la Société Haut-Marnaise des études locales*, 1927–30, pp. 499–505.

[18]Malzey: department of Meurthe-et-Moselle, commune of Aingeray, canton of Toul.

[19]P. Marthelot, "Géographie et histoire agraires," *Mémoires des Annales de l'Est* 21, p. 42.

[20]An article to be published in the volume on deserted villages by the Ecole Pratique des Hautes Etudes (see n. 1, above) will cite a certain number of villages destroyed by floods, glaciers, or sand.

that in the close vicinity of such abandoned villages there are other localities that were just as brutally destroyed by passing armies or emptied of their population by the plague and yet recovered and flourish to this day? In the final analysis, then, we must endeavor to explain a differential evolution, a process of natural selection in which certain centers of settlement fell by the wayside, while others survived. The villages deserted in times of war were not the only ones destroyed, but they were forgotten when it came to rebuilding. Other causes were working against them, but of these we hear nothing in the texts.

If we wish to shed some light on these causes, we must first make sure that we know when a village was abandoned. A date will enable us to focus on the circumstances, the combination of factors that led to the death of the village. Yet even if we have established at least the approximate date of a desertion, we may still be off the mark, for villages die slowly. It is therefore important to find out when the process of desertion began. In Artois, the village of Mussent, near Aire-sur-La-Lys, had been replaced by a single farm by the end of the nineteenth century. On the Cassini map [late eighteenth century] it is shown as a hamlet, but in 1739 it was still the center of a parish. In 1698 the intendant Bignon reported that this village had only twenty-five inhabitants. A text of 1475 tells us that Mussent was "poor; there used to be 12 or 16 households, but now there are only 5 or 6 households of poor people."[21] But then, twelve or sixteen households is not very much for a parish either. Earlier texts still speak of the *villa* of "Mussehem" in 1304, and even in 1181, although there are no indications as to its size. Where, then, shall we place the decisive date? In the eighteenth century when the parish was abolished? In the fifteenth century, when its population declined by half or even two-thirds? Or in an even earlier period, since the parish was already very small in the fifteenth century? Shall we say that war marked the beginning of the end, or was the migration to the cities at the end of the nineteenth century the determining factor?

The fact is that it is not easy to kill a village; it often takes a whole series of causes, all converging on the same spot. Take the case of Milly, a village in Poitou, which had definitively disappeared by 1872. At that date, Milly consisted of a single house, which was in turn abandoned in 1896. This village was an enclave in the province of Poitou, but it belonged to the duchy of Anjou. For this reason it was difficult to obtain salt there, and according to a document of the eighteenth century, this is why a certain number of inhabitants left. Another plausible motive is Milly's location at the bottom of a valley, which was a flood plain and, furthermore, had an unhealthy climate. It should be added that while the most important resource of the inhabitants was sheep raising, the pastures were on a plateau rather far from the village. Finally, the roads that were built in the nineteenth century avoided deep

---

[21]Cited by Bocquet, *Recherches sur la population de l'Artois.*

valleys and passed along the plateau, thus favoring the neighboring village of Liniers, which eventually absorbed the population of Milly.[22] All of these causes played their part, but only their combination spelled the end of the village.

But this case concerns a recent period; the risk of error is obviously much greater for desertions that were completed at earlier dates. Nonetheless we must not permit this risk, compounded by the gaps in our information, to deter us. Our next task consists in outlining a chronology of the desertion of villages in France.

Villages Deserted before the Beginning of the Fourteenth Century

The earliest desertions (before the fourteenth century) are the least well known. The scarcity and the disparate nature of the documentary material practically rule out any statistical evaluation and only provide us with circumstantial evidence concerning the causes, dates, and geographical distribution of the phenomenon. There is reason to believe that the incidence of these earliest desertions has hitherto been underestimated. Such information as we do have for a very few regions indicates that the number of cases is rather considerable.[23]

The centuries during which clearing took place on a large scale were, above all, a time that saw the creation of new settlements, when new villages sprang up everywhere and the population was rising. But sometimes this great movement of conquest went hand in hand with the demise of existing localities. New settlements were often created in an atmosphere of anarchy and aroused as much suspicion and hostility as enthusiasm. Moreover, they were not always very well planned. In the thirteenth century there were areas that recent settlers on cleared lands eventually abandoned in order to return to their place of origin. Altogether, such settlements lasted as long as the mobility of the rural world. Most of the earliest desertions can be attributed to this mobility of peasant society which, in turn, must be seen as a corollary to the widespread clearing undertaken at that period.

"New towns" [villeneuves], for example, took in more than merely the surplus population of the existing villages. And they had more to offer than new land. Indeed, in many cases the conquest of new land had nothing to do with their creation. The founder of such a settlement was interested in augmenting his revenues by increasing the number of inhabitants paying dues and taxes, even to the detriment of neighboring seigneurs and existing localities. The freedoms offered to the inhabitants of new villages were granted for this

---

[22]Cf. A. Dernier, "Un village disparu au xixe siècle: Milly," *Bulletin de la Société des antiquaires de l'Ouest* 9 (1931): 50–56.
[23]Cf. table 5.2, p. 86.

purpose. New towns thus offered advantages that were apt to diminish the population of neighboring villages. Were such localized migrations enough to lead to the complete desertion of villages? One hesitates to say so. All we can say is that we do see the disappearance of villages located near new towns or *bastides* [farms, or granges] at the very time when new towns were founded.

A rather sizable number of new towns and *bastides* also disappeared; and even though they were not all abandoned at the same period, one is tempted to place them in a separate category. For it is likely that, because they were founded at so late a date, they were rather fragile and thus more apt to fall prey to the various factors of destruction.

Abandoned villages in the vicinity of new towns, and abandoned or simply aborted new towns, are among the types of deserted village frequently found in Champagne.

On the immediate outskirts of Reims, two new towns sprang up about 1240. La Neuville-les-Pomacle was founded by the cathedral chapter of Notre-Dame, and Beaumetz was founded by Thomas de Beaumetz, provost of the chapter and future archbishop of Reims.[24] In the same region several villages disappeared in the thirteenth century, namely Bavisy near Brimont, Anserières near Fresne and Pomacle, and Mairy in the territory of Witry; and near Caurel, Coulevreux, as well as probably Courtmartin, which was still mentioned in 1263 but does not appear in the list of villages drawn up at the beginning of the fourteenth century.[25] We cannot assert categorically that the competition of these two new settlements killed the five villages, since we have no proof for such a statement. But we do know that these new settlements were founded rather late and that they are among the very last cases of collective clearing by means of the creation of new towns. Moreover, these new towns were located in a particularly densely populated area, especially at that period. In addition to the five villages cited above, ten others disappeared at a later date (while fifteen are still in existence). In this manner the two new towns could only prosper at the expense of neighboring settlements.

We also know that the creation of these towns led to serious disputes between the founders and other seigneurs, who were masters of the existing villages. The Benedictine fathers of Saint-Thierry, in particular, lodged a complaint protesting the departure of twenty of the peasants belonging to their manse who had moved to the new village of Beaumetz.

In any case, the settlements founded toward the end of this period often did not last very long. By 1278 Beaumetz was reduced to a *villula,* and after that date it disappeared from the texts altogether. La Neuville was to survive

[24]La Neuville-les-Pomacle (or les-Burigny): department of Marne, commune of Caurel, canton of Bourgogne; Beaumetz: department of Marne, commune of Merfy, canton of Bourgogne.
[25]For these villages, see A. Longnon, ed., *Dictionnaire topographique* (Paris, 1874), as well as H. Jadart and L. Demaison, *Répertoire archéologique de l'arrondissement de Reims,* 2 vols. (Reims, 1911, 1933), and especially the study by Abbé Dessailly, *Histoire de Witry-les-Reims et les villages détruits qui relevaient de son église* (Reims, 1867).

longer, but between 1522 and 1533 it too disappeared.[26] Nor were these the only deserted new towns. The topographical dictionary of the department of Marne permits us to note at least five additional cases.[27] No doubt some of these new villages had too little land to withstand the crises of the fourteenth and fifteenth centuries. But others probably never amounted to real villages; they were still-born, as it were, since they did not fulfill the expectations of their founding seigneurs and thus came to grief in short order.

This must have been the fate of some of the deserted villages of Haute-Marne. The village of Montcignon, for example, is only known to us from the partnership contract concluded between the cathedral chapter of Langres and the priory of Saint-Geosmes in view of its founding.[28] In the twelfth century, Poisat near Langres was founded conjointly by the seigneur of Marac, the Knights Templar of Morment, and the bishop of Langres. But these seigneurs, or their heirs, had a falling out, and Poisat appears for the last time in a contract of 1269, which attempts to settle their differences. Shortly thereafter the inhabitants left the village and settled at Marac.[29] Saint-Julien-sur-Rognon is a new town that is known to us only through its foundation by the Abbey of La Crète between 1220 and 1240. Again, this town was created late in the period.[30] Finally, in 1220 the countess of Champagne and the abbot of Septfontaines concluded an agreement for the building of two new villages on the site of the granges of Bugnémont and Roidon; but it appears that these plans came to nothing, since these two localities were never known to be anything but farms.[31] This, then, is a matter of clearings that were not carried out, which is not surprising in view of the chilly environment of the plateaus of Langres and the region of Bassigny, both still largely covered with forests to this day.

Also on the forbidding heights of Haute-Marne we find evidence, even in the twelfth century, of the most important factor leading to the desertion of villages, namely domain building. In this area, which clearly belonged to the sphere of influence of Clairvaux and Morimond, the domain builder was none other than the Cistercian order. We know that as early as the thirteenth century the White Friars were accused of hoarding land and driving away those who

[26]It no longer existed in 1539. Cf. A.D. [Archives départementales], Marne, G. 1101 (according to the printed inventory).

[27]La Neuville near Villiers-en-Argonne; La Neuville near Herpont; La Neuville near Sept-Saulx; La Neuville near Warmeriville; and La Neuville-au-Temple, in the territory of Dampierre.

[28]Abraham, "Anciens villages en Haute-Marne" (Montcignon near Saint-Vallier-sur-Marne; department of Haute-Marne, canton of Langres).

[29]Ibid. (Poisat: department of Haute-Marne, commune of Marac, canton of Langres).

[30]R. A. Bouillevaux, *Notice historique sur Benoitvaux et les villages du Val-de-Rognon* (Chaumont, 1851). Saint-Julien-sur-Rognon: department of Haute-Marne, commune of Bourdons-sur-Rognon, canton of Andelot.

[31]Abraham, "Anciens villages en Haute-Marne." Bugnémont: department of Haute-Marne, commune of Roche-sur-Rognon, canton of Doulaincourt; Roidon: commune of Rochefort, canton of Andelot.

lived around their granges. In a recent study,[32] Jean Batany has shown that the Cluniacs, in their prolonged quarrel with the Cistercians, were particularly resentful of these activities, accusing the White Friars of doing away with parishes in order to build their granges.

A thousand churches I can count
Where their granges now are found,

wrote the monk Guiot. Is this more than a polemical argument? In England, at least, this accusation was perfectly justified.[33] We think it is justified for France, too. It is not enough, of course, to find a deserted site in the proximity of an abbey to attribute the entire responsibility to the friars.[34] But if after a certain date what used to be a village appears in the charters as a simple grange, such an assumption would seem to be justified, although conclusive proof is lacking. This is also true if a village disappears shortly after having been given to an abbey (*post hoc, ergo propter hoc?*). Part of the land belonging to the village of Chavagne,[35] for instance, was given to the abbey of Auberive in 1136; and at the very beginning of the thirteenth century we no longer hear of a village or parish but only of the land which, by that time, belonged almost entirely to Auberive. Part of the hamlet of Espauthères, situated near Chavagne, was given to the same abbey in 1198; it is no longer mentioned in the texts after 1214. Magnil, a village belonging to the Abbey of La Crète in 1121, was destroyed at the end of the twelfth century.[36] In the immediate vicinity of Clairvaux, the village of Perrecin, which had belonged to the abbey since 1145, disappears from the sources after 1189.[37] The parish

---

[32]Jean Batany, "Les moines blancs dans les états du monde (XIIIᵉ–XIVᵉ siècles)," *Cîteaux* 15 (1964): 10 ff.

[33]Cf. R. A. Donkin, "Settlement and Depopulation on Cistercian Estates during the Twelfth and Thirteenth Centuries, Especially in Yorkshire," *Bulletin of the Institute of Historical Research*, 1960. Germany also saw the depopulation of certain villages by the Cistercians. Cf. Georges Duby, *L'économie rurale et la vie des campagnes dans l'Occident médiéval* (1962), who cites the findings of Epperlein. Similar cases can also be found in Italy, at least in the San Pietro Patrimony (according to P. Toubert), and in Poland. Cf. S. Trawkowski, *Gospodarka wiekiej wlasnosci cysterskiej na dolnum slasku w XIII wieku* [The Management of the Cicercian Landed Estates in Lower Silesia in the Thirteenth Century] (Warsaw, 1959).

[34]When it was founded in 1131, the Cistercian Abbey of La Buissière (La Bussière, department of Côte-d'Or, canton of Pouilly-en-Auxois) was established on the site of an old village. Had this village totally disappeared by that date? Subsequently, the abbey moved to another location, and the site was occupied by one of its granges. Similarly, the Abbey of Fontenay (department of Côte-d'Or, commune of Marmagne, canton of Montbard) seems to have taken over the terrain of an older village. This village had a church and at least one chapel, which was dedicated to Saint Laurence. Cf. J. Richard, "Les débuts de la Buissière et de Fontenay," *Les débuts des abbayes cisterciennes* (XXIVe congrès de l'Association bourguignonne des Sociétés Savantes, 1953).

[35]Department of Haute-Marne, near Chameroy.

[36]Department of Haute-Marne, commune of Bourdons-sur-Rognon.

[37]R. Fossier, "Le plateau de Langres et la fondation de Clairvaux," *Bernard de Clairvaux*, vol. 3 (Paris: commission d'histoire de l'ordre de Cîteaux, 1953). The author cites this old village among a number of others but does not feel that the friars of Clairvaux were responsible for its disappearance.

of Villenesse was given first to Molesne and then to the Cistercian abbey of
Mores,[38] located very close to the village. By the end of the twelfth century
the documents mention only the *finage* [cultivated land] of Villenesse. There
are even more clear-cut cases; Vière is mentioned as a village with a church in
the cartulary of Montiers-en-Argonne; by 1148 it no longer exists, and in its
place we find a grange called Outrivière belonging to the same abbey
("grangia que dicitur Ultravera").[39] We also know of Saint-Porcaire, a village in the vicinity of the Abbey of Pontigny, present department of Yonne.
The village was destroyed in 1119 and reduced to a grange of the abbey. The
monk Guiot may have exaggerated, but his charges against the Cistercian
friars were not unfounded.[40]

There is reason to believe that some of the earlier desertions must be laid
not to the failure of clearing but, on the contrary, to its success. The villages
that disappeared from the old frontiers of colonization may have fallen victim
to temporary halts or even setbacks in that conquest. But it is equally possible
that the great waves of colonization swept away these marginal settlements,
which proved to be no more than way stations in the conquest of new land.

In northern Artois the waterbound region of the coastal plain was not
colonized before the twelfth century; the first abbeys were built there only at
the very end of the eleventh century (La Capelle, 1090). By the twelfth
century, villages were already beginning to disappear from this region. Today
there are four parishes in the region of Bredenarde: Audruicq, Nortkerke,
Zutkerque, and Polincove. A charter of Count Charles the Good reveals the
existence of a fifth parish in 1119: "in parochiis de Bredenarda, scilicet de
Nortkerke, de Sudkerke, de Ouderwich, de Pullingahove et de Furfres." This
is the only known reference to this "Furfres." Moreover, de Loisne believes
that before it designated the small "pagus" of Audruicq, *Bredenarde* was also
the name of a parish, and he cites two charters from the beginning of the
eleventh century to prove his contention.[41] These two villages, then, which
were founded about 1090 at the earliest, must have disappeared again by the
twelfth century. They fell victim, not so much to aggressive clearing as to
human mobility, which carried the population further and further north into

---

[38]Mores: department of Aube, commune of Celles. Another village, Chenevières, whose
church was still mentioned in the cartulary of Montiers in 1233, had become one grange, with a
house and a chapel, in the fourteenth century. (Department of Marne, commune of Givry-en-
Argonne).

[39]*Dictionnaire topographique de la Marne*, s.v. "Outrivière" and "Vière." (Outrivière: department of Marne, commune of Noirlieu).

[40]There are some isolated cases of desertions due to domain building in which lay seigneurs
played the most important role. Some examples of this can be found in the study of the Woëvre
region of Lorraine by Marcel Grosdidier de Matons, *Bulletin de géographie du Comité des
Travaux historiques et scientifiques* 40 (1925). The fate of the villages of Woëvre cited there
shows certain similarities to the lost English villages studied by Maurice Beresford. In England,
the village land was converted to pastures; in the Woëvre, the fields were irrigated.

[41]De Loisne, "Les anciennes localités disparues du Pas-de-Calais," *Mémoires de la Société
des antiquaires de France*, 1906, pp. 57–133.

the heart of the marshes. These are not aborted new towns, but villages that were left behind by the advancing frontier of colonization. Further to the west, in the region of Guines and Ardres, colonized land was part of a narrow strip wedged between the forest of Guines and Licques and the marshes of the coastal zone. Here again, such hamlets as Courtalon, Rorichove, Ophove, Rigewogue, and Selnesse disappeared very early.[42] Later, that is in the fourteenth and fifteenth centuries, other hamlets, and even parishes, disappeared as well, so that the total number of deserted settlements comes to more than twenty. And yet this region continued to show a remarkably high concentration of villages. It therefore seems likely that with the advancing colonization of the marshes, settlements became less concentrated as the population moved toward the newly conquered areas.

Desertions of the Fourteenth and Fifteenth Centuries

Beginning with the fourteenth century, our documentation is more plentiful. We have lists of households and also parish censuses that permit us to draw up lists of villages and to locate the gaps created in the course of time. The documents of the early fourteenth century show the patterns of settlement prior to the great crisis of the end of the Middle Ages, an economic crisis compounded by famines, the Black Death, and the Hundred Years' War. One might expect that these scourges, especially the loss of population, would have brought about a considerable contraction in the pattern of settlement. On the strength of this assumption, Wilhelm Abel included the French countryside in his treatment of the *Wüstungen* [deserted countryside].[43] It appears, however, that in the main Abel's documentation applies almost exclusively to Alsace, where the disappearance of a significant number of villages in the fourteenth and fifteenth centuries is indeed an incontestable fact.

There is every indication that, even at the end of the Middle Ages, the phenomenon of the deserted village was far from uniform throughout France. The present investigation is admittedly incomplete; due to the lack of data that can be easily systematized and the absence of previous research, it does not shed light on such provinces as Brittany, Auvergne, and even parts of Burgundy. Yet it has enabled us to notice a rather marked contrast between two types of region. On the one hand, we have the areas beyond the medieval limits of the kingdom—that is, the eastern regions, especially Alsace, and the southeastern regions, especially Provence—where the fourteenth and fifteenth centuries witnessed massive desertions that claimed even large villages and parishes. On the other hand, there were the old provinces of the kingdom,

---

[42]Department of Pas-de-Calais, communes of Guines, Ardres, and Brêmes.
[43]Wilhelm Abel, *Die Wüstungen des ausgehenden Mittelalters* (Stuttgart, 1955).

where the network of parishes remained essentially intact, and in those few cases where parishes disappeared permanently, they were usually hamlets. For Artois and Champagne we have a sufficient quantity of statistical data to establish a chronology. Table 5.2 shows that in these two provinces, in contrast to the trend in Alsace, desertions before and after the local events of the Hundred Years' War were far more frequent than in the fourteenth and fifteenth centuries.

To be sure, this is true only if we limit ourselves to permanent desertions. For the provinces within the kingdom were affected as severely as Alsace and Provence—sometimes more severely—by economic depression, the ravages of war, and demographic decline. They too experienced ruined or deserted villages, wastelands, and overgrown fields. But sooner or later—usually sooner, by the end of the fifteenth century—the ruins were rebuilt, the villages resettled, and the overgrown fields cultivated once again. In short, what we have found is not regional diversity due to the varying severity of the crises, but rather an uneven pattern of reconstruction.

In Alsace, any research in local history is bound to encounter traces of abandoned localities, if only in the guise of the *"vieux bans"* that preserve the names of deserted villages from century to century. As far as we know, Schoepflin was the first to establish a list of the *loci destructi* of Alsace. The many studies devoted to our subject since then by Alsatian scholars leave no doubt that most of these desertions took place at the end of the Middle Ages: 137 of the 213 desertions that can be dated occurred in the fourteenth and fifteenth centuries.[44]

In Alsace, the geographical distribution of abandoned localities does not seem related to any recognizable physical considerations; there is no evidence for a process of natural selection of sites by which the most unfavorable locations were eliminated. It is not even clear that there was such a thing as a "flight from the countryside," for villages were forsaken as frequently for other villages as for towns. We do know, however, that market towns and fortified villages, such as Ingwiller, Soutch, Sainte-Croix, Eguisheim, and Ammerschwihr, gradually came to be surrounded by a belt of deserted sites, and this makes it likely that it was the quest for security that usually prompted the inhabitants to abandon their villages. No doubt they felt that the rough-hewn walls of a fortified village would afford sufficient protection against roving bands of mercenaries and highwaymen, for these were by and large the only kind of armies that troubled fourteenth- and fifteenth-century Alsace.

But then we must also explain why the peasants did not return to their

[44]We have essentially used the following studies: L. G. Werner, "Les villages disparus de la Haute-Alsace," *Bulletin de la Société industrielle de Mulhouse*, 1914–21, for Haute-Alsace, and for Basse-Alsace, A. Humm and A. Wollbrett, *De la Bruche à la Sarre, des Vosges à la forêt d'Haguenau, villages disparus d'Alsace* (Société d'histoire et d'archéologie de Saverne), nos. 37–39, 1962. Two other studies are based on older research, whose findings they confirm for two regions adjoining Alsace: J. Thilloy, "Les ruines du comté de Bitche," *Mémoires de l'Académie de Metz* 10 (1861–62), and C. D., *Les villages ruinés du comté de Montbéliard* (Arbois, 1847).

Table 5.2—Desertion of Villages in Selected Areas of France

Department or Region	Number of Villages Lost				
	before 1340	between 1340 and end of 15th century	between beginning of 15th century and 1800	at Indeterminate Period	Total
Haut-Rhin	9	90	42	15	156
Basse-Alsace[1]	4	47	15	12	78
Comté de Montbéliard[2]	2	13	3		18
Pas-de-Calais	28	29	73	23	183
Aube	6	10	54	8	78
Marne	13	40	73	16	142
Haute-Marne	14	11	16	14	55

1. The section of the department of Bas-Rhin that lies north of the Bruche River, including the cantons west of the Vosges Mountains and some land belonging to communities in the department of Moselle.

2. Approximately, the cantons of Montbéliard, Audincourt, and Hérmincourt in the department of Doubs, and the canton of Héricourt in the department of Haute-Saône.

abandoned villages once security had been restored. Can we invoke a tendency toward a more concentrated pattern of settlement, which must be considered a permanent feature of the rural societies of eastern France? And would such a tendency be the response to the collective organization of the land and its cultivation,[45] or to some mysterious psychological need that impels people to live in groups?[46] It is an established fact that in Alsace the crises of the fourteenth and fifteenth centuries led to an accentuated concentration of the rural settlement; but this concentration entailed not only the abandonment of hamlets but also the disappearance of full-fledged villages.[47] There is a considerable difference between these two kinds of desertions, and psychological tendencies or the constraining power of rural traditions will not do as an explanation. But it may help to invoke the power of the peasant community. This power expressed itself in the imperialism of the village community, which was always ready to take over vacant land in its vicinity. Historians have noted the exceptional extent of common land in Alsace.[48] Is it possible that this tradition prompted villages to take over the arable land of other localities as soon as these were deserted, thus increasing their own pasture? Whatever the fate of such land, whether the *vieux ban* remained under cultivation or was converted to pasture, whether it became the joint property of several communities, was annexed by a single village or distributed among a number of them, the fact that a deserted village had officially lost its land was almost certain to preclude its future restoration. The annexation of the *ban* prematurely confirmed the desertion and consequently made it permanent. It therefore appears that fourteenth- and fifteenth-century Alsace, like other areas in other periods, underwent a process of territorial consolidation which, in this case, was not the work of an individual domain builder but of a collectivity, namely, the village community.

In Provence, as in Alsace, the gaps left in the pattern of settlement by the crises of the fourteenth and fifteenth centuries can be explained by the conditions under which the reconstruction took place. But in Provence the situation was compounded by the emergence of a number of long-range trends, whose full impact was felt by the end of the fifteenth century. They included a more dispersed pattern of settlement in the valleys than in the mountains, the (at least temporary) predominance of large domains, the rapid development of

---

[45]E. Juillard, *La vie rurale dans la plaine de Basse-Alsace* (Paris, 1952), p. 131.

[46]Grosdidier de Matons, "Woëvre," cited at n. 40, above.

[47]In the seventeenth and eighteenth centuries more hamlets than villages disappeared. This was another stage in the evolution leading to concentration. Cf. F. J. Himly, "Les conséquences de la guerre de Trente Ans dans les campagnes alsaciennes," in *Deux siècles d'Alsace française* (Strasbourg, 1948).

[48]Juillard, *La vie rurale en Basse-Alsace*. While the author is mainly concerned with the nineteenth and twentieth centuries, he also shows that the common lands were even more extensive in the past, as indicated by areas with *German* place names, all of which are under private ownership today.

transhumant herds, and deforestation. These trends were obstacles to the complete restoration of all the deserted villages.

The results of the exhaustive research conducted by Georges Duby and Gabrielle Demians d'Archimbaud are not yet available, but a study by Edouard Baratier already provides us with the data for a preliminary statistical evaluation.[49] Baratier suggests that the Provençal *Wüstungen* are very clearly localized, indicating that the populations migrated toward the lowlands.[50] Baratier has shown that the desertions essentially involved the mountainous regions of eastern Provence. Within that area, they affected the coastal and subcoastal mountains, i.e., the regions of Esterel, Maures, and the Alpes-Maritimes, all of which were located in the *vigueries** of Grasse and Draguignan, where 19 out of 107 communities disappeared from the lists between the fourteenth and the eighteenth centuries. Above all, desertions affected the highlands of the interior toward the north, wedged between the Mercantour range, the Lure Mountains, and the plateau of Valensole; in the *vigueries* of Castellane and Digne, as well as in the valley of Barrême, the attrition rate claimed 45 out of 121 villages (37 percent) between 1315 and 1765. This is the highest rate we have found anywhere within the present boundaries of France; indeed, this percentage comes close to the proportion of *Wüstungen* to be found in Germany.

During the reconstruction of the early modern period, the rapid increase in outlying farms and *bastides* in Provence sometimes tended to disperse the village settlement to the point of sapping the vitality of its central core. In 1471 and especially in 1540 the royal commissioners [*enquêteurs*] often found the old medieval agglomeration still crumbling and uninhabited—gutted towers, houses in ruins, broken-down ramparts; but scattered around the ancient, dead site, they noted a profusion of new settlements. These were grain-producing *bastides* or, in areas where animal husbandry was prevalent, "granges for keeping livestock." Quite often, the local or nonresident owners of transhumant herds were unwilling to admit that these granges had been erected without permission on the land belonging to an extinct community. This was the case at Esperel, Aurent, Aubenas, Beaudument, Niozelles, Troins, Chandol, Saumelongue, Bezaudun, and Favas.[51]

In Provence, another factor likely to prevent the rebirth of a village was also at work; it was the consolidation of land in large domains which, between 1450 and 1550, were established in places that had been cleared of peasant settlements by the crises. Thus at Pontevès, which had counted sixty-three households in 1350 and was deserted by 1471, there was still no village in

---

[49]Edouard Baratier, *La démographie provençale du XIIIᵉ au XVIᵉ siècle* (Paris, 1961).
[50]Cf. table 5.3.
**Viguerie* is the area under the jurisdiction of a *viguier,* or provost.—Trans.
[51]Cf. Sclafert, *Cultures en Haute-Provence* (Paris, 1959), p. 103, for the grain-producing *bastides* of Aubenas, and also pp. 162 ff. and *passim.* Cf. also Baratier, *La démographie provençale,* pp. 90, 168 ff.

Table 5.3—Desertion of Villages in Provence

Circumscription (Baillie or Viguerie)	Number of Villages in 1315	Number of Villages Still Inhabited in 1471	Number of Villages in 1765	Difference 1765–1315
Bayons	27	11	26	− 1
Hyères	11	2	11	0
Toulon	5	1	7	+ 2
Aix	90	22	88	− 2
Apt	44	20	44	0
Tarascon	27	4	26	− 1
Saint-Maximin	17	3	16	− 1
Colmars	4	0	4	0
Seyne	12	0	11	− 1
Moustiers	30 or 31	9	27	−3 or 4
Forcalquier	58	16	54	− 4
Sisteron	52	8	49	− 3
Brignoles	18	3	16	− 2
Grasse	43	14	35	− 8
Draguignan	65	25	53	−12
Castellane	44	16	35	− 9
Dîgne	68	19	35	−33
Val-de-Barrême	10	4	6	− 4
	625 or 626	177	543	82 or 83

SOURCE: Edouard Baratier, *La démographie provençale du XIII* au XVI siècle (Paris, 1961).

SOURCE: Edouard Baratier, *La démographie provençale du XIIIe au XVIe siècle* (Paris, 1961).

1540; but by that time the seigneur, who was the only resident, had built a *bastide* to lodge his sharecroppers.[52] The same seigneurial monopoly is found at Cadarache, where all the village land belonged to the seigneur by 1540. Only one-eighth of this land was under cultivation, but that was worked by the tenant farmers of the château.[53]

The rise in transhumant livestock-raising may also have contributed to the disruption of the pattern of settlement in Provence. One striking fact can be noted: the very areas where depopulation seemed to be final, and also those where formerly clustered villages suffered a long eclipse and then broke into little pieces, as it were, gradually came back to life around 1540 as *bastides,* or "granges for keeping livestock." These areas correspond precisely to the major areas of summer pasture (Digne, Méailles), winter pasture (Pontevès) or *relargage* for the transhumant herds;[54] pastures serving as rest-stops [*pâturages relarguiers*] are found around Digne, Entrevaux, and Castellane.[55]

Lastly, while it is true that in the fifteenth century the desertion of villages

[52]Baratier, *La démographie provençale,* pp. 89 n. 1, 92, 145; Sclafert, *Cultures en Haute-Provence,* p. 104.
[53]Baratier, *La démographie provençale,* p. 137; Sclafert, *Cultures en Haute-Provence,* p. 102.
[54]*Relargage:* a rest stop on the way from the summer pasture to the winter pasture.
[55]Sclafert, *Cultures en Haute-Provence,* pp. 133–40 and maps, pp. 134–35, to be compared with the revealing maps of the department in Upper Provence, in Baratier, *La démographie provençale,* pp. 206–7.

sometimes permitted the forest to reconquer the land, the irrational clearing of forests that went hand in hand with the economic revival destroyed the soil and did irreparable damage to the higher regions. Beginning with the sixteenth century, the forests of Provence were robbed of all vitality, mercilessly destroyed by voracious goats, by timber merchants, by the harvesters of tanning bark, by chalk-ovens and charcoal-burners; and where solid masses of trees had once stood we now find, not good wheatland, but barren, burnt ground— *la terre gaste*—only occasionally dotted by the ephemeral clearings of the *rompides*.

By ruining the source of humus, this deforestation destroyed one capital asset without creating another in its place. There can be no doubt that in the very long run, deforestation was a factor in the "inter-secular" demographic decline of the mountainous, rocky regions of Provence; it is also clear that once this decline reached its lowest point, the definitive desertion of certain sites was bound to ensue.

In contrast to Alsace and Provence, where the crises of the fourteenth and fifteenth centuries have left indelible traces, let us now turn to the provinces where the *Wüstungen* of the late Middle Ages, though not completely absent, did not amount to very much.

Artois may have been by-passed by the Black Death, but it did experience various murderous outbreaks of plague and was spared neither by the agricultural crisis, nor by the stagnation of the textile industry, nor, above all, by war: every one of the English raids on or out of Calais passed through Artois; in this province, moreover, the Hundred Years' War continued as France struggled with the House of Burgundy and waged almost uninterrupted war against the House of Austria.[56] A remarkable study of the population of Artois at the time of the Burgundian domination shows the extent of its demographic decline.[57] This study documents a catastrophic depopulation between the end of the thirteenth and the middle of the fifteenth century: one cluster of thirty-one villages, for instance, went from 2,067 to 1,149 households between 1299 and 1469.

Yet, on the whole, the crises of the fourteenth and fifteenth centuries left the pattern of villages in Artois intact; in particular we note that the disappearance of parishes was rare. Only the region of Calais and the small seigneurial jurisdictions in its immediate vicinity, such as the Ardrésis, the county of Guines, the regions of Bredenarde and Langle, and the northern part of the *bailliage* of Saint-Omer—and all of these were directly affected by the continuous incursions of the English—witnessed the definitive end of an appreciable number of villages, and even most of these, namely, Bonham, Edequines, Ernonval, and Hebergues, were hamlets; only one parish, Mar-

---

[56]Cf. A. Verhulst, "Economie rurale de la Flandre au Moyen Age," *Etudes rurales,* 1963, pp. 70, 72.
[57]Bocquet, *Recherches sur la population de l'Artois.*

kène, near Guines, was definitively wiped out.[58] We should probably add five villages near Calais to this list, although the parishes of Bodericke, Sclives, and Espellecke and the hamlets of Bowere and Dirlingthun definitively disappeared only by the middle of the sixteenth century.[59] It is quite likely that these villages, in very poor condition in 1556 and gone by 1566, had been seriously traumatized in the fifteenth century and finally died in the following century.

But for the rest of the province, we can attribute only about ten definitive desertions to the difficulties of the last two centuries of the Middle Ages; most of them are not well documented, and none of them involved a parish.

Yet several fifteenth-century documents—a tally of 1414, a census of 1469, and especially, an investigation of 1475[60]—attest that many of the villages of Artois were totally abandoned by their inhabitants at one time or another. In 1414, there were fifty-two deserted villages; in 1475, thirty-one other villages were razed and abandoned. But these were no more than vicissitudes without lasting consequences. The devastated regions were completely rebuilt by the untiring efforts of the peasants. In 1475, we hear that a sizable number of the razed villages had been destroyed once before, only three years earlier. After the second wave of destruction, as early as 1476, the tax receiver of Hesdin was able to report that the inhabitants were already returning and beginning the work of reconstruction.[61]

Robert Boutruche has given another very convincing example of this vitality of the village.[62] He has shown that not even the many episodes of war, which the region of Bordeaux experienced at the time of the Hundred Years' War, were able to overcome the determination of the peasants, even when the disasters of war were compounded by repeated outbreaks of epidemics. Boutruche notes only one case of definitive desertion: the parish of Guibon, abandoned by its inhabitants in 1377, never came back to life.

Located in the Southwest also, fourteenth-century Quercy was undoubtedly the French province most severely affected by depopulation. This, at least, is the conclusion of Father Denifle, who bases his opinion on the study of a pontifical investigation of 1387 and similar documents.[63] Completing the data of this *informatio caturcensis* with the marginal notations found on the lists of

---

[58]De Loisne, "Anciennes localités," and Bocquet, *Recherches sur la population de l'Artois,* p. 260 (Bonham: commune of Sainte-Marie-Kerque; Edequines: commune of Wisernes; Ernonval: commune of Enguinegatte; Hebergues: commune of Nordausques (department of Pas-de-Calais).

[59]De Loisne, "Anciennes localités" (Boderike: commune of Coquelles; Sclives, Bowere, and Dirlingthun: commune of Sangatte; Espellecke: commune of Guines [departement of Pas-de-Calais]).

[60]Cf. Bocquet, *Recherches sur la population de l'Artois,* and, for the tally of 1475, E. Mannier, ed., *Chroniques de Flandres et d'Artois* (Paris, 1880).

[61]Bocquet, *Recherches sur la population de l'Artois,* pp. 123–24.

[62]Robert Boutruche, *La crise d'une société: Seigneurs et paysans du Bordelais pendant la guerre de Cent Ans* (Strasbourg, 1947).

[63]H. Denifle, *La guerre de Cent Ans et la désolation des églises en France* (Paris, 1899), pp. 600, 607, 625, 821 ff.

the ecclesiastic tithes, Father Denifle has drawn up a list of 150 parishes or church establishments that were abandoned or destroyed in the diocese of Cahors. Counting only the parishes, since we can be certain that they represented a village, we find that seventy-eight of them were deserted or ruined during the years 1380–90. And yet it is easy to find seventy-six of these villages on contemporary maps or at least in a seventeenth-century parish census for the diocese of Cahors.[64]

We therefore have reason to believe that in spite of massacres, epidemics, and emigration, Quercy experienced practically no definitive desertions.[65] The reason is that this province in its turn benefited from the emigration of the inhabitants of neighboring provinces. Notarized documents, especially concerning the purchases of land, shed considerable light on this migratory movement. The abandoned land of the *Causse* [high plateau] of Quercy attracted large numbers of peasants from the dioceses of Mende, Saint-Flour, and especially Rodez. And while the people from Rouergue came to resettle Upper Quercy, those from the *Causse*—from Caylus, La Capelle, Doze, and Saint-Projet—went to cultivate the land of the plain.[66] This, then, was a migratory movement that amounted to a descent from the unproductive highlands of the Massif Central to the more fertile plains along the Garonne River.[67]

Most historians are well aware of the facts studied by Robert Boutruche for the region of Bordeaux.[68] The Entre-Deux-Mers, in particular, a winegrowing region and the hinterland of an important port, attracted an immense number of new settlers throughout the Hundred Years' War. New inhabitants came from as far as Spain, but especially from Saintonge, Poitou, and Brittany. In the end, their number was sufficient to repopulate all the deserted parishes, though not to return all the fallow fields to the plough.

Resettling by immigrants did not, of course, immediately restore these localities to their former importance; but even a handful of people was enough to bring life back to a deserted village and to prevent its disappearance. But what if we follow the current of immigration back to its sources, to the provinces from which the new settlers of Quercy or the Bordeaux regions had come, namely the Massif Central and the west-central regions? We would expect that in these areas emigration compounded the depopulation and created gaps in the pattern of parishes and villages. This does not seem to have

[64]Longnon, ed., *Dictionnaire topographique*.
[65]It is rather significant that deserted villages are not even mentioned in the thesis by Robert Latouche, *La vie en Bas-Quercy du XVIᵉ au XVIIIᵉ siècle* (Toulouse, 1923).
[66]Galabert, "Le repeuplement du Bas-Quercy après la guerre de Cent Ans," *Bulletin de la Société archéologique du Tarn-et-Garonne*, 1881. See also L. d'Alauzier, "Le repeuplement de Carouac au xvᵉ siècle," *Bulletin de la Société des études du Lot*, 1960.
[67]Cf. C. Higounet, "Mouvements de population dans le Midi de la France du xiᵉ au xvᵉ siecle," *Annales, E.S.C.* 8 (1953): 1–24, especially the map, p. 23.
[68]Robert Boutruche, "Les courants de peuplement dans l'Entre-Deux-Mers," *Annales d'Histoire économique et sociale*, 1935.

been the case, at least in Rouergue. The list of all the localities of Rouergue on the eve of the Hundred Years' War and the Black Death has come down to us in the *Etat des Feux,* or list of households, of 1341.[69] (This listing was, in fact, drawn up twenty years earlier and is probably one of the documents that served to establish the *Etat général des paroisses*—general listing of parishes—of 1328). There are very few villages on this list that cannot be found on modern ordnance survey maps or on the Cassini maps of the eighteenth century.[70] While it is true that the loose pattern of settlement during the Middle Ages makes it impossible to keep track of every one of the smallest population centers—the hamlets (which were called villages in the Southeast) and outlying farms—it is possible to assert that parishes have indeed survived.

It appears that Normandy was to the region of Paris what the Massif Central was to the Southwest. Normandy, like the Massif Central, was greatly diminished by the ravages of war and mortality. And yet here, too, repopulation and reconstruction were, all told, complete and effective. Fiscal documents that were brought to light by Michel Nortier give the list of fifty-two rural parishes for the viscounty of Coutances, 199 for the viscounty of Caen, 374 for the viscounty of Falaise.[71] Several of these 625 parishes subsequently shrunk to hamlets, many more were eventually merged with neighboring parishes (usually about the beginning of the nineteenth century), but none of them has physically disappeared.

But the date 1365 came *after* a critical period, which may be the reason for a contrast with the preceding period. While desertions of Norman villages virtually never occurred between 1365 and the end of the nineteenth century, it does appear that this phenomenon was not absolutely negligible during the period between the end of the thirteenth century and 1365, short as it was. For the viscounties of Caen and Falaise, Michel Nortier is in a position to compare the figures of the fourteenth century with a list of parishes he found in a collection of the customary laws of Normandy dating, most probably, from the preceding century.[72] This comparison does show a certain "falling off," since fourteen localities that were alive in the thirteenth century were no longer counted in 1365. But here again, caution is indicated, for some of these localities are difficult to identify, and we cannot be sure that all of them were actual parishes. Moreover, the proportion of villages lost between the thirteenth century and 1365 would be quite small in any case, amounting to only 2.5 percent.

[69]Auguste Molinier, ed., in *Bibliothèque de l'Ecole des Chartes* 44 (1883).

[70]This may be the case for Manhaval (region of Mur-de-Barrez ?), Aynières (near Sainte-Radegonde), and La Roumière (near Montjaux).

[71]Michel Nortier, "Aperçus sur la population de la vicomté de Coutances vers 1365–1368," *Notices, mémoires, et documents publiés par la Société d'archéologie et d'histoire naturelle de la Manche* 65 (1957). See also M. Nortier, "Recherches sur l'étendue, les subdivisions, et la population des vicomtés de Caen et de Falaise au xive siècle," *Bulletin de la Société des antiquaires de Normandie* 54 (1957–58).

[72]Bibliothèque Nationale, ms. latin 4651.

The situation in the countryside of the Paris region in the last centuries of the Middle Ages is beginning to be quite well known to us, thanks to some important research in history and geography on the economy and the physical characteristics of these rural areas.[73] Yet data relevant to our present purpose are quite rare, no doubt because definitive desertions were extremely unusual. Here again, reconstruction was much more frequent than terminal destruction.

Guy Fourquin has reported only one case of a collective settlement that was replaced by a single farming unit, namely that of the hamlet of Vignole.[74] For the plateaus east and north of the Paris region, Pierre Brunet's book offers a somewhat greater number of examples, but even they represent only a very small proportion.[75] The localities that disappeared were mostly hamlets that were either totally stricken from the map or replaced by outlying farms. In the Montois region, near Egligny,[76] for instance, the hamlets of Le Jardel, Beaulieu, and Le Petit Chanzy were deserted in the fourteenth or fifteenth century. This modification in the pattern of settlement (in Brie as in the Montois and Multien regions) went hand in hand with a transformation of the countryside itself, since the long, narrow fields gave way to a loosely woven open-field pattern. The regrouping of land by capitalistic seigneurs, bourgeois, or working tenant farmers was undoubtedly involved here. On the other hand, here as elsewhere,[77] the destruction of the fifteenth century played only a preliminary role; the actual regrouping of the land was to take place later, at the end of the sixteenth and in the seventeenth centuries.

The case of Languedoc appears to lie midway between the massive extinction of villages in Provence and the virtual absence of desertions in the Paris region. The *Wüstungen* of Languedoc are located in certain marginal areas, such as marshy lowlands and the barren soil of the *garrigues* and the mountains. Limited though they are as a percentage of the total number of parishes, these *Wüstungen* are nonetheless found in appreciable numbers.

[73]Y. Bézard, *La vie rurale dans le sud de la région parisienne de 1450 à 1560* (Paris, 1929); Guy Fourquin, *Les campagnes de la région parisienne à la fin du Moyen Age* (Paris, 1964); Pierre Brunet, *Structure agraire et économie rurale des plateaux tertiaires entre la Seine et l'Oise* (Caen, 1960).

[74]Vignole, near Andresy, canton of Poissy (department of Seine-et-Marne). Despite the fact that almost all the inhabitants left Magny-les-Hameaux during the fifteenth century, none of the hamlets were permanently deserted before 1570. The only places not resettled after the fifteenth century were two farms, La Mare Cochereau and La Croix Brisée. Cf. O. Tulippe, *L'habitat rural en Seine-et-Oise* (Liège, 1934).

[75]Pierre Brunet's data are of great interest, but—and this is only normal in a geographical study—they are not directly based on archival sources. They are usually taken from sometimes unreliable nineteenth-century authors who practically never provide any references to their sources. Among these works are the following: L. Graves, *Essai sur la topographie géognostique du départment de l'Oise* (Beauvais, 1847); F. A. Denis, *Lectures sur l'histoire de l'agriculture dans le départment de Seine-et-Marne* (Meaux, 1880); Delettre, *Histoire de la province du Montois* (Nogent-sur-Seine, 1849); R. Benoist, *Notice historique et statistique sur May-en-Multien* (Meaux, 1884); Réthoré, *Recherches historiques sur Jouarre et ses environs* (Meaux, 1895).

[76]Department of Seine-et-Marne.

[77]Especially at Magny-les-Hameaux.

In the coastal areas of Languedoc it appears that the inhabitants were most likely to abandon land that was subject to "salt-bite" and where settlements were infected by "bad air." Such land was very close to the sea or to lakes and ponds and suffered from salinity, mosquitoes, and fever. Here parishes that had been born or confirmed in the course of the great expansion of the eleventh century disappeared or shrank to outlying farms beginning with the fourteenth century. This was the case with Exindre, Saint-Michel-de-Grémian, Saint-Jean-de-Cocon, Maurin, Saint-Marcel-de-Fréjorgues, Saint-Denis, Ginestet, and Coussergues.[78]

A *mas* [farm] often sprang up or remained as the sole dwelling at the site of a dead village; this is what happened at Cocon, Maurin, Fréjorgues, and Coussergues; in the sixteenth or seventeenth century these *mas* were to become the residences from which robe nobles or canons, who were often avid domain builders, took their titles.

In the other end-zone of the old clearings, in the *garrigues* and in the mountains, the *Wüstungen* of the fourteenth and fifteenth centuries usually did not affect the major village centers but often claimed the smaller hamlets. In 1374, six outlying hamlets were listed for Cessenon-sur-Orb: Casedarnes, Prades, Lugne, Berilles, Chavardes, and Vessatz. In the *compoix* [tax roll] of the sixteenth century—1560—the first three are still mentioned, while the last three have totally disappeared.

The examples we have rapidly cited thus far show one thing very clearly: a demographic crisis, even in conjunction with the ravages of war, will not kill a village completely. It will only create the conditions that permit the other factors leading to desertion to do their work; and these are essentially domain building and displacement of the population. Why have these factors had so little impact in France? The seigneurs could not take advantage of a long-run improvement in the rural economy; they did not have enough money to buy land, and they also had lost too much of their power to evict the peasants. No doubt one should also mention the fact that the land had been settled for a very long time. Even if they were deserted for ten, twenty, or thirty years, the old villages were never forgotten; church censuses and tax rolls kept them alive, if only on paper. All the texts indicate that even the old distribution of the land was never lost from sight and that it was very difficult to alter the respective rights of seigneur and cultivator. Nor must the extraordinary density of population in the French countryside prior to the crises be overlooked. General studies and regional research[79] show that French population density at the time of the *Etat des Feux* of 1328 was much higher than that of neighboring

---

[78]Exindre, Saint-Jean-de-Cocon, and Maurin: commune of Lattes; Saint-Michel-de-Gremian: commune of Cournonsec; Saint-Marcel-de-Frejorgues: commune of Mauguio; Obilion: commune of Lunel; Saint-Denis-de-Ginestet: commune of Saint-Nazaire-de-Pezan; Coussergues: commune of Montblanc (department of Hérault). For Coussergues, see A. Chéron and G. de Sarret de Coussergues, *Coussergues et les Sarret* (Brussels, 1963).

[79]For the kingdom as a whole, see Lot, "L'état des paroisses et des feux de 1328," cited in n. 2, above. For Normandy, see R. Strayer, "Economic conditions in Beaumont-le-Roger,"

countries and that the rural population of France was almost as large at the beginning of the fourteenth century as it was to be in the eighteenth century. To be sure, the demographic crisis of the fourteenth and fifteenth centuries more than wiped out the surplus population, but it did not depopulate enough areas to leave any appreciable or permanent gaps in the pattern of settlement.

The Early Modern Period

Once the time of plagues, of repeated crisis and war with the English was behind them, the French peasants saw the beginning of a period of relative ease. It was the Renaissance, the welcome sixteenth century. At that time, the disappearance of group settlements was extremely rare, or, if you prefer, the mortality of villages dropped to almost zero.

Nor is this surprising. The period spanning roughly the years 1480–1560 was favorable to the peasant. It was a time when the forest was pushed back again, when great strides were made in clearing, when wheat-land was expanded at the expense of animal husbandry, and when wheat became more important than wool or meat.

The tendency toward subdivision of individual properties persisted for a long time; indeed, this trend was to be lastingly reversed only in the last third of the sixteenth century, sometimes even later.[80] And to speak of the proliferation of peasants who owned a small plot of land also means to speak of villages that were, if not happy, at least solid and well entrenched.

As for taxation under François I, and even under Henri II, it did not represent too heavy a burden. The curve of taxes, at least direct taxes, trails along the bottom of the graph, and when it begins to rise it cannot always keep up with the curve of nominal prices that rose under the impact of the inflation of the century.[81] Similarly, the burden of peasant indebtedness (at least with respect to debts stipulating money, for there is also the vast problem of debts of grain) gradually eased between 1530 and 1570, owing to the price revolution. In this manner, peasant land was to a large extent not exposed to foreclosure.

These relatively favorable conditions gradually deteriorated after about

---

Speculum, 1951, pp. 277–87; and for Languedoc, see L. J. Thomas, "La population du Bas-Languedoc (xiiie–xviiie siècle)," *Annales du Midi,* 1908. For Rouergue, the listing of households [*état des feux*] of 1341 shows that in the fourteenth century the population of that province was almost as large as at the time of the 1801 census.

[80]For the reversal of this trend, see J. Jacquart, "Propriété et exploitation rurales au sud de Paris, dans la seconde moitié du xvie siècle," *Bulletin de la Société d'histoire moderne* (6 November 1960); Marc Vénard, *Bourgeois et paysans au XVIIe siècle* (Paris, 1957); J. Jacquart, "Livres récents sur les paysans du Hurepoix," *Bulletin de la Société d'histoire et d'archéologie de Corbeil,* 1959. For the enduring tendency toward division of property even at the beginning of the sixteenth century, see Fourquin, *Les campagnes de la région parisienne.*

[81]M. Baulant and J. Meuvret, *Prix des céréales, extraits de la mercuriale de Paris* (Paris, 1962); J. J. Clamageran, *Histoire de l'impôt en France,* 3 vols. (Paris, 1867–76).

1560–70. The reasons for this shift are related to the destruction wrought by a succession of wars.

Among the provinces left in ruins in the wake of the wars of the seventeenth century, northern Champagne was probably the most cruelly ravaged. Especially hard hit was the entire region between the Vesle and the Aisne rivers, stretching from Reims and Châlons in the south to Rethel and Vouziers in the north. In the course of the princely Fronde, compounded by the simultaneous prosecution of war against Spain, northern Champagne experienced a fate similar to that of the Palatinate a few years later (except that in the case of Champagne the worst destruction was wrought by its own defenders). When the Peace of the Pyrenees [1659] finally ended the fighting and the movement of troups, northern Champagne was reduced to exhaustion, covered with ruins, and more than half deserted.

Most of the historians of Champagne agree that the region never completely recovered and that its impoverishment and depopulation go back to the seventeenth century. What we know of its definitively deserted villages attests to this difficult and incomplete recovery:[82] fourteen or sixteen villages destroyed during that period never came back to life.[83] In itself, this is not very much, since this same region still includes one hundred fifty villages today; but it is a great deal by comparison with the very low level of desertion in France as a whole and in view of the negligible rate at which desertions in the seventeenth century usually occurred.

It is possible, of course, to blame the poor soil of the Pouilly region of Champagne for these desertions, as well as the attraction of a town like Reims and the familiar interaction between poverty and emigration. But one must also realize that people often migrated from village to village, and that these were one-way moves which emptied one locality to the advantage of a neighboring one. This happened, for example, at Gerson, whose inhabitants moved to Barby. It is interesting to note that Gerson followed the customary law of Reims, while all the neighboring villages, and especially the nearest one, Barby, still followed the customary law of Vitry. A number of other deserted villages—Warny, Somme-Arne, Ardenay, and Puiseaux—were in a

---

[82]See the studies by Abbé Dessailly and by H. Jadart and L. Demaison cited in n. 25, above. See also H. Jadart, "Recherches sur le village natal du chancelier Gerson," *Travaux de l'Académie de Reims*, (1879–1880); Varin, *Archives législatives de la ville de Reims* 1 (1847): 804, n. 1; also the articles by Drs. Vincent and Guelliot on "Les localitiés ardennaises disparues," *Revue historique ardennaise*, vols. 1, 3, 8, 17.

[83]The names of these villages in the department of Marne were Ardenay (commune of Prosnes), Brimontel (commune of Brimont), Burigny (commune of Witry-les-Reims), Marqueuse (commune of Fresne-les-Reims), Mouchery (commune of Beine), Sainte-Anne (commune of Saint-Thierry), Saint-Aubeuf (commune of Bouvancourt), Tourizet (commune of Betheny). In the Department of Ardennes, there were Germiny (commune of La Neuville-en-Tourne-à-Fuy), Gerson (commune of Barby), Nepellier (commune of Nanteuil-sur-Aisne), Somme-Arne (commune of Saint-Etienne-à-Arnes), Theline (commune of Sainte-Marie-sous-Bourcq), and Warny or Warigny (commune of Machault). More doubtful are the cases of Heudreliscourt (department of Marne, commune of Pontfaverger) and Puiseaux (communes of Dontrien and Saint-Souplet).

very similar situation, being located either at the outer limits of the jurisdiction of the customary law of Reims or in enclaves of that law within the jurisdiction of Vitry.

As it happened, it made a great deal of difference to what juridical district one belonged. The customary law of Reims was considered to be the more severe of the two.[84] Most notably, the inhabitants of the parishes where it applied, unlike those of neighboring villages, were obliged to pay rights of *lods et ventes.** These were onerous charges, which the inhabitants resented bitterly, as we can see from the *cahiers de doléances* of 1789.[85] A more detailed comparative study of the two bodies of customary law would undoubtedly bring to light other differences, all of them unfavorable to the customary law of Reims. The condition of people with respect to their legal status and their liability to taxes varied from one parish to the next; indeed, the borderline between two legal systems sometimes passed right through the territory of one village. Under these circumstances it would be a serious mistake to neglect this essential feature of the Ancien Régime in studying the deserted villages.

At the time of the great clearings, the desire to escape from bondage and to free themselves from the most arbitrary charges had prompted the peasants to flee their original villages. In the early modern period the memory of old injustices may have dissuaded the rural people from rebuilding a village destroyed by war. Taxes levied too soon after the disaster, a tax rate calculated without sufficient allowance for the losses sustained, or renewed poverty could easily have driven the inhabitants away from a ruined site forever. One can also visualize a community diminished by massacre, plague, or famine that was unable to meet its obligations. Arrears begin to accumulate, foreclosures further impoverish the inhabitants, until the villager simply flees from his doomed parish and moves to one that has suffered less, trying to become part of a more fortunate community. As more and more of the inhabitants move away, the burden becomes even heavier for those who remain; and the village gradually loses all of its population.[86]

For, much more than in any previous period, taxation must be held responsible for the situation of the seventeenth century, especially after Richelieu had come to power. Despite the stagnation in the "gross national product," the demands of the tax collector had become much more stringent, especially after the Cardinal had so drastically "tightened the vise." On the other hand, tax relief for disaster areas and individual tax reductions—both measures that the monarchy, having become more responsive and more enlightened, was to

[84]Except with respect to the legal status of women. This body of customary law was sometimes referred to as "the women's law."

*Lods et ventes were mutation fees paid to the seigneur when a property changed hands.— Trans.

[85]G. Laurent, *Reims et la région rémoise à la veille de la Révolution* (Reims, 1930), p. 239.

[86]This scenario is borrowed from Bocquet, *Recherches sur la population de l'Artois.* However, Bocquet applies it to fifteenth-century Artois, and it is difficult to see how it would explain the small number of villages deserted in that province at that time.

accord freely in the Enlightenment—were still granted only exceptionally in the seventeenth century.

But we do not wish to propose a single-cause explanation. Taxation alone could not empty a village. But in certain cases it represented "the last straw," which transformed a whole range of serious ailments into a mortal disease.

In Champagne, domain building was not involved in the process that led to the desertion of villages.[87] By contrast, we do see such an involvement in the Paris region.

In the vicinity of Paris the situation of the peasants had been deteriorating ever since the beginning of the seventeenth century. This deterioration was, first of all, of a demographic nature. Certain preliminary indications make it appear likely that the Paris region experienced a steep decline in population after the high point of the sixteenth century.[88]

Moreover, certain financial burdens became more onerous. This was clearly the case with taxes. For a long time, the [royal] taxes, at least the direct tax, or *taille,* had approximately followed the price curve of wheat in the Paris market. Under Richelieu the curve of the *taille* detached itself from the price curve. In real value, the *taille* had almost doubled by 1635–40.

And lastly, there was the problem of the increasing burden of indebtedness. Payments for rented land, it is true, rose only slowly during the seventeenth century, at least in areas where the *taille* was "personal,"* since rents were predicated on the tenant's payment of the royal taxes. But the same cannot be said of payments on borrowed capital. Throughout the sixteenth century, the burden of debts owed by peasants had become increasingly lighter, thanks to that century's galloping inflation. In the seventeenth century, however, grain prices rose very slowly, indeed declined at certain times. Under these circumstances, anyone who calculated these monetary debts in relation to their real value, namely in terms of grain, was in a very good position. When prices "bottomed out" under Colbert, creditors brought their claims up to date, reevaluated them, and temporarily inflated them.[89]

Loss of population, taxes, indebtedness, deficits in agricultural operations—all of these misfortunes opened the way for an attack from the city. The disintegration of certain hamlets was closely tied to the great leap forward in domain building. The most important domain builders were Parisian bourgeois, robe magistrates, and wealthy merchants who bought land in order to become seigneurs[90]; some of them were monasteries, such as Port-

[87]Was this "great culprit" really absent, or is it just that the historians of Champagne and our own research have failed to find the evidence on this point?

[88]J. Jacquart, "Morangis aux xvi⁰ et xvii⁰ siècles," *Paris et Ile de France,* 1956, p. 197.

*That is, assessed on the person rather than on the land.—Trans.

[89]The curve of nominal prices for wheat in the Paris wholesale market shows that a break in the "intersecular" trend occurred, broadly speaking, about 1585–95. As for the "Colbertian" deflation (to use this shorthand term), it affected the region of Paris between 1662 and 1690. Cf. Baulant and Meuvret, *Prix des céréales,* 2:152–53. The graph shows prices in *livres tournois* for each harvest year.

[90]Jacquart, "Propriété et exploitation rurales."

Royal, and there was also a minority of nonurban buyers, such as well-to-do working tenant farmers, grain merchants, or village officials. The landed imperialism of all these groups seems to have become particularly acute at the end of the sixteenth century, at the time of the crises and conflicts of Wars of the League.[91] One particularly enlightening example is the case of Magny-les-Hameaux.[92] On the eve of the Hundred Years' War, Magny-les-Hameaux had been a classic "atom," one among several types of old-style settlements. It consisted of an old central "nucleus" (Magny), surrounded by outlying hamlets, some of which were of rather recent origin, having been created by the great clearings. Altogether, twelve localities still constituted the village in about 1400.

This whole complex was abandoned in the middle of the fifteenth century; during the early sixteenth century it was resettled in a touching manner that exactly reproduced the normal medieval pattern of settlement. But this was no more than a false start, a brief interlude. The age of property *par excellence*—the age of bourgeois domain builders who aspired to nobility, of large-scale farms and châteaux—was rapidly approaching. After 1560, the movement of domain building wrought havoc among the hamlets of Magny. Five of the oldest outlying hamlets—and these are already documented in the Middle Ages—disappeared first. Nor did the newer hamlets (end of the fifteenth–beginning of the sixteenth century) fare any better. Of the twenty-eight localities that made up Magny between 1520 and 1550, seventeen disappeared between 1550 and 1702, with most of the losses occurring between 1550 and 1600–1612.

Whenever the documents permit us to analyze the process of desertion—as in the case of La Couperie, Broissy-le-Vieil, Les Granges de Port-Royal, and Cressely—we are able to point to a responsible party. Sometimes it was a small nonresident landowner; more often it was a bourgeois or a seigneur, like the seigneur of Buloyer or the seigneur of Mérautais. But the most important domain builder in the region of Magny was none other than the Abbey of Port-Royal, which now became the direct owner of the land over which it had long held seigneurial rights.

The construction of châteaux and the creation and expansion of private pleasure parks also threatened the peasant settlements. Of the eighteen parishes in the jurisdiction of Saint-Cloud documented for 1370, two disappeared when they were taken over by the masters of a château or by the king. One was La Marche,[93] which was replaced by the château of that name; the other was Trianon, which was obliterated by the palace of Grand Trianon. Nor was Trianon the only victim of the royal pleasure; the villages of Choisy-aux-Boeufs and Versailles and the hamlet of Musceloue were also eliminated when Versailles became a building site.

---

[91]Vénard, *Bourgeois et paysans au XVIIe siècle.*
[92]Cf. Tulippe, *L'habitat rural.*
[93]Near Vaucresson.

The eradication of these villages by the architects and landscape artists of Louis XIV was more than the result of an aesthetic venture; it was part of a long-range plan, similar to the projects of the domain-building bourgeois. By erasing villages and consolidating their lands, the kings of France, like other domain builders, were finally able in the early modern period to assemble vast blocks of landed property. At an even later date, Louis XV ordered the razing of the parish of Retz, which "inconvenienced the King"; the site was eventually converted to an English garden by François de Monville.[94] By 1778, this block of royal domains comprised thirty-four farms and ten thousand arpents [approximately three thousand acres], producing an annual revenue of 1,600,000 livres.

Conversely, the taste for luxurious residences was not confined to the kings. Private individuals could also live like minor potentates. The village of Rouillon, for instance, totally disappeared between 1621 and 1652 because the master of the château of Plessis-Saint-Père had the remains of the village razed in order to use the land for the pleasure park and avenues leading to his château.

Whenever we hear of the demise of a village or a hamlet in western France—where pastures interspersed with small woods make up the bocage country—we frequently also hear of new small farms and at times of new large farms. As in the Paris Basin, these changes took place after 1550, at the end of the sixteenth and throughout the seventeenth centuries. But in western France this development was brought about not only, or not primarily, by a rising bourgeoisie (as it was elsewhere, by the Parisian bourgeoisie), but by the local nobility, including its most "feudal" members. For this nobility had recently come into money, having accumulated during the sixteenth century a surplus of wealth due to the rise of agricultural prices and the influx of specie. Despite its vitality, this old nobility remained wedded to certain juridical institutions of the past and was by no means inclined to encourage the more modern forms of capitalist leaseholding that were practiced in the Beauce or Brie regions. The nobility of western France adhered to the old "half-fruits" contracts, to sharecropping, and to the small-scale leaseholds that characterized less-developed societies until the twentieth century. The seventeenth century was the golden age of this nobility, which was old in title but new in its aggressive policy of domain building.

The peasants of western France who sold their little plots to domain-building nobles or notables in this manner were compelled to do so by debts or even by hunger. An example of this desperate need for money or bread is the harvest year 1630–31.

<hr>

[94]Lefevre, "Le jardin anglais et la singulière habitation de Monville au désert de Retz (1785)," *Commission des antiquités et des arts de Seine-et-Oise* (1916), pp. 63 ff; Deligny, "Un Anglais et sa maison du désert de Retz," *Revue de l'histoire de Versailles* (1932). Retz: department of Seine-et-Oise, commune of Chambourcy. On this subject, see also *Conférence des Sociétés littéraires et artistiques de Seine-et-Oise, 1910* (1912), pp. 61, 132–34.

The unhealthy demographic situation of the seventeenth century undoubtedly also played its part in the *Wüstungen*. Thanks to new research, the
demographic fluctuations of western France in the early modern period are
beginning to emerge from the shadow. Certain trends are already appearing,
namely, a probable rise in population in the sixteenth century until 1580 and
then a decline, which is visible in the curves of births, deaths, and marriages
of Maine-et-Loire and Calvados.[95]

Broadly speaking, then, the *Wüstungen* of western France in the seventeenth century may be seen as the combined effect of an offensive of domain
building and a retreat in population density. Nevertheless, at least insofar as
we can determine in our present state of knowledge, the settlements that fell
victim to this evolution were neither numerous nor particularly important.

In the department of Vienne, the hamlet of La Reygondonnière was acquired and then destroyed by certain domain builders about 1600.[96] The
hamlet or village of Rouflamme, which had been inhabited by independent,
small holders in 1563, 1571, and 1596, became an outlying farm after 1600.
The hamlet of L'Herpinière was inhabited by five to six peasant families, all
of them small owners, until 1601; it was subsequently transformed into a large
domain. The commune* of Saulgé,[97] which included Rouflamme and L'Herpinière, appears to have been particularly prone to changes in the pattern of
settlement, for a third "village" (Les Gats) also became an outlying farm
sometime between 1600 and 1620.

In the present commune of Secondigny,[98] two hamlets (or villages?) were
wiped out: La Poussonière was incorporated into the farm of La Gaschère and
another farm, La Mortière, inflicted the same fate on the "village" or "settlement" of La Tillardière sometime between 1520 and 1540.[99] The hamlet of
La Petite Barre was exposed to the assault of a domain builder as early as
1458.[100] After a long period of latency, La Petite Barre again came under
attack from the same quarter after 1595; its ruin was completed between 1662
and 1719, the date when it had finally been "phagocytized" by the Légier
family, the seigneurs of La Barre-Poivreau.[101] The hamlet of L'Ecutadière
(six households in about 1520) was reduced, or "consolidated," by a series of
legal documents dated 1529, 1604, and 1650.[102] At the end of this process,

[95]Pierre Goubert, *Beauvais et le Beauvaisis au XVIIe siècle* (Paris, 1960), maps on pp. 48, 52.
Also, Gouhier, "Port-en-Bessin (1596–1792)," *Cahiers des Annales de Normandie* 1 (1962).
[96]Parish of Saint-Rémy, region of Montmorillon (department of Vienne).
Commune is the term used today to designate the smallest administrative unit. It corresponds
approximately to a parish.—Trans.
[97]Department of Vienne, canton of Montmorillon.
[98]Department of Deux-Sèvres, cantonal seat.
[99]Merle, *La métairie et l'évolution agraire de la Gâtine poitevine, de la fin du Moyen Age à la
Révolution* (Paris, 1958).
[100]Commune and canton of Menigoute (department of Deux-Sèvres).
[101]Merle, *Gâtine poitevine,* pp. 56–59.
[102]Commune of Azay-sur-Thouet, canton of Secondigny (department of Deux-Sèvres).

instead of a number of different occupiers we find a single sharecropper in the service of a clan of determined domain builders, the Darrot family.[103]

These diverse examples from the bocage [wooded region] of western France seem rather significantly like English enclosures, for here too we see the familiar spread of hedgerows.[104] But we must qualify such a comparison, for these were not the *extensive* enclosures for sheep raising that were laid out in England at the end of the fifteenth century and that often led to the disappearance of a dozen parishes at a time. Their place in time (essentially the seventeenth century) and their economic purpose make these enclosures, the destruction of outlying hamlets, and the creation of farms in western France much more similar to the *intensive* enclosures for the cultivation of wheat about which we hear in England in the seventeenth and eighteenth centuries. Like the newly enclosed English farms of that period, most of the consolidated farms of the marshy region of Poitou consisted of grain land.[105]

In Languedoc the desertion of villages and settlements was rather clearly related to certain precise factors, some of which were interconnected, while others operated independently. Among these factors were epidemics of malaria in marshy zones; the failure to cultivate fields (which resulted in reduced *finages*, or cultivated areas, around villages) due to the decline of agricultural markets between 1675 and 1720; the decline in small-scale ownership beginning about 1670–90 and lasting until about 1760–70, as well as the corresponding advance in domain building (relatively modest though it was by comparison with that in England or even in the Ile-de-France region); the wave of depopulation that affected Languedoc between 1677 and 1740, although it, too, was relatively limited in scope; and lastly, the deliberate destruction of villages carried out upon orders from Versailles by the royal army in the Camisard strongholds of the Cévennes Mountains.[106] One or several of these factors played a causative role in every major desertion of a settlement.

The typology of the lost villages of Languedoc often implicitly shows two distinct phases in the process of desertion. First, in an initial stage of demographic or economic decline, the village is reduced to a mere hamlet (stage 1), which eventually—sometimes much later—becomes so feeble that it succumbs to a final deathblow. At that point, the village either disappears altogether or is transformed into an outlying farm by a process of consolidation (stage 2).

As for the crisis besetting the France of Louis XIV, its nefarious effects

---

[103]Merle, *Gâtine poitevine,* pp. 61–62.

[104]Merle, ibid; Raveau, *L'agriculture, les classes paysannes, la transformation de la propriété dans le Haut-Poitou au XVIe siècle* (Paris, 1926).

[105]Merle, *Gâtine poitevine,* p. 133.

[106]In 1703, fifty-three villages, which also included hundreds of hamlets, were systematically demolished by the troups of Marshall Montrevel. Twenty of these fifty-three names did not reappear and were striken from the map forever.

sometimes became evident in the first stage, sometimes in the second. This crisis could spell the end of a dying village by permitting it to succumb to a capitalist or seigneurial "phagocytosis" (Buadelles, Sainte-Colombe); it could also infect a still healthy village with a languishing malady that reduced it to the status of a hamlet, in which case the shriveled-up settlement might somehow keep alive for another century (Montels). The three examples alluded to above will have to suffice to illustrate this point. In the department of Aude, at Buadelles,[107] the desertion of the village (which had already shrunk considerably during the Hundred Years' War) went hand in hand with a capitalist operation mounted by a powerful seigneur, the Abbot of Lagrasse. In 1666 the abbot obliged all the freeholders of Buadelles to get rid of all the land they owned and merged their land with the manse of the abbey, thus transforming the village into an outlying farm. (The Abbot of Lagrasse, incidentally, was by tradition a stout consumer of parishes; his predecessor had already absorbed Tréviac, probably during the sixteenth century, and his successor was to merge Bubal with the lands of the abbey in the beginning of the eighteenth century.)

Sainte-Colombe-de-Nissargues,[108] a substantial medieval village (eleventh century), was already very much diminished in about 1440. By 1520 it counted no more than five houses and forty-eight *taille* payers, and its wheatland was very fragmented. The village still existed in 1654, for we know that a *compoix* [tax roll] was drawn up at that date. By 1720, however, desertion and consolidation had done their work; the peasants were dead or had moved away, and an extensive farm had swallowed up all of the village territory. This farm, by the way, found it very difficult to pay its taxes, which continued to be assessed on the wealth of the extinct village.

At Montels the chronology of events unfolds somewhat later.[109] Around 1520 Montels still had a church, ten houses, thirty-six *taille* payers, and a fragmented grain-producing territory. In the following century the village remained quite alive (despite a rather sluggish demographic trend over the long run). Early in the seventeenth century the land of Montels was converted to vineyards. The parish had forty-five active members in 1657, even fifty in 1677.

Then, between 1677 and 1689, a sudden catastrophe. The village lost four-fifths of its inhabitants, declining from fifty parishioners in 1677 to ten (belonging to three families) in 1689, and this number remained more or less constant until about 1777. What had happened? The Revocation of the Edict of Nantes? No indeed. There was only one Huguenot listed for Montels, the seigneur of Farges, and he did not even live there. What, then? Food shortages? Epidemics? A high death rate? A crisis in the wine market? Economic

---

[107]Buadelles: department of Aude, commune and canton of Lagrasse.
[108]Department of Hérault, commune of Saint-Geniès-des-Mourgues, canton of Castries.
[109]Montels: department of Hérault, near Lunel.

stagnation due to the Revocation of the Edict of Nantes that sapped the strength of commerce in neighboring Protestant regions? All of these factors were undoubtedly involved to a certain extent. But one thing is certain: death and migration emptied this village during the terrible years of the 1680s. Montels was to eke out a precarious existence for another century, finally to be absorbed by a domain builder around 1860.

After the happy interlude of the Renaissance, the desertions of the early modern period occurred essentially between 1560 and 1720. In the first analysis they often appear to be the result of the disasters of war (the conflicts of the Catholic League, the Fronde, the Thirty Years' War, the War of the Camisards); at the same time, they must also be seen as part of a vast complex of adversity that made life increasingly more difficult for the peasantry, beginning with the last third of the sixteenth century. The most important adverse factors were a frequently declining birth rate; the stagnation of prices and production, which made the weight of financial obligations and debts more difficult to bear; and the increasing burden of an antipeasant tax structure.

But against this background of unfavorable circumstances, we also see the conscious desire of landlords to rationalize and simplify the traditional patterns of settlement. The English methods of agriculture were adopted in early modern France, albeit after a time-lag of several generations (the usual delay of the Continent) and not without substantial modifications. Châteaux, seigneurial or royal pleasure parks, extensive farms in the bogs of northeastern France, small farms in the bocage of western France, and substantial *mas* [farms] in the South took the place of dozens of hamlets and even parishes. In terms of France's agrarian well-being and the temptations inherent in landed capitalism, the damage was considerable. Yet it could have been worse, for the network of villages did not break down. The mass of the peasantry received a severe blow, but by and large, it withstood the assault.

The peasantry held together by reason of its very size, because its demographic dimension was not even comparable with the much more restricted number of peasants in England or Germany. After all, from the fifteenth to the nineteenth century, France was always one great grain factory and, to a lesser extent, a wine factory, with an enormous need for agricultural labor. The heavily populated villages of France were incomparably more solid than those of wool-producing nations such as England and Spain at certain periods of their history.

Moreover, the hard times did not last. After the dark century of Louis XIV came a long period that was easier for the villager. There were certain stimulating factors that brought new life to the countryside, among them an economic upswing that gradually took shape beginning with the Law boom; a rise in the birthrate after 1740–50; greater freedom for the peasant and also the social achievements of the French Revolution; the wider distribution of small-scale ownership in the nineteenth century; and lastly the solicitude of successive governments from Turgot to Méline, which were often willing to grant price support for grain. Each of these factors infused the French village with new vigor.

Since the end of the nineteenth century a new wave of village desertions has been under way, brought about essentially by the flight from the countryside. This movement is responsible for an increasing number of empty villages and deserted hamlets in the Alps, the Jura, and the Massif Central; in all probability their number is greater than that of sites deserted in earlier periods.

But here again compensating factors—this time of a totally new variety—are beginning to play their part: city dwellers of 1964 are buying up dilapidated houses and fixing up old shacks whose roofs have fallen in. In this manner, many a defunct settlement has been artificially resuscitated. For the impact of the city has changed. In the seventeenth century, domain builders from the city killed the villages and hamlets of the countryside, transforming them into fields, meadows, estates, châteaux, or pleasure parks. Now, in the twentieth century, it can happen under particularly favorable circumstances that a dying village will survive, owing its good fortune to the need for relaxation of the great urban centers, to the widespread desire for a vacation home, or to the snobbery of the city-dwelling bourgeoisie.

6
Power and Ideology in the Village Community of Picardy: Past and Present

Alain Morel

In the village community of Picardy, there is no open conflict between the small group of farmers who own or lease considerable amounts of land and the large group of proletarians who own nothing but their labor. Originating in the relations of production, the relations between employers and employees are not played out on the level of class. But within that relationship, there are certain relations of dependence of the patron-client variety—personal acquaintance, paternalism, prestige—that shape the strategies of both parties. The strategy of the patron-employer is aimed not only at preserving his own importance but also at maintaining the status quo, in other words, at preventing the workers from taking any action against a system that works to their disadvantage. It is obvious that the patron-employer can preserve the power he wields over those he employs in the economic sphere—by means of working conditions, wages, and promotions—only if he extends that power to other spheres of social life. In order to do this, he earmarks some of his extensive property, consisting of land, pastures, various machinery, financial resources, for creating obligations among a clientele. In this manner, he is able to win the loyalty of the workers, who constitute the majority of the population, and thereby consolidate the system that gives him power. He thus preserves his position of hegemony by playing on two boards at the same time, as it were. Patron-client relations add a dimension that is apt to mask the existence of class relations. Conflict, therefore, does not take place on the collective level, between the exploiter and the exploited, but on the level of the individual. Everyone asks: "How can I get the most out of the

Annales, E.S.C. 30 (January–February 1975): 161–76. Translated by Elborg Forster.

game?'' and most of the time the answer will be something like: "It's best to trust in the boss."

As for the strategy of the workers, the individual ties linking them to the employer permit them to obtain special treatment from him without violating the principles of an ideology of effort that considers work to be the measure of all things. Like the employer, the workers manipulate the patron-client relationship, attempting to protect themselves against the power of an omnipotent employer who, for his part, feels called upon to make compromises and to extend protection and favors to those who support the system. One of the aims pursued by the clients is to make the patron-employer reluctant, in terms of his own ideology, to drop a client who has often been of service to him.

Today, while such ties are falling into disuse and while the workers no longer avail themselves of the generosity and the aid of their employer, it is still true that the traditional ideology—inspired by the social Catholicism that enjoyed considerable vogue among the employer class of northern France—continues to shape the attitudes and the behavior of the villagers, who still look upon the wealthy farmers of middle-class background as their village lords, at once their master and their employer.

This essay is based on a study of Vercourt, a small village of the Marquenterre region, located in the district of Rue, twenty-five kilometers from Abbeville. Following a short description of the social structure of the village, I shall analyze the ideology of the client relations and the mutual exchanges to which they give rise. I shall also try to show the uniqueness of the model that obtains here, comparing it with other types of relations based on dependence.

Social Groups and Their Interrelation

Two classes coexist in the village, farmers and farm workers. However, the first of these is far from homogeneous, and it is impossible to advance the same reasons for the behavior of the small-scale farmer and for that of the wealthy landowner. We must therefore distinguish a number of smaller groups, each of which pursues its own strategies.

RURAL NOTABLES

At the top of the hierarchy we find the rural notables. Rural notables, although occasionally of noble origin, are for the most part the sons of modest rural families that have made their fortune. At Vercourt, only one man falls into this category. He lives in the château and also owns and manages the largest agricultural enterprise. His grandfather, a modest farmer, settled in the village at the beginning of the nineteenth century. The family gradually accumulated a considerable amount of land; as a result, it built a large house about 1860, and this house soon came to be called the château. Today, the châtelain commands an agricultural enterprise of 170 hectares (420 acres), which amounts to 27 percent of the land in the community. What are the characteristics that distinguish the rural notables from the other farmers and, more generally, from the rest of the villagers? Since they own much of the means of production—land, buildings (among them the workers' dwellings), capital, and machinery—they enjoy a privileged position in the economic system. They do not have to work with their hands. Their incomes are those of capitalist entrepreneurs. Inheritances of various kinds consolidate and stabilize their privileged position. In fact, a major portion of the land they own had been handed down in the family. This stability, however, is founded not exclusively on the transmission of material property but also on a whole complex of inherited cultural values. On the one hand, this involves a bourgeois family upbringing that transmits models of behavior for members of the ruling class. On the other hand, it involves schooling that gives access to technical knowledge, enabling the rural notables to interpret economic trends, engage in scientific agriculture, and ensure the rational management of their enterprise. This schooling also gives them access to French culture. All of these things are a mystery to the average villager, who is impressed by such accomplishments and feels that the scion of a good family is more than a master—namely, a *Monsieur,* to whom they owe not only obedience, but respect.[1]

These advantages give the notables dominance in the land market. They are always able to stay in the game when a leasor tries to drive his rents up by competitive bidding. But the situation is favorable to them in any case; whether they bid the highest rents and obtain the lease or whether they let a small householder have it, they cannot lose. For the small leaseholder will have to work for the notables part of the time anyway—and he will not have to be paid for the entire year—since he will be unable to live on the income from his tiny farm.

Their social environment and way of life also distinguish the rural notables from the rest of the villagers. They belong to a bourgeoisie that lives in châteaux, is waited on by servants, and frequents "high society." They often travel, and they have close ties with the urban bourgeoisie. In short, theirs is a milieu where one has connections, sometimes very useful ones, so that the villagers say that the master of the château has "a long arm." Furthermore, notables have power of more than one kind, for they are often mayors. At Vercourt, the grandfather of the châtelain was even councillor general [in the Departmental Council], a position that brought him great prestige. As the employers of numerous heads of families in the village, notables have indirect

[1]He is also the only one to be addressed as *Monsieur.*

ways of influencing these families as well. In 1901, the T. family employed
29 persons and could thus exert direct influence over 67 of the village's 167
inhabitants.

In short, the portrait of the rural notable of this region is one of a capitalist
entrepreneur of bourgeois upbringing and extensive local power.

LARGE-SCALE FARMERS

At Vercourt, two agricultural entrepreneurs fall into the category of large-
scale farmer; their farms comprise 74 and 40 hectares (183 and 99 acres),
respectively. This type of farm is spacious, the buildings are impressive, and a
dovecote in the center of the courtyard confers a certain status on the place.
These large-scale farmers employ a number of agricultural workers; the more
important of the two used to employ eight persons, not counting the seasonal
help. Like the notables, they have accumulated a considerable share of the
means of production, and the size of their enterprises, the number of hectares
under direct cultivation, and also the revenues derived from the farms differentiate them from smaller operations. Because they pay wages to a work
force and own the dwellings of their workers, these farmers are "bosses"
[patrons], and their relations with others, who show less aggressiveness toward
them than toward their peers, reflect their social position. They are, therefore,
treated with a certain respect. The old people of the village, who have seen
these men grow up, do not address them as *tu,* the way they normally address
younger people.

Yet these agricultural entrepreneurs are clearly distinguished from the notable and châtelain. Since they have not received any special education, their
manners are similar to those of the other villagers, and their circle of acquain-
tances remains very restricted, although it might extend to a neighboring
market town. Furthermore, these farmers cultivate their land in the traditional
manner and also participate personally in the farm work, or at least some of it.
Because these men have grown up in the village, there is much more familiarity between them and the villagers, including their workers, with whom they
take a daily coffee break. Insofar as the village is concerned, the farmers of
this social category are "bosses," to be sure; but, unlike the châtelain, they
are not perceived as notables.

MEDIUM-SCALE FARMERS

The two medium-scale farmers, who own 21 and 18 hectares (52 and 44
acres), respectively, also employ a seasonal labor force, yet they are not
perceived as "bosses." They have very little capital, and although they do use
a tractor, their farm equipment is rather rudimentary, so that they are some-

times obliged to borrow machinery from the large-scale farmers. Generally speaking, their buying power is about that of an agricultural worker. In short, they have nothing to offer.

SMALL FARMERS

There are only two small farmers at Vercourt, both of whom farm about 8 hectares [20 acres]. They are former farm workers who have achieved this ownership by dint of hard work and tenacity, but for all that their existence is still as harsh as that of the farm workers. They cultivate with one horse and work nine hours a day, often on Sundays. They have some compensation in the satisfaction of being independent. Their precarious position obliges them to seek help from the larger farmers.

FARM WORKERS AND RETIRED WORKERS

The largest group within the village consists of farm workers and retired workers. Aside from a house and garden that some of them have been able to acquire, they own nothing but their labor and long years of experience in farm work. Hemmed in by a class structure in which they occupy the weakest position, they must accept a personal relation of dependence with their notable-employer in the hope that it will bring some advantages, and, in a general sense, protect them from the insecurity of their position.

Dependent Relationships and the Power of the Patron-Employer

Members of all social categories are clients of the châtelain; all of them, in varying degrees, expect something from a more powerful man whom they consider to be their representative. Obviously, the independent farmers are less vulnerable than the others and expect less tangible advantages.

But even the large-scale farmers enter into this client relation, even though they also play the part of patron vis-à-vis their own workers. The difference is that their exchanges with their workers imply an exchange of goods and services that gives a special dimension to their class-based relationship, even though it lacks the ideological content characteristic of the relations between the châtelain and the village as a whole. The villagers' ideology views the châtelain as protector, model, and guide, while the notable, immersed in his own ideology, feels that he has a special mission. While these ideologies reflect the traditional technological and economic structures, they have not kept pace with their evolution. Today, the villagers are in a much less dependent position vis-à-vis the patron-employer, but the relative independence they are enjoying has done very little to change their mentality. They behave more like commoners toward a seigneur than like proletarians toward management. In this context, the following facts are significant:

—Villagers are proud if they are personally acquainted with the châtelain or with members of his family; they take pride in having been a servant in his household or a game carrier at one of his hunting parties.

—They take pride in having known him when he was a little boy or in having played with him as a child.

—Conversely, they are proud to be known by him. Those who call on him leave their bicycles at the gate of the park and remove their berets.

—Those who work for him are most reluctant to ask for their wages on payday if the patron has forgotten to pay them.

Such submission reflects the situation during the nineteenth century, when the mayor-employer-notable had his way for a number of reasons:

—There was an oversupply of labor, and the rural notable was the main employer (of workers and household servants).

—Since he owned many houses in the village, he was also the largest land-lord.

—His influence with the rural and industrial bourgeoisie of the area gave him the power to find jobs for workers or to block their opportunities.

—Due to the isolation of the rural population, he was the principal source of information concerning the outside world.

—The so-called householders[2] (minifarmers with 1 to 5 hectares (2.4 to 12 acres), who had been very numerous in the past, could only survive with the help of the large-scale farmers, who lent them farm equipment and also gave them work.

—Whenever the villagers were faced with illness, accident, or legal difficul-ties, they called on the mayor-employer-notable for help, which might take the form of mediation, financial aid, transportation, and so forth.

—In case of conflict among villagers, the notable assumed the role of arbiter.

—Finally, as mayor, he also directed the affairs of the community, appointing rural officials, selecting and supervising families qualified to take in foster children for the public welfare (Law of 23 December 1874), verifying the level of indigence of those who applied for free medical service (the deci-sion was made by the municipal council, which he headed) and for all other welfare benefits (these decisions were made by the cantonal council, Law of February 1934, art. 55).

---

[2]P. Pinchenel, *Structures sociales et dépopulation rurale dans les campagnes picardes de 1836 à 1936* (Paris: A. Colin, 1956), p. 86: "The householder [*ménager*] is a very small farmer who cultivates a few small plots totaling between one and five hectares. He makes up for his lack of equipment by trading his labor."

The Ideology of Hard Work

Faced with the power of the village notable, the villager could assume one of two attitudes. *He could make the best of it,* and this meant accepting the law of the strongest, namely the employer, and trying to obtain, by means of a two-way relationship, a redistribution of his wealth and power in the form of favors. This was the individual solution, one that relied on paternalistic patronage and did not question the system in any way.

The villager could also combat that power. This meant taking part in union activities, joining the socialist movement—the party of those who "want their share"—and fighting the omnipotence of the employer class. This collective solution, however, ran counter to the peasant ideology of hard work, which is based on the principle that the individual can only be judged by the work he performs, by his personal efforts to overcome every obstacle. This ideology compels peasants to be busy at all times, never to stop even for a moment. Peasants work for the sake of working. The villagers say of themselves that they can do only one thing—produce; this goes so far that they refuse to admit that eating and sleeping can be anything but functional necessities, maintenance for a machine that is made for work. Eating for pleasure? That would be gluttony, a costly sin! In this perspective, failure can only be explained by a lack of zeal. Capacity for hard work and energy are, therefore, important factors for the social standing of an individual, especially when his labor power is the only thing he owns; for the more well-to-do farmers can fall back on their wealth and their power.

For this reason, the workers see a solution to their problems only in work, where rivalries can be fierce. Some even feel acute frustration when they are unable to participate in an activity where they can demonstrate their outstanding skill. "They always take me, because I am the fastest worker. . . . I have done this kind of work all my life. I can hardly stand it when I see the others go out to do the sugar beets," says a woman who is a seasonal farm worker and who is unable to participate in digging the sugar beets because of illness. The respect workers can earn by hard work is not limited to the fields; it spreads to the village as well. Thus, in the days when a worker could still find a wife in the village, girls were often advised: "Take him, he is a good worker."

The desire to appear energetic is more than a matter of social standing. As the advice given to girls indicates, proof that one is a good worker, a hardworking man, is also proof of other qualities that are implicitly linked to energy. Behavior at work is the criterion by which an individual's entire personality, not just his aptitude for physical labor, is judged.

What are the themes of this ideology? Failure must be laid to insufficient effort. In the face of accident or bad luck, there is only one way out: more hard work. "I'll work extra hard tomorrow," says a worker in order to comfort his wife who has had an accident. Old people feel that economic changes and the modern way of life are signs of decadence, which they attribute to the laziness of the new generation: "People don't want to work any more. Look at the workers today; they don't raise a cow, or even a pig, any more."

Here are some of the characteristic expressions that reflect people's attitudes toward work:

—*Heuré* [punctual], A synonym of "orderly," it means as much as "organized": "One who sees to his work from morning till night" is the opposite of one who is impetuous and "works in spurts and then sits back" or is "capricious" or "changes his mind all the time," as well as of the "putterer," who "does useless jobs." One who is "punctual" does not dawdle (by reading the newspaper on the side, for example).

—*Paisible* [steady] is the quality of one who "works without stopping and never looks right or left."

—*Patient* [patient] means able "to do things right and carefully" and is the opposite of "sloppy" [*foufteux*], said of "one who does poor work, who does the second hoeing without pulling the weeds."

—*Vaillant* [strong, persistent] describes "one who is always ready to work." This goes with "energetic"—"works himself to the bone"—and with "persistent"; it is the opposite of "slow-poke" [*podak*]—"one who doesn't move much"—of "loafer" [*fainéant*], and of "dreamer": "always in the clouds, doesn't do anything."

—*Subtil* [keen] is a synonym of "clever," means "to work rapidly," and goes with "spontaneous": "one who is always ready to do what is asked of him." It is the opposite of "fooling around" [*amusette*]: "one who doesn't watch the time and has fun with a lot of little things," of slow [*nunu*], "one who starts all kinds of things and never sees them through," of "slow," of "dopey" [*étombi*], "one who doesn't see what must be done, doesn't get it, can't follow directions, doesn't understand anything," and of "pudding-head" [*tourte*], a synonym of the preceding term. A "keen" person does not "sit around" [*lantipone*] like one whose nerves lack that keen edge.

—*Fameux* [first-rate] is stronger than "keen"; it designates one who "can't be stopped." It is the opposite of "goof" [*losse*]: "Does everything badly, you can't make him do anything right," and of "worthless" [*indigne*]: "He botches every job, worse than not working at all."

There are other themes. Those who work hard "don't have time to think up trouble"; those who have time on their hands will get into mischief. Work confers rights. Severe criticism is leveled at those who try to obtain by ruse what is normally due to those who have worked hard. Seen from this angle, the acquisition of property can only be seen as the reward for hard work and is open to criticism if it is obtained with a loan. This principle has also inspired the following joke: "He who does not work does not eat," says the head of the family to his wife when the machine has broken down.

Finally, this ideology implicitly associates work with life and rest with death, which is therefore called eternal rest. Death, by the way, is a theme that frequently appears in the speech of the people of Picardy. Always present in their minds, it becomes a very familiar phenomenon which, aside from its tragic aspects, also connotes an aspect of liberation. "The accounts are settled on the last day" is a phrase that is frequently heard; in other words, the account will be closed, I will have worked enough, the time will come to stop and enjoy eternal rest. That is why idleness has a taste of death for old people; it tells them that their end is near.

As a result, this ideology of effort compels people to let everyone know that they are hard at work at all times, at home as well as in public. Anyone who takes a few moments to chat with a neighbor or an acquaintance in the street will always be sure to accuse himself of "wasting people's time" and will not admit to the pleasure this has given him. One must also be careful, however, not to carry this attitude too far, for it could mean that one is "restless," a person who is always running about, does not honor the Sabbath, and especially, does not feel that he can afford the time for a few words with his fellow villagers. Nonetheless, it is better to be "restless" than a "goof."

The villagers trot out this attitude whenever possible and try to use it to maximum advantage. Having nothing to show in terms of wealth and power, they compensate by judging people solely in terms of their energy, a quality they themselves do possess in ample measure. To obtain something by means other than personal struggle would not even be desirable under the terms of this ideology of effort.

The Ideology of the Employer Class

Meanwhile, the employer class elaborated its own ideology. It tried to implement the ideas of social Catholicism inspired by Frédéric Le Play who, at the end of the nineteenth century, had formulated the basic themes of an ideology of patronage; these ideas could also be used to oppose the spread of socialism. What are the principal points of this ideology?

—Relations based on force must be avoided. To this end, it is necessary to promote the idea of a social contract that would assign to each segment of society a specific role as well as its duty to society as a whole. "Le Play sees the most fruitful aspect of the patronage system in the fact that the clear awareness of mutual interests and obligations will maintain an excellent relationship [between workers and employers]. He also feels that the obligation to live up to agreements will result in well-being and harmony for everyone."[3]

—This ideology implied an elitist concept of society. Some people ("the

---

[3]Fontanille, *L'oeuvre sociale d'Albert de Mun* (Paris, 1926), p. 40.

social authorities'') are born to command, others are born to obey. "Some persons are marked by Providence, and they must fulfill a particular function in society," wrote Albert de Mun.[4] What is this function? To guide the people, to point out what is good for them. "This regime enables the employer class to carry out its social duty, which is to improve the morality and the lot of the workers, for history proves that the emancipation of the people has always been the work of the social authorities. . . . The fish dies when its head is chopped off."[5]

—Great emphasis is placed on charity. Self-sacrifice, a Christian virtue, alleviates the conscience of the employer class and improves the lot of the proletariat.

—Paternalism is an important aspect of this ideology. The employer must educate the workers by teaching them how to honor a contract and how to accept their station in life. By doing this, he establishes a moral connection between his personal interests and the great values of society for which he is responsible: The people will only revolt if they cease to trust the elites.

—The workers do not suffer because of poverty, but because of their lack of moral satisfactions. There is therefore no reason to raise wages; money must be given a human dimension. Under these circumstances, charity makes it possible to establish a human bond, which will bring the social partners closer together. The Christian order of things, based as it is on religion, family, and property, will provide the workers with moral satisfactions. These values, which are threatened by the development of the industrial society, must be preserved.

Large-scale agricultural entrepreneurs who felt threatened by the spread of socialist ideas also adopted this ideology of patronage, although it had been created for the use of the industrial employer class. The activities of a large-scale agricultural entrepreneur in Picardy who employed eighty workers and was considered to be a pioneer because of his social ideas have been described in great detail and with considerable enthusiasm by M. Pisseau. "Monsieur Eugène B. realized that it is the duty of the rich to extend a brotherly hand to those who might need his help and that, properly understood, it was in his interest to initiate a social movement in order to direct it according to his own enlightened principles. By the same token he also realized that he must not permit the movement to get out of hand by showing any reluctance in supporting it."[6] To this end he created permanent employment by financing a brick factory; he also accorded his workers benefits in kind—housing, bedding, food, hot soup in winter. He instituted a bonus system and founded a religious school for girls, a mutual benefit fund, and a retirement fund. Furthermore, he supported special charitable institutions, such as the "trousseau society," in

[4]Ibid., p. 97.
[5]Ibid., p. 40.
[6]M. Pisseau, *L'oeuvre sociale d'un grand propriétaire agricole: Le domaine de Moyenneville*. Thèse de droit (Paris, 1927), p. 12.

which his wife helped girls to assemble a trousseau. "When Monsieur Eugène
B. started his endeavors, the region had long been subjected to revolutionary
propaganda and had always sent a clear majority of radical socialist deputies
to Parliament" (p. 14). "As we have seen, Monsieur B. did not conquer the
hearts of the inhabitants of Moyenneville right away . . . but his ceaseless
efforts finally bore fruit, and his protegés thanked him by electing him mayor
of Moyenneville, long before the war. . . . Today, there is only one political
list in Moyenneville, that of Monsieur B." Monsieur B.'s son was able to
muster the votes of the socialists, which was something his father had never
been able to accomplish. In this connection, M. Pisseau notes: "All of
Monsieur B.'s sons were perfectly willing to take a worker who needed to go
to Compiègne in their personal car and to have him sitting next to them" (p.
136). For Pisseau, the "social idea" is the best prophylaxis (sic) against
socialism. It must be put into practice by the employer class, which will thus
be able to reward the good workers and leave out the others. In order to
benefit from the charitable institutions, for example, a worker had to stay
away from politics. M. Pisseau found it necessary to conclude: "Needless to
say, no strike or lockout ever took place in Moyenneville" (p. 101), the
reason being that "while the workers know that Monsieur B.'s income is
incomparably greater than their own, they also know that such gentlemen
have enormous expenses and that their generosity redeems their wealth" (p.
87).

Today certain themes in the ideas of social Catholicism—charity for
example—have fallen into disuse, but essentially this ideology of patronage
still inspires the employer class. The employer feels it to be his duty to assume
moral leadership and to set a good example; thus, he will head a drive to
combat alcoholism, attend mass regularly, show proper behavior at all times
and speak up for work and the salutary effects of effort. Since the village is
one big family, he must assume a specific role there; he must give orders and
see to it that they are carried out, and he must supervise and see that everything is done properly. As long as everyone knows his place, things are bound
to go well.

Why does the patron-employer manage the villagers in this manner? What
is the reason for this paternalism? He feels that there is no other way, for he
considers the villagers to be big children, often lazy, and apt to fall into bad
habits. It is the patron-employer's role to give them work, to guide them, and
to reprimand them if need be. He may even dress them down in public;
"Don't make so much noise," he may sternly say at the village café. Obviously, the workers, treated like children in this manner and totally without
power, must draw the logical conclusion from the situation and regard the
patron-employer more often as a father than as an employer. Hence, their
self-censoring attitude in any dealings with him, their frequent spying on
fellow workers, their hatred of the patron's favorites, their endeavors to curry
favor, and their show of respect at all times. Everyone always asks for his

wages politely. Some even fear the hypothetical situation in which there might be no patron-employer at all. Who would give them work? In their situation they cannot even conceive of a different role for themselves.

Objectives of the Two Parties

These two ideologies, that of the "deserving worker" and that of the patron-employer as "father of the village," are part of a consensus, a framework that permits both parties to develop their strategies, since each can count on certain predictable reactions. Both ideologies are manipulated by the patron or by the client, as the case may be, to justify their particular objectives.

THE OBJECTIVES OF THE
PATRON-EMPLOYER

The objectives of the patron-employer are defined by two major considerations. On the one hand, he wants to maintain prestige and reputation based on the devotion and allegiance of a large number of clients. Prestige permits him to identify with the image of his forebears and gives him a sense of power that compensates for a feeling of inferiority owing to his marginal position in present-day industrial society. On the other hand, he wants to continue to exert his influence in order to manipulate the villagers' political behavior, thereby guaranteeing the willing cooperation of his work force. In other words, he wants to uphold the status quo in every respect, and to this end it is particularly important to preserve the fundamental values. Thus, the patron-employer wants to be esteemed and respected as the incarnation of goodness, as one who works for the good of others. In this respect, he has clearly reached his objective and can easily interpret his workers' attitudes in a sense favorable to him. Respect mixed with fear is expressed in various forms of behavior; men take off their berets when they enter the grounds of the château, which they always cross on foot rather than on their bicycle; they address their patron-employer as *vous*, while he calls them *tu*. Of course, disrespectful jokes are freely made behind his back; some of the workers refer to him as *Monseigneur*, for example.

Admiration is expressed in conversations among villagers for, as I have already pointed out, people take pride in their personal acquaintance with "the château." While severe personal criticism may well be expressed in such conversations, the patron-employer is still admired as châtelain and notable. In other words, the admiration is for the public personage rather than for the man himself. Presents from the closest clients—the finest products of their vegetable gardens, fruit, blood sausage when the pig has been slaughtered—give concrete expression to their interest in his existence.

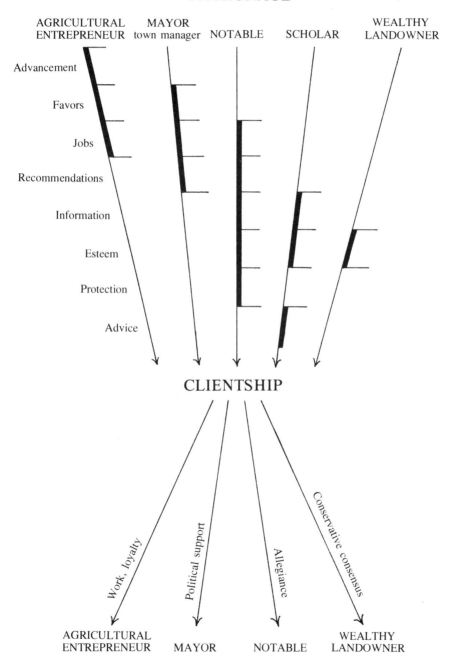

Figure 6.1. The Patron-Client Relationship

But the patron-employer wants more than the personal satisfaction he derives from the attitude of his clients; he also expects tangible services from them. His first priority is to keep a constant supply of faithful, devoted, and disciplined labor in the village. In Picardy, dissatisfied workers are traditionally free to leave their employer, who will neither hinder their departure nor contact other employers in order to prevent such workers from finding work elsewhere. As long as a recalcitrant worker does not engage in open defiance or in clandestine activities, the employer does not interfere. Thus some workers have sought work within a radius of ten to fifteen kilometers from the village.[7] If the patron-employer wants to keep his labor force without having to raise wages, which differ from farm to farm (hence creating a potentially competitive situation for the employers), he must offer his permanent workers special advantages. In this manner he will establish a preferential relationship, based on mutual assurances, with the most loyal workers. To that extent it is to the workers' advantage to remain in the service of a powerful man, for in case of need they can call on him for help rather than face the risks of the unknown. In this manner the employer hopes to create a reliable work force for himself, and indeed, the results bear him out. This policy was completely successful in the past and still works for the generation over forty. It is no longer convincing to younger people, but then they no longer wish to live in the village in any case.

Finally, the patron-employer seeks to use these client families as a source of inexpensive substitute labor. Whenever extra help is needed (a sudden rush, illness, etc.) he can ask a son or the wife of a client to come to work, and the client will not dare to refuse, even if he himself may have to do without the help he needs. Until very recently, this solution was always easily available to the patron-employer. Now that money plays a much more important role than it did in the past, however, the peasant attaches a price tag to situations that were never part of any accounting system before, and when he lends out his son, he calculates his benefits and weighs the advantages he derives against the services he renders.

Another objective of the patron-employer is control of the municipality. Such control will enable him to steer the decisions of the town council in a direction favorable to him, thus extending his power even further. His interests are not the same as those of the villagers, who wish for the modernization of the community. They want such things as a public water supply, street lighting, tarring of cart roads, and so forth, all of which demand an increased budget. As the largest landowner, the notable is interested in keeping the communal budget as low as possible. (In an effort to reduce "wages," by far the largest item in the communal budget, the mayor of Vercourt took over the job of secretary to the mayor himself and put off the appointment of a new

---

[7]Alain Morel, "L'espace social d'un village picard," *Etudes rurales* 45 (January–March 1972): 73.

field warden, having dismissed the old one for professional misconduct.) Recall that any increase in the budget is financed by a rise in the property tax, which means higher taxes for the largest property owners. Once the employer-patron-notable has become mayor, he wields twofold power. As mayor he is the only link between the government and the local inhabitants; it is he who transmits and comments on information from the outside; it is he who passes on the demands of his constituents, he who advises them. Furthermore, he is responsible for the appointment of rural officials and is therefore in a position to favor his own clients. Finally, he represents authority, and this fact alone brings him obedience and respect.

Under these circumstances, the notable will always have his way, since his competence and his qualifications are above doubt. But even if he does not seek the office of mayor, scorning a power he does not need and one that would also impose certain obligations; even if he prefers to leave the villagers with the illusion that they are governing themselves, he will be able to exert a very considerable influence over the decisions of the municipality through the channel of certain of his clients who are members of the municipal council. In any case, being the "Monsieur," he has no need to solicit the votes of his clients. On the one occasion when this did happen, two employers of equal importance were running for mayor, and both of their "teams" were very firmly advised to vote properly. In some cases there were actual threats of dismissal. In this particular case, however, neither of the candidates could indisputably be defined as a notable. The notable "from way back" does not have to campaign, since he has a large number of the villagers in his pocket already, either directly or through family connections.

Lastly, the patron-employer has one less obvious objective. He wants to have some trustworthy associates who will bring him information on village affairs that might otherwise escape his attention and who will disseminate his religious, political, and social ideas, all of which are of course conservative. Usually, his most loyal clients take over this function and tell him what X, Y, and Z are doing, or who has been caught stealing. They also report workers who are considered to be unreliable. In this manner the patron-employer knows what is going on in his community, so that he can more easily manipulate people and be ready with arguments that do not deal in generalities, but are tailored to their own, personal concerns.

The notable also counts on his informants for the dissemination of his own propaganda through the network of family relations, through conversations at the café, and so forth. For he feels it his duty to counteract the communist propaganda, for which he holds the schoolteacher responsible.

Even today the patron-employer benefits from these various services. But his influence has diminished to the point that it no longer affects anyone but his own workers and certain people who derive special advantages from him. The decline of his clientele has gone hand in hand with the decrease in the number of villagers who earn their livelihood in agriculture. Those who work in other occupations have different concerns; they either have needs that the local notable cannot fulfill or that they can satisfy by other means.

THE OBJECTIVES OF THE CLIENTS

For their part, the clients essentially have two objectives. On the one hand, they want to increase their material well-being by obtaining special privileges or services. On the other hand, they seek security in a position that permits them to call on their patron-employer for help if necessary. But while the patron is the main source of benefits, he cannot be expected to fulfill every need. He is therefore called upon only to the extent that he has something to give. For this reason, the expectations of the clients should be seen as a function of the services a patron can render. He can "give" work, and a good job is a major asset. Workers also used to ask their employer for help when it came to raising a cow or a pig. Depending on the circumstances, the patron would let his clients use a plot of ground where they could grow grain and beets; he would lend them farm equipment or even give them permission to pasture a cow in his own meadows. Workers would also borrow the patron's vehicles for various cartage needs, such as the transport of manure, firewood, etc. This service was called "the boss's corvée."

In another type of exchange the worker cultivated a piece of land belonging to the notable and gave him part of the crop. Being able to borrow equipment was vitally important to the "householder."[8] This kind of dependence is concrete evidence of the power of the patron, for the very accession to the status of householder, the first step in a worker's upward social mobility, depended on the patron's goodwill. Even today the châtelain renders such services. He has, for example, lent a meadow to one of his clients, a small farmer. Similarly, he sometimes gives clients who have leased a farm from him the use of his equipment. Compared with the past, only the objects have changed; it is no longer a horse, but a lawn mower that is borrowed.

Traditionally, unruly workers, the "independent ones" who had little use for personal loyalty and went to work elsewhere if "things didn't work out," obviously could not hope to avail themselves of the patron's services to the same extent as the loyal workers did. Since the notable owned the homes of some of his workers, many workers tried to buy their houses so that they would not have to move in case of dismissal. But no one can buy something that is not for sale. If the landlord decided to sell, it was not as a special favor to one of his workers, but as a recompense to a client who had been loyal for many years.

A patron can perform many other services. He can quickly drive a sick person or the victim of an accident to the hospital; he can act as a banker,

[8]See n. 2.

either by extending a loan or by withholding the wages of a worker who is afraid of spending them! He can give advice on the use of a new piece of machinery or on the interpretation of a new government regulation. When the farmers were urged to adopt the T.V.A. [Value-added tax], for example, they naturally turned to their notable for an explanation of the advantages and disadvantages of the new system. Thanks to his connections among the rural notables as well as among public officials and manufacturers, the notable was in a position to find jobs for his people, especially domestic jobs for women. By the same token, he was also able to intervene in case of difficulties with the police. Here again, his influence has diminished considerably. In the past, such connections also gave the notable access to the latest news. "Passing on the word" was another favor he would bestow on his clients, who derived special status from their knowledgeability. For some time now, the mass media have taken over this function.

Today, new needs have arisen, and they are of such a nature that the patron-employer can no longer respond to them. If, for example, the son of one of his workers wants to learn a trade and live in the city, that worker can call upon relatives who have already migrated to the city, and they will receive the young man and help him find a job. As for the clients, they are increasingly interested in the blessings of the consumer society. They want a car, they want television, they want modern conveniences, and they must harness their resources to achieve these goals. These needs can only be fulfilled by an increase in wages or in revenue, and that can only be accomplished by an organized effort to break the power of the patron-employer. Individual "arrangements" will no longer do.

Before comparing these relations with others of the patron-client variety, we should try to find out which features are characteristic of Picardy. Here the ties between patron and client are direct: the patron knows every one of his clients. Theirs is an enduring relationship, which may continue over several generations. It is also voluntary, although the margin of maneuverability is not the same for the two parties. The patron can easily get along without those who might be unwilling to accept his conditions, while the villager will think twice before turning his back on a patron who, after all, is the only person who can provide certain services. In addition, this relation is open, for anyone who lives in the village can become a client; on the other hand, some of the local patron's clients work at Vercourt, but do not live there. And while this relationship is, generally speaking, of the contractual type—both parties pledge themselves to furnish the equivalent of what they have received—it is also informal. The terms of the exchange are arrived at by tacit agreement rather than by legal contract. Finally, this relation is multifunctional. It is not designed to fulfill one specific need, but rather to respond to the entire range of both parties' concerns.

A comparison with other systems of relations of dependence will make it

easier to grasp the originality of the model obtaining in Picardy. This comparison will involve Castile, Umbria, and Sicily.[9] Generally speaking, the
respective needs and the goods and services exchanged are the same in each of
these systems. It is also possible to give a general definition of roles. On the
one hand, there is a patron who acts as mediator and protector; on the other,
there are his clients, who play his game in the areas of politics, economics,
and ideology. Yet by carrying the analysis further, one realizes that these
relations are designed to fulfill comparable but not identical needs, since these
various societies have neither the same rules nor the same values.

In Castile and Sicily, for example, the duty to provide help and protection
for family and friends takes precedence over the sense of duty toward the
employer or the state. This rule has fostered the opinion that all public officials are corrupt, and necessarily so. It is therefore a general conviction that
"to straighten out one's affairs in the city," one must know the person in
charge and have an "entry." Here the role of mediator, which is rather muted
in Picardy, assumes capital importance. Indeed, in Castile and Sicily, where
agricultural societies have the structure of an urban environment, the needs
and the services to be rendered are more diversified. In this situation, we find
much more complex and extended, pyramid-shaped networks of relations, in
which the man who is seen as a patron by his clients is himself the client of
more powerful patrons. Everyone wants to be a chief and attempts to surround
himself with a network of influence and support that will enable him to wield
maximum power. Clients who have achieved status and position will in their
turn exercise authority and influence, distribute favors, or act as inter-
mediaries. At that point, they too will be courted by those who have less
influence. This is not a possibility for the client of Picardy. Hemmed in by the
structure of his village, he does not demand services of this kind from his
patron. For this reason the patron of Picardy is more interested in relations of
the lateral type, friends in town, for example, so that his field of activity is
more restricted than that of his Mediterranean counterpart.

The situation in central Italy, on the other hand, resembles the situation in
Picardy. In Umbria the patrons form a local group and play an active role in
the lives of the villagers. The relation between the patron and his client has
strong paternalist overtones. Both patron and client feel that they belong to the
same world, the same family, and they will always stress their mutual friend-
ship. The role of mediator between urban and rural society, the national and
the local culture, and different social classes is here seen not so much as that
of an intermediary who has "a long arm" as that of the repository of knowledge who belongs to a different milieu and is competent to administer, interpret, inform, counsel, intercede, and help. In this way the client deals with

[9]Sydel F. Silverman, "Patronage and Community-Nation Relationship in Central Italy,"
Ethnology 4 (1965): 172–89; M. Kenny, "Patterns of Patronage in Spain," *Anthropological
Quarterly* 33 (1960): 14–23; J. Boissevain, "Poverty and Politics in a Sicilian Agrotown,"
International Archives of Ethnography 1, no. 2 (1966).

one general mediator rather than with a series of specialized mediators. As in Picardy, such patrons are confirmed notables, and the client cannot become a patron himself, for wealth alone is not sufficient; the real prerequisite is notability. In Umbria the relation between patron and client is based on the same ideology as in Picardy, for it is an extension of the relation between landlord and tenant farmer, which was created by the system of land tenure.

Yet, in contrast to the less urbanized society of Picardy, Umbrian society has produced notables who are not only landowners, but also priests, mayors, militia officers, physicians, or pharmacists. Thus, the clients are in a position to choose the most useful individual among several patrons. In this case the distribution of power is obviously more favorable to the client than in a situation where all power is in the hands of a single individual. Here, too, there is a hierarchy of patrons, since some patrons are themselves clients of other patrons. In this system the villagers are the last link in a chain that extends to the highest powers of the nation.

All of these societies have two points in common. On the one hand, the patron, whether Sicilian, Umbrian, Castilian, or Picard, has one basic objective: he wants to mask the class structure and maintain the status quo by controlling the opposing forces that might jeopardize the consensus. This objective is most openly expressed in Sicily, where the patrons direct violent repressive actions against militant labor leaders. Between 1946 and 1948, fourteen labor leaders were murdered in several cities of western Sicily. It was not a concerted action, but rather the spontaneous expression of a general conflict that had its origin in the tension between the powerful landowning interests and the increasingly fierce struggle of the better and better organized workers who were determined to take over the land. Thus we see that the patron seeks to maintain his material situation, which is one of the foundations of his social position. But at the same time, he also pursues another objective: he wants to preserve his power and increase his influence. To this end, he tries to take over several sources of power in several areas of life, thereby creating the illusion that his power is innate, a permanent attribute against which there is no revolt. Such power resembles that of the father, who has the authority to decide what is good and what is not good and who can set a course and make his "innocent protegés" follow it. In order to attain this kind of power, the patron voluntarily creates for himself obligations toward his clients, who, in return, give him their support and render him a variety of services. In other words, the patron's power can only be maintained by a process of exchanges.

But now the system is crumbling. Today the sources of the patron's power—information and work—are beyond his control, indeed beyond his reach, and his power ends at the limits of the village.

7
Tillers of the Fields and Woodspeople*

Tina Jolas
and Françoise Zonabend

The village of Minot is situated on a plateau.[1] Clustered at the center of the village land, it opens on the plain,[2] a cultivated area divided into small plots and almost entirely surrounded by the solid mass of the communal forest. Outlying farms are wedged between the tilled fields and the forest. This configuration, visibly inscribed, as it were, in the very outlines of the land and its various uses, immediately points to a contrast between the periphery and the center, the wild and the cultivated, the communal and the private.

At the time of the 1876 census, Minot had 523 inhabitants: 50 heads of farming families, 49 artisans,[3] 11 tradesmen, 47 agricultural workers, day laborers, or farm hands, 35 *rentiers* [people living on an income], 7 government or municipal employees, 1 physician, and 2 beggars. The recession that so severely affected the region of Châtillon at the turn of the century further accentuated the population decline that had begun as early as at the end of the

---

Annales, E.S.C. 28 (January–February 1973): 285–305. Translated by Elborg Forster.

*Unfortunately it is impossible to reproduce the striking parallel construction of the French title *Gens du finage, gens du bois,* since there is no one English word for *finage. Tillers of the fields* and *woodspeople,* then, is the best that can be done—Trans.

[1]This study of the village of Minot (Northern Burgundy) was a group project carried out under the auspices of the Laboratoire d'Anthropologie sociale by Tina Jolas, Marie-Claude Pingaud, Yvonne Verdier, and Françoise Zonabend.

[2]In Minot the word *plain* designates the *finage,* the cultivated area of the land belonging to the village.

[3]By 1876, the real tradition of the independent craftsman had already ceased to exist at Minot. Craftsmen were tied either to agriculture (there were 3 shoeing smiths, 2 cartwrights, and 2 harness makers) or to the building trades (6 masons, 1 plasterer, 1 bricklayer) or to the forest (11 woodcutters, 6 sawyers, 1 log splitter). There were also 3 barrel makers and 2 coopers who worked for the vintners of the Burgundian wine-country, in addition to 4 sabot makers and 2 shoemakers. The presence of 5 weavers, finally, serves as a reminder of an activity that had flourished earlier. The women were menders, seamstresses, hatters, and laundresses.

nineteenth century.[4] By 1921, the census registered only 292 inhabitants. Recovery was slow. The 1968 census registered 359 inhabitants, namely, 25 heads of farming families, 1 artisan, 2 tradesmen, 29 laborers, 22 retired persons, 7 public employees, 7 small entrepreneurs, and 2 agricultural laborers.

Yet this distribution of occupations cannot hope to capture the real situation, which the oldest inhabitants of the village describe in terms of a double cleavage.

First, these villagers speak in terms of a cleavage between the "poor" and the "rich." "Until the last war the village was split into two parts: on the one hand, the *Messieurs*, or the "haves," on the other, the "have-nots", essentially consisting of the entire community, which, as a result of these tensions, had a strong sense of identity and solidarity. "Minot used to be one big family . . . everybody was poor." But this poverty, shared as it was by everyone (the farmers were not much better off than the woodcutters or the laborers), was seen as a virtue; in the people's memory that time of general poverty is remembered as a time of mutual help and understanding. "Then life was better than it is today; now people are too proud and everyone looks out for himself. In those days neighbors would help each other out and everyone got together. Nowadays, people stay at home; times have changed. It's because we were not rich."

The Messieurs

In 1876, the *Messieurs*—the rich—were essentially represented by two families, Potey and Villerey.[5] "We did not eat meat more than two or three times a year. The butcher came through once a week, and he really had only three customers, the château, the Villerey family, and the schoolteachers." The food of the *Messieurs* was characterized by the fact that it was purchased. They would even buy the wild fruits of the land that could be gathered—a bounty not usually sold or even given away. "We used to search for truffles under the oak trees; the *Messieurs* wanted to buy them." Later, the *Messieurs* were even credited with introducing the tomato. They also read the newspapers. "The postman used to bring three newspapers here; they were for Monsieur Potey, for Monsieur Villerey's place, and for the schoolteachers."[6]

[4]On the economy of the region of Châtillon at the end of the nineteenth century, see P. Mathal and P. Evrard, "L'évolution en longue période de l'agriculture d'une petite région: le Châtillonnais" (Paris: Institut de la recherche agronomique, 1967), mimeographed, no pagination. Chapter 2, in particular, analyzes the causes and the effects of the economic crisis, namely, the decline in the sale of wool and grain and the loss of markets for the local iron and wood.

[5]Most of the statements reproduced here refer to the period of time between the youth of our oldest informants—around 1880—and the postwar years and the technological upheaval of the 1950s. We started our analysis of the censuses with the year 1876 in order to cover the entire period.

[6]Note the different manner of referring to these two individuals. The term *Monsieur* translates the very clear-cut distance between Potey, a notable of long standing, and the community. By

The *Messieurs* were the repositories of written knowledge, the bringers of new techniques, and such, precisely, are the traditional attributes of those who hold power in the village.

The Potey family lived at Le Mont [the Hill] in the old seigneurial château; the Villerey family lived at Le Vaux [the Valley] in the "Big House," which is called the "lower château" to this day.

Georges Potey's maternal great-grandfather was Joseph Joly, chief stewart of the last seigneur of Minot and heir to part of his land. After Joseph Joly had become a rent-collecting landowner [*rentier-propriétaire*], he married his daughter to Louis Guillemin, doctor of medicine, a scion of the regional bourgeoisie. Their daughter Marie also married a physician, Pierre Potey. That couple's son, Georges, steeped himself in local history and archaeology; although he had inherited the château and the land belonging to it, he took very little interest in the management of his fortune. Married to Marie Saunier, the daughter of a wealthy landowning family, he died without offspring in 1916, leaving his widow in straitened circumstances.

The Villereys were descended from a modest family of artisans. Jean-François Villerey, who had been a shoemaker in 1808, was referred to as *propriétaire-rentier* in the census of 1836. In 1847 his son Jean acquired the office of notary at Aignay and, due to the favorable economic circumstances of that period, was able to build up, piece by piece, a considerable landed estate. His son Etienne was to do likewise. "In those days, all the farmers were very poor. M. Villerey's father was a notary, and he lent out a lot of money. But the farmers couldn't pay back, so they gave him their fields, and then their houses." There is a striking parallel between the rise of the Mairetet family,[7] the last seigneurs of Minot, in the seventeenth century, and that of the Villerey family in the eighteenth. The founders of both families were originally artisans, both bought land, and both acquired the office of notary, which helped them to consolidate their landed fortune. The only difference is that in this process of domain building, Denis Mairetet was able to avail himself of seigneurial prerogatives in addition to the prerogatives of money.

As the social ascent of the Villerey family was becoming more definite, matrimonial alliances within the community gradually came to an end. While Etienne Villerey still married a remote cousin of Minot's rich wine merchant, his daughters broke with past traditions and contracted alliances outside the matrimonial confines of the community; indeed, they no longer lived permanently in the area. After Etienne Villerey's death in 1919 there were no longer any *Messieurs* in the village.

---

contrast, Villerey, whose social standing is of more recent origin, is also designated as *Monsieur*, but this term is still used in conjunction with "place" (*chez*), which is also used to refer to all the other families of the village.

[7]On the history of the Mairetet family, see G. Roupnel, *La ville et la campagne au* XVIIIe *siècle. Etude sur les populations du pays dijonnais* (Paris, 1955), pp. 221–73.

Physically occupying the opposite ends of the village, the *Messieurs* were antagonists in every possible way. For almost a century, from 1830 to 1920, the political history of Minot was dominated by the constant rivalry between the two families. There was the struggle for power in the municipal government and conflict in the vestry board of the church, and there were ideological differences. In 1870 one family was in favor of the Empire, the other of the Republic; later, one was pro-Dreyfus, the other anti-Dreyfus.[8] This rivalry reproduced a much older conflict, in which Le Mont represented lay power, the seigneurie, and Le Vaux, religious power—for the church stood in the lower village. It is possible that this antagonism favored an early development of communal power. Today the location of power has changed. The mayor lives in the center of the village, across the street from the school and the town hall, and both the upper and the lower châteaux stand empty most of the year. One is a youth camp and the other a private summer residence.

Although united against this twofold power, the community was less homogeneous than might appear at first sight. There was a second cleavage, which was expressed in terms of a certain relationship with the land and livestock: "My father had neither land nor a cow; he had a goat, a pig, and a few chickens, that's all."

Those who had "land and cows" were the *tillers of the fields.* They either lived in the village, in which case their fields were scattered throughout the area, or they lived in the outlying areas of the plain, in which case their farms formed large continuous blocks of fields. But some of them were artisan-shopkeepers who, in addition to their multiple activities—the blacksmith also kept the inn, the barrel maker tended the tobacco shop, the cabinetmaker sold groceries, the tinsmith ran the café ("he sells wine by the glass"), the cartwright helped deliver the mail—owned a few pieces of land, one or two cows, a small flock of sheep, and some pigs and fowl. "My father-in-law ran a grocery store and bakery; he had two cows, a horse, and two or three hectares under cultivation."

As for those who had only "a goat, a pig, and a few chickens," they were *woodspeople,* who also used to be called "cutters in the forest." This term refers to woodcutters, charcoal burners, sawyers, and log splitters, but also to workmen, day laborers, road menders or, to use a more modern term, "workers." " 'Workers' means all the people who do not work their own land; woodcutters, farm hands, and day laborers are all workers." They were all people who, since they did not even own a cow, *bought their milk.* This distinction was sanctioned by a custom which, during Lent, required farmers to give free milk "to all those who buy it."

[8]The memory of these political struggles has been preserved for us by L. P. Chaume, schoolteacher in the village, in his "Histoire de Minot," a manuscript written circa 1913. It is in a family archive.

Tillers of the Fields

"We used to make vegetable stew every day: beans, potatoes, cabbage, parsnips, and a piece of fatback. We would eat soup made with that stew in the morning and at noon; at night we had soup with a little cream poured over slices of bread. There wasn't much butter because we would sell it, but cheese was made from curds and whey, and that, we'd keep." The tillers of the fields were practically self-sufficient. "In those days we lived on what we had. We didn't make much money—didn't really need it, except to pay the landlord. The egg-man would give us coffee, sugar, and salt for eggs or butter."

Each item of their food was related to an aspect of their "land and cows"—to the vegetable garden, the hemp field, and the various pieces of field-land in different areas. When Didier Lachaud, a weaver, died in 1879, he owned the following properties: a dwelling and farm buildings, including a barn, a stable, and a courtyard in one location; a separate garden of 2.4 ares in the village proper; 27 ares at Pré Piard; 10.8 ares at Froide-Fontaine; 33.20 ares at Grande Rente; and 7.40 ares at Petits Vaux, in the outlying area. His ownership was marked upon the land itself, but it was also laid down in writing, for these people not only appeared in the land records [*cadastre*] but also notarized their marriage contracts and the arrangements for the division of their property.

This cultivated space was regulated by an immemorial way of doing things which, in this area of open fields and scattered properties but clustered dwellings, maintained a balance between communal and private activities.

There was a certain way of doing things in the village and its immediate vicinity; one had to be careful not to "run into" the marked but unenclosed pastures, and one had to wait one's turn before leading one's animals to their designated watering spots. "One was always careful not to cross another herd, for that would have mixed up the animals. Every herd had a lead cow that was wearing a bell; and we knew each other's bells. And as they could be heard from far away, we would say, depending on the sound: 'These are the cows from Tribolet's place, these are the ones from Camuset's place'."

There was also a certain way of doing things in the outlying areas of tilled fields, where one had to be careful not to "overstep," not to disturb a dividing line ("a furrow that has not been touched for a hundred years and serves as a divider between two fields"); here everyone was enjoined to see to it that the fields not be "broken up, left untended, or planted out of rotation," as the leases put it until the last war; likewise, it was forbidden to hinder anyone from exercising his communal right, namely grazing livestock after the harvest, gathering, and gleaning.

The evolution of grazing practices shows the constraints inherent in this way of doing things. In the past, all the livestock of the village grazed on the uncultivated communal land and on any temporarily fallow fields under the care of the village herdsman. By the end of the nineteenth century the gradual changeover from fallow fields to forage crops no longer permitted the pasturing of communal herds. The last contract with a communal herdsman was drawn up in 1885. Ever since then, each farm has raised its own forage crops and pastured its animals on its own land. The herding of livestock is now entrusted to children—and all the children of the community[9] "take the cows to the fields"—but in the intricate mosaic of this open-field system, where the fields take the shapes of curves, corners, and points, this is not an easy task. The children must learn to recognize the boundaries of all the properties and be sure that the animals do not "cause damage." "We were forever pushing the cows to the right or the left to keep them within a field, so that they wouldn't do any damage." There was a whole parajudicial system for transgressions: "If any damage had been done, the field warden would send us to the proprietor to say that we were sorry." Until World War II, and even until the land reorganization of 1959, the tillers of the fields experienced "taking the cows to the fields" as a conflict caused by the changeover from the collective to the individual herd without a concomitant change in the structure and organization of the traditional open-field system. The excessive fragmentation of inheritances and the variety of crops in each area made the enclosure of fields impossible;[10] "you couldn't have a cow pasture in the middle of the beet or wheat fields; people simply had to use different areas. We had a triennial rotation, so that the fields were big enough to take the animals without doing damage. Enclosures really started only in 1950." This is why the herds had to be constantly shifted about and why they were divided and scattered all over the individual fields. This restlessness, as it were, of animals constantly wandering through the fields in every direction forms a stark contrast with the slow movement of the big herd under the communal system, and also with the immobile existence herds now lead in their newly enclosed pastures.

This finite sphere of subsistence, where everything has its name and its order, has its counterpart in a sphere of relationships which, while not finite, but circumscribed, is equally named and ordered. For to have a place in one sphere automatically means to be genealogically situated—and traceable—in the other. "His wife was a Couperet, whose brother married a girl by the

[9]All the children, those of the tillers of the fields as well as those of the woodspeople, "learned" the land in this manner. But while this was an immediate economic necessity for one group ("the children of the woodcutters were hired out by the time they were six years old; they watched the cows; in this way they were at least fed and earned their wooden shoes"), it was seen as an educational experience for others: "The children (of farmers and craftsmen) were placed with an uncle, so that they would learn to work." "Watching the animals in the fields" was an experience common to everyone, almost an initiation, which later, when it had ceased to respond to an economic need, took on the character of a normative value. "Albert Cochois (a mason) came here asking me to take on his children. He said: 'I took the cows to the fields when I was a youngster, and I want my kids to do it too.'"

[10]The first enclosures are attributed to the people from the Morvan, and the inhabitants of Minot still make fun of them: "In the old days, the only enclosure for a pasture was at Desgranges' place. They sure went to a lot of trouble to build a wall all around a field!"

name of Alice Chauvirot. Alice's brother, Albert, is a pharmacist at Is-sur-Tille, and he is married to a Lamarche. Some others are from that family, too. Albert and Alice's mother was Marie Bergeret, the sister of Jeanne, who was married to Jean Lanier; they were the maternal grandparents of my mother-in-law. My oldest daughter, who lives near Is-sur-Tille, went to the pharmacist there, and when she gave her name, he said: 'How about that, I know we have some relatives by that name; we should try to find out how you are related to us.' My daughter spoke to me about it, and of course the connection is easy to make; it is through the Bergerets.''

Clearly, these people know that they are all related by marriage or direct descent to the few founding families of the village whose names appear in the community's first written documents, the religious census (1642) and the records of seigneurial justice (1686); furthermore, their kinship ties are duly confirmed by the genealogies. They know that they belong to families which, as they say, ''are related from way back,'' keep up their ties of alliance and descent, and carefully preserve all written records, such as contracts, announcements, leases, the family arrangements of their forebears, and so forth.

This means ''cousining'' with just about everybody: ''I am a cousin to half the village, and we all know each other very well.... We call each other cousin.'' Such cousinship does not refer to a precise kinship relation as much as to a certain status. This status implies that one belongs to a regulated universe, one that brings with it the obligation of mutual help, an etiquette of kinship, and matrimonial constraints.

The obligation of mutual help applies to the ''cousins'' in the village who are often neighbors in the same part of the village or live along the same street. ''In the rue Paluet there were Toussaints at every door.'' These cousin-neighbors may be both farmers and artisans, for in every generation each group of brothers splits up into different occupational categories. Of the seven children of Nicholas Lachaud, the owner of the farm of Buxerolles, only the eldest son went into farming. Nicholas became a weaver, Didier a shoemaker, Jean-Baptiste a cartwright; and of the three daughters, Anne married Pierre Lafol, a small independent farmer, keeping Madeleine, who did not marry, with her, and Victorine married a farmer at Poiseul-lès-Saulx, where she went to live. The mutual help concerned mainly the ''land and cows.'' The few small plots of land belonging to the artisans were cultivated by a relative who was a farmer in exchange for ''a hand with the hay and the harvest''; hence the meeting of the clans at harvest time. ''For the threshing with the steam thresher (1920) we would need at least twenty guys, so we would get together with Fleurot, my brother-in-law, with the fellows from Tribolet's place, and with those from Mairet's place; those from Chanut's place, who were relatives of my cousin who ran the dry-goods store, would also come to help.'' The same was true for the livestock: ''Old mother Morelot, the dressmaker, she had a cow, which she put with the herd of the farmer next door. He let her have milk, her butter, her cheese, and in exchange she gave him a calf.'' Even today, Clémence Bernigaud, who used to work a farm, keeps her cow with those of her nephew who is a farmer, but she also does the milking for his herd. Between these close cousin-neighbors, milk assumes the function of an almost unbreakable tie: "For our milk, we would always go to someone in the family." No money was involved in any of these transactions, which always took the form of exchanges of goods and services. "We lend things . . . we give something in return . . . we help each other out." The harness maker borrowed a horse from a farming cousin when he had to make the rounds to oil his customers' harnesses. "In exchange, I kept his harnesses in repair. . . . Sometimes, I was paid in kind, with a part of a slaughtered pig, five kilos of melting-butter, or potatoes." Nonetheless, there was never a pooling of resources: "Everyone was on his own."

The etiquette of kinship, which applies to relatives scattered throughout the region, involves a much larger network of relationships. "We visit the family graves twice a year. On Palm Sunday I take green branches to the graves of our relatives at Frolois, Etalente, Blaisy-Bas, and Poiseul-la-Ville. My brother goes at All Saints' Day." People also participate in family reunions outside the village: "We are invited to a wedding at Echalot." In this manner, ties between communities are established: "We usually go to three festivals every year, that of our own village and those of our two grandfathers' villages." These obligations lead to a kind of pseudo-kinship: "Madame Fresnaud and I used to meet at every family reunion. She was a relative on the uncle's side, I on the aunt's, so we would always meet and we would act like cousins; but really, we are not related at all."

This sphere of cousinship coincides with the area over which the family has spread; it is the area within which the members visit, take part in village festivals, and find their marriage partners. For it is at weddings and festivals that couples meet. There is, then, a definite sphere of marriage possibilities, which can be placed within certain geographical boundaries and which is also confirmed by and clearly visible in the records of the public registry. In this respect, Minot is open in almost every direction over a radius of some fifty kilometers, but it closes itself off toward the north-northwest, in the vicinity of Aignay-le-Duc, the cantonal seat, and Châtillon. The standoffish, almost hostile attitude of the villagers toward the people of Aignay is expressed in many ways; in particular, there is a great deal of criticism of their casual attitude toward death: "I once saw a funeral there that was attended by no more than fifteen people." And besides, "for marriages we don't go any further than Moitron," a village halfway between Minot and Aignay. This whole tradition is justified in meteorological terms: "From the direction of Moitron came neither good winds nor good people." Even though the contours of Minot's land and its water table are sloped toward the northeast, this village of the plateau keeps in contact with only those communities that show the same physical features, the same lay of the land, the same balance between field and forest. Whatever lies beyond, Minot neither wants to know nor to marry.

But even within these limits, the people of Minot are faced with matrimo-

nial constraints. Marriage "says something" about people. Men and women
know and say what they do, or should be doing, when they marry. What does
a marriage "say"? "One always married the same people. It used to be that
we married among ourselves; it would not do really to go outside the family;
the money shouldn't leave it." To be sure, the phrase "among ourselves"
could be taken in a larger sense: "They were people in the same line of work,
both families were equally as well-off, so that was a proper match."[11] Or,
even better: People married "for the land; it was always a matter of fields."
Such a twofold exigency dictated a matrimonial strategy that combined two
terms, namely, genealogical as well as spatial proximity—kinship and the
land.

Genealogical proximity is the main reason for marriage between consanguineous relatives and members of previously allied families in the village and
within the matrimonial sphere.[12] Spatial proximity is the reason for marriage
between people of the same village. When both of these conditions are present, a marriage will take place between people who are from both the same
family and the same village, when only one is present, they will be from either
the same family or the same village. When neither of them is present, in other
words, when neither kinship nor the land is involved, one is left with the
reference to the sphere of matrimonial possibilities.

However, these two exigencies do not carry the same weight. The land is
considered the more important.[13] "How we loved that land, you wouldn't
believe it! It meant more than anything else. But you must understand that it
was hard to come by. It was bought piece by piece, and one had to give up
everything else to get some land together; so one really loved it and wouldn't
have given it up for anything!" Love of the land was used to explain marriages within the village:[14] "In the old days, people hardly ever left the village
to get married. Today the young people don't care about the land any longer.
They don't mind going away, even those who own property. They go to drive

---

[11]And yet marriages were not strictly homogamous. Alliances between craftsmen and farmers
were quite frequent, provided there was "a little something" on both sides and an heir to take
over a family farm. "My father did not give his consent to my marriage; he did not want me to
marry a shopkeeper. I was an only child, and there was no one else to take over the farm," the
retired keeper of the drygoods store related.

[12]A description of these marriages can be found in "Parler famille. . . ," *L'Homme* 10, no. 3
(1970): 5–26.

[13]On the transmission of landed property see M. C. Pingaud, "Terres et familles dans un
village du Châtillonnais," *Etudes rurales* 42 (April–June 1971).

[14]The relationship with the land, expressed in terms of an obligation to "stay," to "work it,"
sheds light on the high value attached to endogamy within the village—a phenomenon we had
already noted in an earlier study. And indeed, the level of endogamy has remained practically
unchanged. In the course of the century (1880–1970) 38 percent of the tillers of the fields married
people from the outside. At most, we can observe an expansion of the area of marriage possibilities since the use of the automobile has become more widespread. Yet this development has
served not so much to open up new possibilities as to renew contact with branches of the family
that had been lost from view. "With the car, we see a lot more marriages between cousins." The
change thus pertains only to the concept of endogamy.

a truck and leave everything behind. In the old days they wouldn't have done that; they would have said: 'If you own land, you *have an obligation* to take care of it, you *have an obligation* to stay'."

This recognition of a powerful, constraining bond with the land demonstrates the general tendency and the goal of the system, thus providing us with the elements of a typology.

Within the village of Minot, marriage between first cousins or the children of first cousins appears to fulfill every requirement, for the land is not divided but remains in the possession of the descent-group. In 1909 Theodore Courtot married his first cousin, Marie-Louise Grivot, and by doing this the couple combined the few hectares they had inherited. "We really loved that land more than anything, so we said, if you can marry your cousin, she has ten hectares, you have ten; just think what a nice piece of land that will give you. It will increase the holding of the whole family." In 1904 Mathilde Crochet, the only heiress to a small property, married her second cousin Nicholas Bernigaud, "so that the farm stayed in the family." But such marriages call forth somewhat ambiguous comments, which seem to imply that there was a lack of measure: "They certainly did own that little property of theirs." Here the need for self-sufficiency—that "among ourselves," "on our own"—has become excessive both in terms of blood and in terms of the land, for it is also said that "there is something wrong with the children."

The preferred marriages are those that unite consanguineous relatives (remote cousins) or members of previously allied families, for they preserve the distance between lineages and yet favor the circulation of property within the same group of families. Among such marriages double marriages are particularly favored—"this happened quite often, they'd meet at each other's weddings"—because, among other advantages, they simplified the division of landed property.

Since it was not always possible to unite two families by marriage, one sometimes had to "marry" two fields. "It was a great marriage; think of the two properties that were united. There were 150 guests, nothing but family."

Outside the village, but within the matrimonial sphere, it was a family that one married—"one marries the same kinds of people." And, if there is no family to marry, it is always possible to renew contact with the villages of uncles and grandfathers. Even if the matrimonial potential of such villages had been left fallow, as it were, they could be considered sufficiently familiar to become a terrain of preferential marriage. Such marriages prepare the ground for future marriages between allied families. Antoine Grivot, whose father had left Minot thirty years earlier, returned to marry Louise Ruchet; his uncles and cousins who had stayed behind in the village were his witnesses at the ceremony. Similarly, when she married Félix Pichon, Amandine Colin came back to the village her great-grandparents had left 150 years earlier. "She has brought her family back here."

Conversely, these exigencies rule out, at least in the beginning, marriage with strangers or newcomers, such as people from the Morvan or the Moselle. Such newcomers are relegated to outlying farms and marry among themselves for a generation or two. These outlying farms appear to have served as way stations, where strangers had to stop for a time before they were given access to land and marriage in the village. "Only old families were able to buy land."

Under these circumstances, marriage with the "have-nots," the "woods-people,"[15] is totally out of the question. "A farmer's son would not have married a worker's daughter; there had to be a little something behind her, a small inheritance, a cow or two. Marriage between woodcutters and farmers just wasn't possible. The girl had to have some money. The boy was waiting for it to buy things with."

The tillers of the fields keep up their kinship relations and store them away just as they keep up and store away their possessions. They are most careful to renew family ties whenever possible and to keep them from breaking down. "For the last-born child, we always ask distant relatives, second cousins or something, to be godparents—that brings the family together." Conventions and obligations enter the picture at every turn: "A lady at Beneuvre asked me to let my daughter be her daughter's partner at first communion, and I couldn't refuse because last year that lady's son had been my son's partner. But now Madame Fleurot, who had also asked me to let my daughter be her daughter's partner, and whom I had to turn down, is mad at me."

Memory of kinship and matrimonial constraints form the characteristic pattern of these genealogies. These lineages are deeply intermingled in their ascendant and collateral lines, where they form knots, cycles, loops, and overlapping patterns: "All these families are related in one way or another." Here we have an image of a family universe that is subtly regulated, of kinship relations that are ordered, even in disorder. Tillers of the fields do not go in for divorce; if absolutely necessary they will eventually go their separate ways, once all questions of inheritance have been settled, taking with them their own cow, a property subject to customary law that accompanies the individual throughout life.[16] "Old man Ferlet could no longer get along with his wife, so he took his cow and came to live with his children."

"The people of the plain had cows. They walked on all fours, just like their animals. Along came some "strangers," who had come down from the mountains (of the Morvan?). These people had learned from their goats, which were the only animals they kept, to walk on two feet, just like the goats do when they want to feed on the lower branches of trees. That is how the owners of the goats taught the owners of the cows to walk upright."[17]

---

[15]Of 162 marriages recorded in the village between 1880 and 1967, only 5 were between tillers of the fields and woodspeople.

[16]The cow, as well as the land, was mentioned in the marriage contract. The young man or the girl brought their cow and its calf into the new home. "When I was married, I had my personal trousseau, a bedroom with wardrobe closet, bed, headboard, dressing table, three cows, a set of pots and pans, and an old brooch."

[17]This story is told by a man from the Morvan.

Woodspeople

"We used to eat herrings cooked in the cinders, wrapped in wet newspapers, and potatoes . . . ; milk was something we'd drink only on holidays."

Whether they were workmen in the village or "cutters" in the woods, or even both at different times,[18] the woodspeople had no sphere of subsistence of their own. They had a tiny garden and the use of furrows between a few rows of hemp or, if they lived in the woods, the cleared space around their shack. The cultivated, privately owned fields, the resources of "land and cows"—vegetables, grain for pig or cow, milk—were thus available to them only in return for their services, sometimes for a small sum of money. "The woodcutters worked in the forest all winter; in the summer they helped with the hay and the harvest; in return they got their vegetables from the farmers, two sacks of potatoes, and maybe half a pig. . . ." If they were given any room at all in the area of tilled fields, the best they could hope for was the space between two furrows. "They used to plant their vegetables in among the beets."

Thus, the woodspeople had access to the tilled land only indirectly, either through the intermediacy of another person (and if there was no such intermediary, if that link was missing, they would steal "potatoes from the fields and cellars, lard from the smokehouses—it couldn't be helped, they were hungry!") or by virtue of collective customs involving cultivated products (gleaned after the harvest), wild products (gathered), and the right of passage ("we'd let the goat graze to the right and the left of the paths"). On the other hand, they did have direct access to the collectively owned, uncultivated land. The forest was their place of work during more than half of the year. Some lived there permanently, and in a sense it was the veritable sphere of subsistence for all of them. It was the place where they hunted, poached, gathered, and even tried to grow things.

Finally, their openness to the "outside" was reflected in the use of a foreign product, the herring, as the principal food staple ("All the woodcutters had a barrel of herrings for the winter").

The woodspeople were constantly moving back and forth between the forest and the fields, the village and the forest; they even moved around in the village itself, where they moved from place to place, although they always stayed grouped together in the same outlying neighborhoods, the Mont [Hill] and the Creux [the Hollow]. There was, however, a definite difference of degree in this mobility, for while the woodcutters, charcoal burners, and sawyers moved seasonally, the workmen, day laborers and handymen moved from day to day.

"My father-in-law was a handyman; he would help out here and there, and

---

[18]Nicholas Mouton appears in the census of 1876 as a woodcutter; five years later he is a worker-woodcutter, in 1886 he is a day laborer. In 1891 he is listed as "in the forest," and toward the end of his life he is again a woodcutter.

he would fix things, anything. There were a lot of people like that. They raised a few crops, they sometimes worked in the forest, they went over to the vineyards on the *côte* [the slopes of the Burgundian vineyard country] for the grape harvest, and they came to help people bring in the grain and tie the straw. They were called handymen or *tainusés*,[19] and these people could do anything.''

Here "doing odd jobs" is contrasted with "working," which was a long-term occupation in a fixed place. Handymen killed the pig, did the gardening, trimmed hedges, repaired enclosures. They often served as helpers to the postman; although, conversely, the postman often became a handyman by virtue of his very mobility. In the summer the handymen "gave a hand" to the farmers at harvest time; in winter "they were all out in the woods cutting." But they did not work for a timber merchant; they "went into the woods to help out," and those whom they "helped out" were invariably the tillers of the fields for whom they cut the communal firewood to which they were entitled. In return, the latter "took care of their cartage." Similarly, their women sewed for people ("for the public," as the census put it),[20] doing little sewing jobs at home or sewing corsets for a commercial enterprise. "My mother stitched the seams, the woman next door did the buttonholes." The work was distributed and later picked up by the *cossonier* [factor] who came by every week and, in exchange, brought oil, washing soda, coffee, and salt. In the village these women did housecleaning and laundry, for which they were paid partly in kind. "At Villerey's place they took in five or six women once a year for the big washing. They were well fed; the vegetable stew was good, and on top of that they took home a liter of milk. It was great!" In the fields these women "picked up the loose sheaves behind the scythe, and they also picked hops; that was money for the mother."

The handyman's knack for being everywhere at the same time was generally acknowledged and even considered an asset: "In those days I used to hire people for one job at a time. These handymen loved to do different kinds of work; they knew how to do everything—a basket, a door. . . . You don't find young people who like to do that any more. Even when they were little children you could see that that's what they wanted to do, they were so clever with their hands." Handymen were credited with special gifts and were sent for when it came to such tasks as capturing a swarm of bees ("the bees like them . . ."). They knew how to play the fiddle, how to whittle, how to play music at dances and weddings. Of one of them who had died recently it was said: "Why yes, André Fleurot; we'll miss him at Minot."

Some handymen attained a certain status of marginal notability, and their wide-ranging knowledge and know-how have become institutionalized. This is the case of the public road mender. It is said that he "does odd jobs," but

[19]In the local dialect, a *tainusé* is a man who "does a lot of useless stuff."

[20]In the 1930s the threshing contractor was a woodcutter turned farmer. He "worked for the public," thus reproducing, in a mechanized form, a typical activity of the woodspeople.

all of these tend in a particular direction. He watches over everything that
connects the village with the outside world—the streets within the village, the
roads through the fields, the paths and cart roads in the forest—and he also
supervises the use and distribution of the collective resources: the water of the
springs and drinking troughs, the sand of the sand pit, the stone and lava of the
quarry, the trees of the forest (for he assists the forest guard with reforesting
the areas that have been denuded by the communal cutting of firewood). In the
same way, he is concerned with everything that connotes change within the
village space; he has a hand in every event that marks transition, beginning or
end, in the life of the community or the individual. Thus, he rings the bells for
births and marriages, but also for deaths and alarms—for the churchbell
connects the village with the outside world by sound. It is he who takes care of
the clock in the tower, who keeps up the cemetery and the war memorial. He
has a special relationship with death and the dead, being the gravedigger and
the designated pallbearer[21] whenever "distant relatives" and "conscripts"[22]
cannot be found. His counterpart is the "helping woman." "Old mother
Marguerite used to go to women in labor; she would deliver the baby and cut
the cord. . . . She did the cooking for first communions and weddings, and
people asked her to watch the dead."[23]

Old man Daniel, the public road mender at the turn of the century, was one
of these marginal personalities. A native of Echalot, he was the son of a
woodcutter and had learned the craft of barrel making, which he still exercised
when people met to spend the evening together. His wife, Mother Daniel,[24]
was the "helping woman," and their youngest daughter has since taken up
that role in the village: "It's sort of a family tradition to go and help out," she
says. Both Father and Mother Daniel did "day work," he during his days off
from the municipality for "haying and harvest," she doing laundry, housecleaning, and digging sugar beets. This couple is a typical example. Father
Daniel, in his activity as road mender and handyman, acted as a mediator
between the fields, the village, and the forest; he was also a mediator between
life and death. In this respect, his role was further reinforced by that of his
wife, who was present and involved in all rites of passage: she washed the
newborn babies as she washed the dead. Their peculiar genealogical
situation—he was from a family of the forest, whereas she belonged, on her
father's side, to a family of small farmers settled at Minot since the eighteenth

[21]Actually, these two roles are incompatible, for while the pallbearer officiates during the
funeral ceremony—between the house and the church and again between the church and the
cemetery—the gravedigger has to leave the ceremony early in order to change his clothes so that
he will be ready to close the grave as soon as the family has left the cemetery.

[22]"Distant relatives" are all the members of the family beyond the second degree of collateral-
ity. "Conscripts" designates the members of the same age group, male and female; it is an
extension of the same "class" of boys who do their military service together.

[23]Children called old women "Aunt"; this was a more respectful term than "old mother,"
which is applied to those who stand out as particularly good or particularly bad.

[24]Women are called by their husbands' first names.

century—legitimized and accentuated their mediatory roles; just as they were at home in both the wild and the cultivated, the communal and the privately owned sphere, so they formed one of the genealogical links between the woodspeople and the tillers of the fields.

The woodcutters, charcoal burners, and sawyers shared a more clearly defined sphere of subsistence than the handymen, and also more regular times of work, namely, two distinct seasons. The woodcutting season lasted from September to May, while charcoal burning took place between May and September. These people did not "help out" the tillers of the fields; they worked for a timber merchant from the outside who had bought a whole stand of trees and who paid them for each cord of wood or sack of charcoal. Their counterpart in the village itself was the mason, who also worked with "wild" material, that is, stone and pumice stone, both of which were also taken from the outlying area. But the mason's rhythm of work was the inverse of the woodsman's: "Between 15 November and 1 March, there was no construction, which had stopped as soon as the frost came. We would work in the forest or cut stone in the quarry, but we'd leave it there. We didn't have any definite jobs, but sometimes there would be some doors or windows to put in."

If the masons went to work in the forest in the winter, those woodcutters who had no steady engagement with a farmer took up masonry in the summer: "In the summer, it was hard; there wasn't any work, so one had to go with the masons; you had to take what you could get." Woodcutters and masons were part of the same world: "These were all people who worked with wood and stone."

Owing to the long duration of their work, the woodcutters had to make their quarters in the forest, where they built shacks—they were also called "shack people"—for the winter, or for the entire year if they also burnt charcoal. The shack was put up next to a spring, often at the location of an old charcoal furnace, which it resembled in many respects. It consisted of a conical framework around a central pole, covered with branches and wads of grass. "We always lived well in the forest; in the shack we had an oven with two openings for cooking, two trunks for putting the linens, a box for the bread, a piece of lard hanging from a rafter, a table, some seats, and wooden bedsteads; for a mattress we had sacks filled with beech leaves, the sheets were made from finer sacks and the covers from several sacks sewn together." Here the woodspeople organized a veritable subsistence economy on the basis of what the forest had to offer. The burnt ground where the furnace had stood was used to raise crops. "We'd plant two or three rows of things, radishes, lettuce, and such. We always had chickens; where you have chickens you don't have snakes. We always took gray ones, too, because the white ones were apt to be eaten by the falcons and the chicken-hawks." Some people even raised a pig. These shacks did not form real hamlets, but they were close enough together for people to "go visiting back and forth of an evening."

On the whole, however, these efforts at agriculture and animal husbandry were only a subordinate aspect of the domestic economy of the forest. The woodcutter, like the handyman, was dependent on the farmer for the products of the land and on the outside world, that is, on commercial channels, for his staple food, the herring. On the other hand, he did have direct access—more systematically and more thoroughly than the handyman—to the wild fruits of the land. He gathered morels around the burning place and in the glens of fir; he picked beechnuts, which he took to the mill—''they made a very good oil''; he also gathered ash branches, which were dried in the shade and fed to the animals in winter, as well as nuts, crab apples, ''which can't be eaten until they are soft,'' the gray fruit of the service tree for the gout, and the red fruit of the dogwood for making jam. The woodcutters knew about the healing powers of plants: ''My grandfather knew about two or three oaks in the woods; under them grew a kind of moss, which he used to make a tea. He gave some to my wife, and she got better, but he didn't give me the secret. . . .'' The woodspeople ''kind of dabbled in sorcery'': ''Old Mother Colas made poultices with pigeon droppings and she knew how to stop bleeding with cobwebs.''

Finally, these people were hunters, especially poachers; but, as the forest warden says, ''they poached intelligently.'' ''When we were little, we used to find blackbirds and thrushes in their nests; we'd find them just as they were about to fly off, pick them from the nest and take them home to our parents; and then we'd eat them. . . . My father, he hunted for fur; he followed the martin from tree to tree until he had found its nest. He could see where a hare had passed through by looking at the broken branches.'' The woodspeople were accused not only of hunting outside the law (''they hunt the boar in the snow'') but also of having dietary habits that lay outside the accepted norm: ''They eat wildcat and fox, and they bury their meat for several says to let it get high.''

Most of what was hunted and poached was consumed directly—''We were never short of meat''—and the rest was used for exchange purposes. The egg-man, who stopped at the cutting area when he passed by on the road that skirted it, accepted game as willingly as he accepted eggs as objects of barter.

Just as their sphere of subsistence is peripheral and wild, so the woodspeople's sphere of kinship is marginal and unregulated. Whenever one talks about photographs of weddings, there is a striking difference between the brevity of the genealogical definitions given by the woodspeople and the richness of those furnished by the tillers of the fields. In the case of the woodspeople, each of the guests is identified in only one term, or in two at most—his relationship to Ego and his position as father, brother, or spouse. ''Emilienne Chapotel was my cousin; she married a fellow by the name of Barlet.'' In the case of the tillers of the fields, each individual is placed within his or her entire network of kinship relations; an example of this operation was given above. Sometimes this goes so far that the woodcutters and workers dispense with genealogical reference altogether. A number of families, all of whom lived in a complex of dilapidated buildings above the village, were simply identified as "the folks from La Grand' Cour."

And yet the woodspeople, too, are connected by ties of blood or marriage to one of the old families of Minot, a group of brothers who were workers and woodcutters living in Minot at the beginning of the nineteenth century. Almost all of the descendants of that family have ever since worked in the woods or as handymen and have founded veritable forest dynasties. One of these is the family of Antoine Maurot and Victoire Martenot, both of whom were from families of woodcutters living in the village in 1876; they had two sons and two daughters who "married into the forest." The older of the two sons was left by his wife and the other died without offspring. The children of the daughters all became woodcutters and charcoal burners, and in the next generation all of them were still working with wood or stone, except for one girl who married a poor tenant farmer from Saint-Broing. In the fourth generation the members of the family left the forest to become workers or small shopkeepers, and they are the people who, even today, belong to a mutual-aid group that meets at Minot every Sunday in order to cut the communal firewood to which everyone is entitled. "We go as a team by car and take along a picnic; we get along very well. My cousin and I work with the chain saw; he runs it and I hold the pole. My father is still very good at tying up bundles of kindling. In September we go to pick up the wood from our section with Follin's tractor; he is a farmer in our neighborhood."

Tillers of the fields and woodspeople constitute two genealogically distinct kinship groups, but at every generation a few marriages establish a connection between them. While such marriages are not necessarily always disapproved of, they are at least considered unusual. The marriage between Daniel Autardet, road mender, and Marie Grivot, helping woman, is a good example, for it marked the beginning of a transition from the forest to the village, a transition that took place over three generations and was helped along by an economic evolution that made it possible for a stonemason to become a contractor. The present mayor of Minot is a descendant of that family.[25] But this transition can also take the opposite direction: Matthieu Vautelot belonged to an old farming family of the village; a Vautelot appears as the signer of one of the oldest acts of incorporation of the community. His is one of the families that "knew each other from way back." Since the Vautelots owned land, they intermarried exclusively with other landowning families until one of Matthieu's daughters, Alice, married a mason and stonecutter from the region of the Morvan. The

---

[25]After the demise of the *Messieurs,* the tillers of the fields held political power in the community for twenty-five years. It was only later, in the early years of the twentieth century, that one or two representatives of the woodspeople gained seats in the municipal council. As a result of discord among the farmers, a mason, who was the one laboring man on the council, became mayor in 1962. Much could be said about this very recent assumption of power by the woodspeople. The mayor is often derided for his ignorance in matters of genealogy: "He doesn't know anything about the old families. . . ."

daughters of that couple married outsiders, one a Spaniard, the other a Breton, and left the village; their son, a mason, married a girl who worked in the fields and whose mother had been raised by the public welfare. Today the son is the public road mender and does odd jobs. "He's always busy; the other day he fixed the gas tank at Louis's place, and Clémence gave him three dozen eggs." The break is complete; there is no communication, no "cousining" between the couple and their relatives who have stayed in the village. The latter never invite them to any celebration and an aunt by marriage even goes so far as to deny that they are related to her at all. A few marriages between the two groups were thus not sufficient to create a network of kinship relations. There is "no cousining" and "we don't talk to each other as relatives."

Of the three rules that regulate the social sphere of the tillers of the fields—obligations of mutual help, etiquette of kinship, and matrimonial constraints—only the first applies to the woodspeople. Relatives whose dwellings face on the same courtyard in the village or on the same cutting section in the forest always help each other out in small ways: "Marguerite Tribolet's mother, who is sort of related to us, and I, we'd lend each other a little money sometimes, and we wouldn't pay it back, and we'd also give a loaf of bread for a little salt or a cupful of oil." By contrast, relationships with relatives scattered throughout the region tend to fall into disuse very rapidly. "We always stayed home and we hardly ever saw the families who had moved away." This loosening of family ties is even more rapid if one of the branches has done well: "In our family (this is a woodcutter–charcoal burner speaking) the girls went into the forest when they were quite young; in the summer they worked as harvest hands. The boys went to school and left to become policemen." In this group success comes only to those who move away.

Etiquette of kinship is still something to be considered, but it has become much reduced and muted. "We are working people, so when it comes to family, we can't afford to invite 150 people, so we don't invite anybody." Furthermore, the events that call for a formal celebration often take place in the forest: "My children were practically born in the forest; I'd go home just a few days before they were born, and I always went back out very soon afterward; we'd put the baby in a basket and the basket on a wheelbarrow." Fathers did not bother to have the bells rung for these forest babies. People also died in the forest: "Old Mother Colas came to see me," the mayor tells us. " 'You have to go and get my husband at the shack,' she told me, 'we'll have to bury my man'." Thus, the forest is not only the woodcutter's sphere of subsistence, the place of his work, but also the sphere of his human relations, the place where he finds his mate. "My husband and I, we met in the forest. He came to finish the section my father did not want to do any more, because my mother had been killed in the forest (hunters had mistaken her for a doe). That's how we first met; after that I helped my father with the charcoal burning, and then I was married." This area of acquaintanceship in the forest is not very extended, for the woodcutters move within a rather narrow compass: "We have always lived at Minot; we never went very far from there, because the cutting was usually close by; the farthest we ever went was to the forest of Barjon." But this relatively fixed existence in a restricted space is amply compensated by the forest's openness to everything "foreign." This area has a long tradition of accepting woodsmen from other parts. Men from Auvergne, most of them sawyers, came around the middle of the nineteenth century, men from the Morvan came in the 1880s, and Portuguese and Spaniards after 1914. These outsiders immediately began to marry into the old local woodcutting families. Over three generations, members of the Mauriot families married, first a sawyer from the Cantal, then a woodcutter from the department of Saône-et-Loire, and finally a girl from the Balearic Islands. Local woodspeople also married people who came from even further away—namely, from "nothing." "She came from nothing, from the public welfare, if you know what I mean. They had to place her as a servant at Minot, and she had a boy; he was born out of wedlock."

Since the group of woodspeople is constantly renewed by newcomers from the outside, its sphere of marriage possibilities is extremely scattered.[26] The genealogical pattern of that group is very different from the closely knit tissue and the characteristic configurations—double marriages, marriages of previously allied families—of the tillers of the fields. Among the woodspeople, entire branches have disappeared from view: "They left the area with their twelve children, and no one knows what has become of them." Certain individuals appear on the scene, stay for a time, and then fade away: "He married a beautiful Italian girl; she left for the forest and he never saw her again." Divorces, remarriages, and concubinage are frequent. In 1876 Alexis Maréchal, a woodcutter, lived on the heights at La Grand' Cour with his wife Jeanne Serrain, a ward of the public welfare, and his five children. Two sons worked in the forest with him. The oldest daughter, Louise, lived in her parents' household with her three children after her husband, a field hand, had deserted her. She divorced him, married a woodcutter–day laborer and moved away, leaving her children in the care of her parents. Her sister, Victorine, was appointed by the public authorities as "nurse" to the children of Henri Curtil, a woodcutter living in a neighboring building, after his wife had died "of exhaustion," as it was said, at the birth of her sixth child. It was not long before Henri Curtil married his children's "nurse." As for old man Maréchal, he lost his wife and, at the age of sixty-seven, immediately remarried. His new wife was Marie Courtot, age thirty-seven, a day laborer. When he died after three months, his widow, "little Marie," went to live with a worker on welfare by the name of Schmidt. Certain abberrant forms of marriage testify to a failure to recognize any pattern of kinship and to a total indifference to the specific role of the individual within the genealogy; Lucie married the brother of her mother's second husband, so that her half-sister called her "aunt."

---

[26]Yet the woodspeople marry residents of the village in about 50 percent of all cases.

"In the forest I was my own master; it was a good life and I miss it. It was lonely, but there was nothing to be afraid of. It's because, in those days, everybody was the same; today, if we were in the forest, people would treat us like wild animals."

This awareness that there was a time when those who lived in the forest preserved their status as human beings, when the sphere of wildness complemented the sphere of cultivation, just as the tillers of the fields and the woodspeople were linked by bonds of solidarity as dwellers in the area as a whole, takes on its full significance if we consider these groups in the context of their year.

There are two seasons that "in the old days" were more clearly distinguished than they are today. "The seasons are not what they used to be. We used to have severe winters with lots of snow. Summer began in March, and it stayed for good. There were long periods of sunshine, with no clouds, when it was really hot. A few thundershowers, then the sun would come out and it would get hot again. We used to put away our woolen vests by Easter and did not bring them out again until fall."

There was a shift in the poles of activity from one season to the next. In the winter, almost everyone went to the forest to cut the firewood to which each household was entitled; in the summer, the harvest brought together large groups of people in the fields. The transition from one space (and one season) to the next was always a time of celebration. There was a short sequence of holidays at the beginning of winter, crowded into the time between All Saints' Day [1 November] and Saint Nicholas's Day [6 December]; there also was a longer, less concentrated period between Mardi Gras and Bastille Day [14 July]. In the village the celebration brought together groups that were defined not in terms of space—tillers of the fields and woodspeople—but, rather, in terms of the time they had in common; they were age groups or, in some cases, family groups conceived in their entire genealogical depth and breadth.

Contracts of sale gave the buyer possession of wheat land on 1 September, and everyone in the village agreed that this was the real beginning of the year. This date marked not only the end of the farming season—the time when the farmer sold the yield of his first threshing ("I saw my brother drive off to Beneuvre with his grain and come back with gold; it was a beautiful sight")—but also the beginning of the woodcutting season: "The woodcutters would hire themselves out at the wood auctions in Châtillon; it was a celebration and they would drink to it from the twentieth to the thirtieth of September. Nowadays, it's all cut and dried." This was the time when the work in the fields was coming to an end, and soon three-quarters of the fields were given over to collective use. People went out to glean and to gather wild plants in the stubble and in the fallow fields, collecting such things as Johnny-jump-ups, meadow saffron, and lamb's lettuce. They also picked the fruits of hedges and wild fruit trees at the edge of the forest, in the fallow fields along the cart roads, and even in the cultivated area itself, where there were always some "clumps of thorns"—enclaves of wildness within the cultivated sphere.

"In those days there were a lot of hedges in the fields; that part was not plowed, and most of the time they included a wild pear tree or, perhaps, some blackthorns. We would pick the wild pears, sloes, and wild apples—most of the farms had a clump of thorns. And then there were the *mounds* [*murgers*]. Most of the time this was just a round heap of stones, and we would find snails there. These things must have been put up by those that came before us.'"[27] At that time of the year the rigorous collective rules in the cultivated area became more relaxed; watching the herds took on the character of a game. The children no longer had to keep their animals strictly separated: "We would meet in the fields and eat together; we would build huts; the countryside was wide open, and we would walk over each other's fields."

In the cultivated area the signs of private ownership gradually disappeared. All Saints' Day was the customary date when all that was still out in the fields was brought in; on Saint Martin's Day [11 November] the children went back to school and the animals went back to the stables. The collective endeavors that during the autumn had taken place mostly in the open country now shifted to the forest, for this was the beginning of the communal firewood season.

In the village it was time to commemorate the dead. The obligation of "visiting the family graves" was the ultimate tie to persist when all others had been broken: "They went back to their own country (Luxembourg), but they still come here to see their mother's grave." And even if the continuity of the family was broken, this obligation was perpetuated because such a grave was an integral part of the village space: "It is not rare that a contract of sale has a clause providing for the upkeep of the family's graves. And if there is no one left to take care of a grave, the neighbors who come to the cemetery will say, 'let's fix it up'."

The eleventh of November (Armistice Day) is the day for commemorating the war dead of the commune; a powerful "communal" symbolism has grown up around this theme. "It was beautiful; a mass for the dead was said with a coffin in the church.'"[28] After mass, a procession, led by a flag bearer, went to the war memorial. The mayor called the roll of the community's dead, and at

---

[27]On the origin of these "mounds": "Edme R. first tried out this idea on one of his father-in-law's fields. Under the stones he had found some rather rich, black soil; Edmond sacrificed the upper part of the field, which was almost too stony to be plowed anyway, to heap up all the stones. That is the most strenuous kind of labor, but he did it with the most untiring courage and also had the hired men help him. He himself built a wall with the large stones around the bottom of the *merger* (for that is what these heaps of stone were called). Then he filled in the interstices between the stones with a little earth and tufts of grain-bearing grasses, up to a height of five or six feet. In this way he not only made a firm foundation for the mound but also provided a pasture for his livestock that was almost equal in wall surface to the area he had been forced to cover. Furthermore, he also made a spiral path to the top, and every year all the stones that had been uncovered by the rain were carried there before the plowing began." See N. Rétif de la Bretonne, *La vie de mon père* (Paris, 1970), p. 71. This scene takes place in 1778 at Sacy, department of Yonne, about eighty kilometers from Minot.

[28]Immediately after World War I, the trappings were even more realistic. A mound of sand was piled in the main street to represent "a grave at the front."

each name the crowd responded: "Died for France." Here the pattern and language of the ceremony concerned an age group; the population was divided by age and by sex. The ceremony ended with the veterans' banquet and ball.

Saint Catherine's and Saint Nicholas's days [25 November and 6 December] also brought together two groups, the "young fellows" and the "unmarried girls," through the custom of "singing for presents" [*passation du chantiau*]. Throughout the year these two groups "went the rounds" and "collected favors," thereby exercising their privilege, almost their duty, of freely roaming through the village on certain institutionalized occasions. In the form of eggs, small coins, and kindling wood, the young people thus levied something like a festive toll on the community as a whole. The end of these "rounds"—and of adolescence—was marked by marriage. On that occasion everyone brought gifts to the homes of the bride and groom. "We had a good custom, that of taking things to weddings. For three or four days, everyone would bring presents; some brought butter, some brought eggs, some brought rabbits. It didn't amount to much when you gave it, but it meant a lot when you received it. People used it to prepare the wedding meal, and the bride and groom had the right to sell what was left." This was the last time that the young couple was on the receiving end of the community's generosity. Once they were married, they became part of those who no longer had the right to "make the rounds" but were expected to "give."

The cutting of the free firewood opened the forest to the whole community. "Everyone went to the town hall on a certain evening in November to find out which section was to be used for the communal firewood." It was a joyous occasion that had certain aspects of a game, for the decision was made by drawing lots. It always ended up at the café. "Everyone took his share of the free firewood. The next day we would all go to the woods to find the spot." The whole community betook itself to the forest, virtually as a body. A note of lost happiness is struck in every reminiscence of that event. "Two or three of us would go out together," the keeper of the dry-goods store recalls, "and fifteen of us would come back together; and out there we would sit down by a fire to eat. In the evening before we went out, we would call for each other; those who lived farthest away would come by to pick up the others, and we would all come back together. It was nice, I always enjoyed it." An old farmer says: "The meal around the fire in the forest, that was really good." People "worked on their wood" until the sap began to rise. As the work progressed, the section of the forest from which the communal firewood was taken became a clearing, a green hall, a well-ordered, luminous space surrounded by the impenetrable darkness of the woods; it became the setting for a celebration. It was a collective endeavor, yet everyone profited from it individually (or as a family). It also took place in a communal, but ephemeral, setting which, the very next year, would again be given over to solitude. Certain constraints, certain obligations, did not apply here; social relations were friendly, since they were not threatened by jealousies. The forest thus was a "warm" place. Meals by a common fire brought together people who never, or very rarely, ate together under ordinary circumstances—tillers of the fields and woodspeople, those from the upper and those from the lower village. In the village, every invitation called for reciprocity, but the informal meal in the woods had no consequences at all; everyone shared a fire and food, things that were usually private. And just as everyone temporarily adopted the woodcutter's tools and his gestures (the sledge hammer and the crosscut saw), so the whole village also tasted his food: "We would make omelettes and cook herrings and potatoes in the cinders." This trucelike situation is corroborated by the absence of conflict among those who were entitled to the free firewood. "We thought it was handled properly." The only protests recorded in the deliberations of the village council resulted from claims made for the firewood. Occasionally one finds a demand by the occupier of an outlying farm for this right, from which he is excluded by tradition. Tied to the notion of "founding a hearth" in the village (the wood is allocated "by hearth"), the right to free firewood and the very act of "cutting one's wood" is a powerful symbol of belonging to the village. Indeed, it has come to signify belonging to an even wider community, namely, France as a whole. "The first year," we were told by a woman who has lived at Minot since 1962 and who is married to an Italian stonemason, "we were not given the right to free firewood. So I didn't go to vote that year, because I said if I am not French enough to keep warm, I'm not French enough to vote, either."

The turning point of the year came between the distilling of the wild fruit brandy at the end of January, an operation that represented the last step in the transformation of the wild fruits of the land, and the arrival of "Carnaval," as the ambulant grain and seed merchant was called. "We never thought about spring before we saw Carnaval."

"Before the war, we would make the rounds on Mardi Gras [*Carnaval*]. Two boys would go as a couple, one dressed as a woman, the other as a man in rags. We would go to people's houses and they would give us goodies, eggs, and coins; that night we always had supper at the postman's house. The following Sunday we would stop at every house, and everyone gave us a bundle of kindling. That night before supper and after the dance, we burnt [an effigy representing] Mardi Gras at Pâquis."[29]

The private order of things, which during this period was gradually beginning to reclaim its rights over the cultivated land, was flouted at Mardi Gras, and even more explicitly at the time of the May Branches, which for one night overthrew the etiquette of kinship and matrimonial constraints. On the evening of 31 April the young men went into the woods to cut branches of

---

[29]The place called Pâquis is situated at the edge of the village at the opposite end from the upper château. This place has negative associations; here were the soaking tubs for wetting the hemp, the basin where the hog intestines were washed, and the fire where the wheelwright beat out his wheels. Today it is a burning garbage dump.

yoke-elm,[30] which they placed at the doors of all the unmarried girls' houses. Later in the night, they collected everything that was loose anywhere in the village and piled it up in the village square; this was done as haphazardly and as noisily as possible. These two sets of gestures formed a contrast in each of their constituent parts; the language addressed to girls was natural (yoke-elm branches), individual (each girl received her own), and quiet, whereas the language addressed to the community was cultural (agricultural implements and household equipment), collective (everything was thrown into a heap), and noisy. ("The young fellows brought the field rollers tumbling down the street, it felt as if they were going to bring the house down!") If the language was twofold, the discourse as a whole had only one meaning: it was a denial of the established order, both with respect to the marriage of girls and the distribution of property.

In the first case, the order based on membership in a family or on social status was replaced by another order based on free choice, on "natural" attraction: "They give them yoke-elm branches [du charme], no doubt in order to say, you charm me." Hence the language of the May Branch has many nuances: a ribbon or a bouquet was attached to it as a sign of matrimonial intention; nettles or thistles were given to those "about whom one has a complaint"; a nanny goat or, worse, a heap of manure was placed by the house of one "whose conduct leaves something to be desired." May Branches were attached only to the houses of those girls who were potential marriage partners, so the granddaughters of the notary Villerey, among others, were excluded.

In the second case, the order of private property and, specifically, that of "land and cows" was dismantled, for among the objects that were expropriated and mixed up together, everything that had to do with houses and fields occupied a prominent place. Shutters and doors were pulled off their hinges, flowerpots, wheelbarrows, brooms and milk cans, carts, harrows, and field rollers were piled up pell-mell. The next morning everyone came to look for his property under the mocking eyes of the young people, and there was always a certain amount of quarreling, since certain "have-nots" were suspected of trying to profit from the situation.

This mock reordering of affairs corresponded to a real reordering, a redistribution of people and things on the land. In the forest the communal cutting of firewood came to an end as the sap began to rise; it customarily closed on the first day of May when the forest itself (in the guise of the branches of yoke-elm) paid a visit to the village. This was also the time when people decided how to deal with the big trees that chance had distributed unevenly among their individual portions. "A big oak we would share like this: We

---

[30]"This year the yoke-elm hadn't put forth its leaves yet; so they cut willow branches. The owner was angry, and they had to pay."

would say: 'if you have it sawed, I give you my share and you just let me have a few boards'.'' During the month of May, saplings were planted in the newly cut section of the forest. And what a bustle of new activity in the village! Saint George's Day [23 April] was the day for assigning new leaseholds, and more or less at the same time, at Easter, the animals were released from the stables, and the children from school, so that they could ''tend the animals in the fields.'' Out in the fields the reappropriation that had begun about the time of Mardi Gras with the March sowing was now complete.

This was the beginning of the harvest season. ''We were celebrating all the time; we helped each other out, and then we had a feast and dancing.'' It began in May with the washing of the sheep: ''We went to the mill, and there was a great spread of food and drink. We drank a lot, and then the men went to the river and passed the sheep down the line. In the end they came back all splattered.'' Haying began the day after the patron saint's feast day, the date of which had to be adjusted somewhat to fit certain exigencies. ''Seventy years ago, the feast day was celebrated on the first Sunday in May; but it was still too cold and, besides, the things that are needed for the celebration aren't ready in May; on the other hand, on Saint Peter's Day [29 June] (and Saint Peter is the patron saint of Minot's church) it's too late for slaughtering the pig and also too late to start the hay; so we made it the first Sunday in June.'' For the patron saint's feast day was above all a family dinner, the Celebration of Meat; in many cases it was the only occasion of the year when beef was eaten. ''The butcher came from Recey with a cow he slaughtered and sold right on the spot. We used to buy a big roast, the best part of which was eaten the day of the feast day, and the rest on the following Sunday.''

The haying lasted all through June. ''We left the new-mown hay in the meadows for a while to give it time to shed its moisture; this also gave the bees a chance to get some more nectar.'' The same rhythm was followed in the cutting of the grains: ''We started with the rye and the oats right after Bastille Day, quite often the propped-up sheaves were left in the fields for two weeks; it was a way to ripen them. We finished the grain harvest by 30 August.''

The celebration of Bastille Day did not differentiate the tillers of the fields from the woodspeople; its language, again, was that of the age group. The minutes of the village council give a detailed account of the various favors and entertainments the municipality provided for the different age groups: sweets and wheel-games for the younger schoolchildren, food baskets for the old people, ninepins and liters of wine for the men, ''knock down the jar'' games for young boys between ten and fourteen, and ''Aunt Sally'' games and small household objects for ''the ladies and girls over fourteen.'' In this way the municipality contributed to the household trousseaux of its daughters;[31] but

---

[31]''The girls are happy when they win something. They pack what they have won in a box, so their mothers won't use it; and they collect these things for when they get married. They always remember that they have won this or that item on the various Bastille Days.''

young men between the ages of fourteen and eighteen were excluded from such distributions. Since they were in a position to ''ask for things'' on their ''rounds,'' it would not do just to treat them.

The big feast of meat on the patron saint's day had its counterpart in the *cagne,* the harvest banquet (although the latter featured rabbit or chicken rather than beef). But this meal was shared by a different group. For the haying and the grain harvest, everyone worked with his own people and with those he had hired by the day. ''Ones's own people'' were a big group: it was the extended family, relatives who worked in other trades, and woodcutters who were in a kind of client position. Most farmers had such long-standing relationships with a family of woodspeople over several generations. To this day, for example, Denis Perron, a worker and the son and grandson of woodcutters, takes leave from his job to help with the haying and the harvest at Clément's farm where his family has ''given a hand'' for two generations.

Throughout the entire harvest season the situation was similar, though in the opposite sense, to that of the cutting of the communal firewood. Now the woodspeople temporarily adopted the gestures, tools, and food of the tillers of the fields. ''The men did the cutting, the women picked up the loose sheaves behind the scythe, the youngsters did the raking or gleaning. The meals were brought out to the field in the big iron kettle, sometimes it was soup, sometimes it was vegetables and fatback; we'd all eat out of the same bowl.'' Even if everyone did not eat together, ''we would get together for the afternoon break, under the trees by a spring.''

Within the sphere of private property, individual groups were relatively closed and locked into a hierarchy; in the language of the tillers of the fields themselves, they stayed ''with their own people,'' ''by themselves,'' ''on their own.'' In the communal, wild sphere, on the other hand, there was no place for dichotomies and hierarchies. Just as the ''hearth''—the self—was absorbed into the communal fire when people cut their firewood, so work in the forest imperceptibly took on the character of a celebration. And while, in the village, celebration involved replacing the categories of space—tillers of the fields, woodspeople—with categories of time—namely, age groups— celebration in the forest abolished categories altogether. The perennial strength of the community, its fundamental sense of time, is inscribed in the trees of the cutting areas: well-grown saplings are notched once every thirty years.

8
Male Space and Female Space within the Provençal Community

Lucienne Roubin

Within each community in the southeastern French province of Provence, a long-established practice subdivided male society into one or more *chambrettes* [literally, "little chambers"]. These elective associations, which zealously fended off any intrusions by females, are a clear indication that the institution of the Men's House, found among most Amerindian and Asiatic groups as well as among certain African ones, was also present along the northwestern shores of the Mediterranean.

My analysis of this contemporary—and poorly understood—institution is based upon an approach combining direct observation, archival research, and comparative methodology. My study has revealed that this institution assumed two forms in the course of time, each supplying complementary data: (a) the traditional form (still found in Upper Provence during the first quarter of the twentieth century), which was woven into the fabric of a Mediterranean way of life and which had been operating for several millennia, thus providing a suitable foundation upon which to base this study; and (b) the present-day form, the *cercle* [club], which functions within a society that is rapidly becoming urbanized and that includes a large number of outsiders who have moved into the area. The club can therefore be used to indicate how male society has evolved and consequently can clarify the mechanisms that assure the longevity of this very flexible institution.

Although communication among the various groups never extended beyond the local center of population, by the nineteenth century the tightly woven

Annales, E.S.C. 25 (March–April 1970): 537–60. Translated by Patricia M. Ranum. The author wishes to thank Robert Mandrou, editor of the series Civilisations et Mentalités, for authorizing the publication in the *Annales, E.S.C.,* of a chapter of her book, *Chambrettes des Provençaux: Une Maison des Hommes en Méditerranée septentrionale* (Paris: Plon, 1970), pp. 157–97.

network of such social gatherings was always based upon a similar pattern of membership, reinforced by strict and unvarying rules involving recruitment and specific practices for admitting new members. These lower-class clubs made up of vineyard workers, artisans, shepherds, sailors, and violet- or mayrose-growers acted as poles that determined the dynamics operating within the village.

Two Universes

"A concrete symbol of the social system,"[1] the chambrette-club is a constant and concrete indication of the existence of male society and emphasizes the distance separating it from female society. If we wish to place the chambrette within the context of society as a whole, we must study it successively in terms of these two markedly different male and female components.

COMPONENTS AND ATTRIBUTES OF MALE
SPACE*

Wine cellars should be put near the top of any list of those parts of the village territory that are closely linked to the male world. During the period when the wine vats were fermenting, menstruating women were expected to keep their distance. In discussing the winter banquet in winegrowing villages I mentioned briefly the role played by the wine cellars;[2] but their social function is a day-to-day one and is not limited to festival days. Cool in summer and comfortable in winter, the wine cellars have always been and remain today a retreat where men frequently meet their friends. Any outsider entering a cellar must first submit to an obligatory endurance test to see how much wine he can drink.

This use of wine cellars as a refuge for male brotherhoods extends as far north as the Val d'Anniviers of Switzerland, where even the bourgeois men

---

[1] André Leroi-Gourhan, *Le geste et la parole* (Paris: Albin Michel, 1964), 2:150.

*"Space," as Natalie Z. Davis, observed in discussing the term with me, "means not only areas where males and females have power to make decisions, but the places where they go, or the spaces thought to be characterized by their presence." Thus, in addition to the various meanings of *space* found in English dictionaries, the French equivalent, *espace,* is also defined as "the milieu within which our perceptions are circumscribed and which consequently includes all finite expanses." *Espace* therefore presents a multiheaded monster to the translator. The words *sphere, world,* and *place* convey the physical milieu; while the word *range* conveys only the perceptual milieu. Perhaps as a result of this double dimension, recent translations from the French have begun to render *espace* by *space.* One of the most striking examples of this is A. M. Sheridan Smith's translation of Michel Foucault's *The Birth of the Clinic: An Archaeology of Medical Perception* (New York, 1973), which Foucault calls "a book about space"; see especially "Spaces and Classes," pp. 3–21.—Trans.

[2] Roubin, *Chambrettes des Provençaux,* p. 132.

of the region still spend considerable time together in the cellars. At the
beginning of this century, men held *veillées* [evening meetings] during the
winter months, in the cellar of one member on one occasion and in that of
another member on the next. In fact, it was in the cellars that the bourgeois of
the Anniviers region secretly prepared their disguises for Mardi Gras.[3] Even
today the wine cellar remains a place in which unobtrusive and sporadic
meetings can be held.

The established places in which male society as a whole could come together openly have always been the village square and the church chancel.
The interior arrangment of the church—as an institution, the church serves to
integrate each individual into village life—reveals this separation of the sexes,
for the men used to occupy the chancel and the choir loft. In the frequent cases
in which the church door opens onto a small square, the square was likewise
reserved for the men.

The village square and its appendages—secondary squares in larger market
towns—constitute the very heart of male space. Long, low stone benches line
the walls of those houses located along the particularly sunny portion of the
square that receives full southern exposure. A man may stop briefly at any
time or stroll at length in the cool of a summer evening or the warmth of a
winter afternoon. The square has served as the site of certain celebrations; for
example, the conclusion of a successful hunting expedition. Even today, in
the upper Verdon valley, if the game is of impressive size or quantity, the
hunters and their dogs enter the square single file. The game, especially if it is
a chamois, is carried in on the shoulders of two men and is briefly placed on
exhibit before the group disbands.

Villagers come to this local agora to exchange the day's news. The women
pass by, coming and going as they do their work, crossing the square and
warming themselves in the sun in small groups along its periphery, but they
do not stop long to chat, unless it is market day.

At the same time, the village square serves as the official public meeting
place.[4] Daily conversation constantly bears this out. "Besides, they said so in
the square," is the usual comment about something that is no longer secret.
On the other hand, if a matter requires discretion, one hears, "It's not something you should shout about in the square." The village square is the scene of

---

[3]In the meetings held today, as in the *veillées* of yesteryear, the men talk and eat pieces of dry,
tangy cheese that often has aged for more than ten years and that must be chewed for a long while.
They drink "glacier wine," prepared with grapes grown on the hillsides of Sierre, along the
Rhone Valley, in vineyards owned by middle-class mountain people. Once prepared, this wine is
carried up into villages with good cellars. It is called glacier wine not because it is made near the
glacier but because it is stored near the glacier, sometimes for more than a century. The cellar of
these bourgeois at Grimentz has two barrels of wine dating from 1886. At the end of the evening,
the men return to spend the night at home. (I found no trace of the permanent winter claustration
of all the men of a household, a custom mentioned to me before my research visit to the Valais
region in 1967.)

[4]See the location of the village square among the Bororos in Claude Lévi-Strauss, *The Raw and
the Cooked* (New York: Harper Torchbooks, 1969), pp. 39–42.

heated debates, spontaneous meetings, and the final ceremonies that bring the village festival to an end.

Within the territory encompassed by the community, but beyond the village perimeter, the fields present us with a more complex situation. They are also a part of the male world, and the heads of the different families used to go out alone to break the soil for the various operations dictated by the agricultural calendar. A few decades ago, each man in the upper Verdon Valley still went alone around his field, sickle in hand, a few days before reaping was due to begin. Nonetheless, women do have access to the plots of land included in the family patrimony, for they will come into the fields during the periods of extended irrigation or when the men need extra help.

Along the outer limits of the village territory the belt of intensive cultivation encounters the *garrigue* [brush] and the forests. From time to time hunters, shepherds, and woodcutters would tramp over this land that had only recently been occupied on a continuous basis. Because these areas were not yet completely under control, they had been transformed into places of evil or had been consecrated as pilgrimage spots; consider, for example, the numerous "Saint John's deserts" located at altitudes suitable only for grazing transhumant flocks.

Thus, male space gradually spreads out from the central village square into the outer limits of the village orbit, but its exclusively male character is clearly less pronounced in some places than in others. Zones of interference are set up around magnetic poles of varying intensity. Each pole bears a magnetic charge and each confers a title upon the individual: "Man," "head of a family," "citizen."

We have just seen how the arrangement of the village tends to juxtapose and to fuse male space with public space in its very center. Throughout his daily life the man of Provence of necessity moves about within this social space dominated by the community. Every foot of the area included within the municipality reminds him of his title "citizen" and makes a permanent appeal to his civic responsibility.

Although a man's relationship to municipal space is one of constant proximity, his relationship to agrarian space is, by contrast, a distant one. The relationship between the individual and the land is of secondary importance. Indeed, in order to work in the fields—an activity by which this relationship is made concrete—a man must pass through the complex of buildings that constitutes the village. As more and more land was cleared to form a wider belt of permanent fields around the village, the relationship between the individual and the land was increasingly influenced by the village center, with its protective ring of threshing floors, vegetable gardens, and orchards. Distance contrasted with proximity, but also discontinuity contrasted with permanence: for the agrarian tasks through which each landowner sees to the management of his own property are strictly determined by the seasons and have a periodic and rhythmic nature. Encapsulated in patrimonial space as a result of cultivating a portion of the community's land, the villager assumes the title "head of a family enterprise" and demonstrates his strength of character and his initiative, or his lack of such qualities. Of these two forces—the municipal pole and the agrarian one—the former is stressed by the community. The Provençal village sees the male world as a world composed of citizens who relegate their role as father to second place. However, a constant state of tension is maintained in Provence, which is situated along the outer limits of the Mediterranean world and is therefore influenced by the North; for the technological and economic imperatives of existence place sufficient emphasis upon a man's role as head of a family to keep this role from being totally subordinated to the political role.

In order to define the male position in its totality, we must first view a man as an individual and then analyze his relationship with the female universe.

COMPONENTS AND ATTRIBUTES OF FEMALE
SPACE

Compared with the extensiveness and diversity of the male world, the woman's domain presents narrow spatial limits and great internal cohesion. Yet I should like to point out that this difference between the two areas of activity does not mean that one is subordinate to the other.

In addition, special attention must be paid to the discrepancy between the patterns of female behavior expected by society and actual female behavior; the latter has yet to be studied. Until now our knowledge of such behavior has chiefly been transmitted by male ethnologists, working on the basis of evidence given by men and conducted without prolonged observations within female society. The official pattern of behavior subjects each woman throughout her life to a series of successive guardianships, all of them male. First there is the guardianship of the father during childhood and adolescence, continued during a woman's young adulthood by the guardianship of the family's oldest son.[5] As soon as his sisters leave childhood behind, the latter claims the right to subject every single activity of their daily lives to his exacting scrutiny. In the early twentieth century, only with this brother as a chaperon could adolescent girls in the mountain communities of Upper Provence attend collective celebrations, especially the annual balls celebrating the patron saint of the village and the saints of neighboring villages, to which they would go on foot in the early afternoon in a large group. When he thought it was time for his sisters to start home—in other words, when he wanted to be free of his responsibilities—the older brother would inform them that it was time to go. On the return trip small groups of girls would cross the fields, and in each house the time of the "girls' return" would be carefully noted.

[5]The observations made by Germaine Tillion (*Le harem et les cousins* [Paris, 1966], p. 13) concerning the elder brother who protects his sisters' honor can be applied to Provence.

Upon her marriage a girl passed from the authority of the men of her bloodline to that of her husband. This new guardianship was proclaimed by the public name that the village conferred upon her. Her own Christian name was laid aside, and she was called by her husband's surname. The wife of Barbaroux, called Gauch, became "la Gauche"; in like manner, "la Bastière" was the wife of Marquis, called Bastier, and "la Renelle" was the wife of Honnoraty, called René.[6]

What was the woman's actual position, hidden behind this permanent legal status as a minor? It was determined by the system of land ownership that made the couple's solid cooperation the prime requirement if the family farm was to prosper. Indeed, although the citizen could consider civic activities and the municipal administration his exclusive prerogative, the head of the farm had to count upon the decisive cooperation of his immediate associate, his wife. Thus, the Provençal couple moved from a legal partnership based upon subordination to an actual one based upon emulation. The equilibrium of the latter type of partnership was not based upon the passive subordination of one partner to the other that could only destroy the subordinate partner's efficacy; rather, it was based upon each partner's capacity to remain competitive and to shoulder all the weary tasks demanded of him or her.

However, the woman's world, while closely circumscribed, was carefully defended and completely dominated by the woman herself. Usurpation by men abounded up to the very frontiers of the female domain, but beyond those borders, women behaved and functioned as sovereigns, conscious of and strengthened by the decisive weight of the contribution they were making.[7]

In addition, in comparison with the male group, which formed an integrated whole, the female group remained a fragmented body. One or several neighboring households might temporarily be united, but these groupings were not characterized by the permanent continuity found in such male associations as the chambrettes. This discontinuity is confirmed by the manner in which female *veillées* were organized. Occurring as regularly as those held by the men, they differed in that they were short-term and were reorganized each winter. There was no permanent meeting place; they would be held first in one stable and then in another. Yet, although the meeting place shifted regularly from one cell to another of this honeycomb, these groups of men or women had clearly stated rules and a carefully observed etiquette.

No one was admitted without the approval of the entire group; each organization was formed at the beginning of winter. Aside from family and neighborly ties, the chief bond among members of the association was the cost of lights. . . . Visits were always requested and announced in advance; the most influential person, the male or female president, was delegated to be in charge of the gathering. Borne on a wooden chair, the

[6]Augustin Roux, *Légendes, moeurs, et coutumes de Colmars-les-Alpes et du Haut-Verdon* (Gap: Vollaire et Cie., 1967), p. 48.

[7]Lucienne A. Roubin, "La montagnarde des lavanderaies," *Arts et traditions populaires,* October 1966, pp. 307–19.

delegated leader, followed by a joyful procession, would arrive at the door behind which the *veillée* would take place. On this special occasion both panels of the double door would be opened to reveal the circle of people about the source of light. The individual presiding would step forward and receive the polite greetings intended for him, then would show the procession in. . . .[8]

The evening gathering described in this text does not conflict with the daily chambrettes held during the winter months, for it was always possible for the head of the household to pass the evening sitting up with the family at a time when another group was expected to pay a visit.

The fragmented nature of female society required the special organization of its own space, which radiated out from each household and which subsequently coalesced into groups of varying sizes.

Le fremo e lou galin
Se perdoun per ana trop alin.[9]

[Women and chickens get lost
When they stray too far from home.]

This proverb reveals the central pivot about which this essentially domestic and private space revolves: the house. I wish to stress the fact that within this region of patrilocal residence, the peasant house actually was controlled by females. The kitchen alone—which was the chief room of the house—represented an organic complex minutely compartmentalized into a maze of storerooms whose contents were fully known only to the *maîtresse* [mistress] of the house,[10] manager of the domestic economy.

The same outlook is evident in the roles played by women in those parts of the church allocated to them: the nave and the side chapels or altars. In the 1950s the hierarchy existing among the women of the various households was still evident in countless village churches. Each woman occupied a specific place in a certain row of benches; these seats were passed on from generation to generation like any other item included in the patrimony. In like manner, in about 1910 the care of the chapels and side altars was still allocated according to a strict system based upon age, as reflected in turn by membership in various religious organizations. The "adornment"[11] of the altar dedicated to the Virgin was assigned to adolescent girls, members of the association called the Children of Mary; the altar to the Souls in Purgatory was cared for by the female Mutual Aid Confraternity, composed of mothers. These tasks, a

[8]Roux, *Légendes, moeurs, et coutumes*, p. 41.
[9]Marie Mauron, *L'Oùro dou souléu* (Fourcalquier: Morel, 1965), p. 45.
[10]This is the title that permanent servants and temporary help gave the mistress of the house in Provence.
[11]The task of "adorning the altars" involves seeing that the proper colors of the liturgical season—based on religious and seasonal cycles—are selected for the cloths and hangings of those altars.

source of competition among the various women of the village, were reorganized periodically, and on each occasion the teams selected were made up of women from families on good terms with one another.

Female space extended beyond the town to the gardens, source of fresh food for the family. These gardens were of two distinct kinds. The first was the ring of small plots—assigned for this purpose by the *cadastre* [land registry]—that encircled the village partially or entirely. The village had established a very strict system of irrigation, each plot being allocated a "round of water" at two- or three-week intervals, on a schedule that alternately permitted owners to irrigate during the day and during the night. The other sort of garden was the much larger type located in the fields. The location of such gardens was changed frequently, and the irrigation schedule applied to them was much more flexible. Only the first kind of garden was tended by women.

The second aspect of the woman's role, that of mother, of bearer of life, involved no extension of this female sphere. Although motherhood restricted the sphere to the confines of the house itself, it conferred a maximum degree of influence upon this sphere. Thus, beyond her duty of perpetuating the lineage, the mother was invested with a power that transformed her into a beneficial force for everything in the domestic area that was living and growing. She supervised the hatching of baby chicks in the poultry yard and cared for the countless dovecotes of Provence. On Saint Barbara's Day (12 December [*sic*]), the beginning of the winter season, she prepared the sprouted wheat and lentils for the "Gardens of Adonis."[12] Each devout family would be represented by these green sprouts about the parish manger scene on Christmas.

A bastion of female space, the Provençal village house has no room exclusively for males. The kitchen, which contains both the hearth and the table, is to the mistress of the house what the public square is to the man.

In the kitchen the woman accumulates her tasks involving the children and the household: this is the very heart of her functional space. With the exception of eating meals and participating in certain family events, the man has no reason to stay there, and he shows little inclination to linger in this domestic universe over which he has no control.

With all this in mind, the full meaning of the chambrette-club is clear. Viewed by the woman as a part of the world of the "others," the chambrette remains totally foreign to her own world. For the man, the chambrette is the meeting place where he feels at home, within that male society from which all participants derive a feeling of unity and cohesion. In addition, it offers the man of Provence—that Mediterranean male who has been stripped of his male

---

[12]They are analogous to those that used to decorate the houses in the mountains of Lebanon during the same era; see M. Dunan, *Byblos, son histoire, ses ruines, ses légendes* (Beirut and Paris, 1965), p. 85.

Figure 8.1.—Integration of Male Space into the Village Territory

As Related to the Municipality	As Related to Agrarian Space
proximity permanence civic solidarity	distance irregularity individual qualities

omnipotence—the means of escaping his wife's orbit when he wishes and, as a result, the assurance that he will be worth more in her opinion, since, even today, she has virtually no control over this sanctuary.

Two Universes United

As a corollary, Provençal society, which was so strict in maintaining the principle that the sexes must be segregated, had to create rules for meetings between the two sexes and had to establish a precise etiquette for them. A series of officers selected annually oversaw the unfolding of these activities. The town held these officials collectively responsible for the ritual followed during the festival; these officers represented a competitive hierarchy organized according to the various age groups, with each generation grouped about its most worthy member.

The picture I am about to present is actually a sort of diptych. On one side panel are the traditional forms that were still in use at the beginning of this century. My information is based upon a series of interviews with individuals who had directed such festivals and upon archival sources covering the past three centuries. The other panel consists of a study of the forms incorporated

Figure 8.2.—Male and Female Spheres of Influence

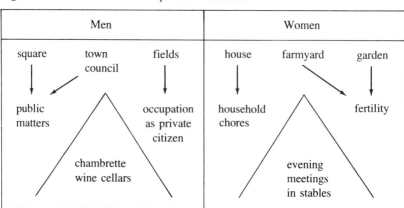

into our mid-twentieth-century society. Direct observation has enabled me to discern the transformations that have occurred and the probable course of future developments.

Elective Offices Based upon Age Groups

THE YOUTH ABBOT AND THE MAY BEAUTY[13]

Young people form an especially distinct group with its own hierarchy and resources. In traditional Provence, boys and girls in small communities formed a single bipartite, but not bisexual, group. In market towns of more than two thousand inhabitants, several groups appeared among the various social strata, each group being subdivided according to neighborhoods.

The youth selected their leader in the autumn from early November to mid-December, according to the village.[14] He bore the title *abbas* [abbot], or *guidou* [guide] of the village youth, and was assisted by a deputy standard-bearer and sometimes by a sub-standard-bearer as well.[15] In Le Lavandou a first slate of candidates was presented and the young men, glasses in hand, held an election in the tavern.[16] Later at the town hall the *viguier* or the *bayle* [local magistrates] chose the most popular of these candidates in the presence

[13]Abbreviations used in my archival research are as follows:
1) V = Departmental archives of the Var at Draguignan;
X = Departmental archives of the Basses-Alpes at Digne;
Y = Departmental archives of the Alpes-Maritimes at Nice;
Z = Departmental archives of the Bouches-du-Rhône at Marseille.
Abbreviations of series [that is, archival collections arranged according to the source of the papers]
Ion = Series M = Miscellaneous instructions
P = Series M = Administrative regulations concerning associations
St = Series M = Official bylaws of clubs (19th and 20th centures)
Tp = Series G = Ecclesiastical courts; episcopal visitations (17th and 18th centuries)
Gf = Series B = Parlements; *sénéchaussées* before 1790
Gf = Series E = Confraternities of Penitents (involved in a judicial proceeding)
Sq = Series C = Statistics
Iv = Catalogs of archivists doing regional studies
2) Municipal archives:
Dc = Series B-B = Debates of town councils
III-G = Series III-G = Episcopal visitations
[14]Z, III, E, Series B-B1, Carry-le-Rouet. The debates of the town council refer to the *élus* on 23 November 1738, 29 November 1739, 30 October 1740, and 5 November 1741.
At Saint-Zacharie in about 1658 the youth and the town council discussed All Saints' Day, which the council wanted to select as the date on which the abbot's term would begin. A. Mailloux, *La Quinzoutite, ou le 15 août à Saint-Zacharie* (Draguignan: Olivier Joulian, 1935), p. 12.
[15]Maurice Agulhon, "La sociabilité méridionale (Confréries et associations dans la vie collective en Provence orientale à la fin du XVIIIe siècle)," *La pensée universitaire* (Aix-en-Provence, 1966), p. 103.
[16]Emmanuel Davin, *Monographie du Lavandou* (Toulon, 1939), p. 107.

of the young men of the village. A two-step process also appeared as early as 1737 at Carry-le-Rouet: "The young men of the aforesaid Carry, having entered this assembly (town council meeting), named and elected Joseph Ollive as youth abbot or *guidou* for the coming year, and Pierre Pavanque as his lieutenant, who were unanimously approved by the Council.''[17] Indeed, it was a widespread custom that each year the community's youth would by acclaim single out a spokesman from among their ranks.[18] We know that the oldest charter for the region of Albi, granted in 1136 by Roger Trancavel, stipulated that the charter itself merely confirmed established practices.[19]

In rural areas this annual officialdom was composed of an *élu* [local tax official] and his lieutenant.[20] In cities, social stratification resulted in the selection of a representative from each of the "estates." Thus, in seventeenth-century Draguignan, four distinct youth groups existed:[21] (a) the *Grand Jouvent* [Great Youth], which united noble boys under the authority of the Prince of Love; (b) the *Basoche,* which included all the clerks in the law courts under their king; (c) the *Groupe des artisans,* which subdivided the numerous artisans into groups for each neighborhood; and (d) the *Bassaquets,* or day laborers, who were organized in a similar fashion.

Each of the latter two groups at Draguignan probably elected its own abbot according to a process analogous to that used in Nice, which has come down to us in a ruling dated 1619. These regulations,[22] in turn referring to an earlier statute of 1539, were drawn up for the Mardi Gras festivities at Nice and codify the election and functions of the abbots of the Ball. These abbots were youth abbots, for among the various rights conferred by their office was that of collecting the charivari dues. There were four such abbots, each accompanied by their monks. One each was elected by the nobility, the merchants, and the artisans; the fourth was chosen by the three combined occupational categories of plowmen, manual laborers, and fishermen. As an emblem of authority, each new officer was given a flag purchased by the municipality.[23]

---

[17]Z, III, E, Series B-B1, Carry-le-Rouet, Dc of 15 December 1737 (sheet 239).

[18]The role of youth leader in the Mediterranean region deserves a study of its own. In Turkey the assembly of young people elects its leader and his aide in a similar manner. Among other functions that these leaders share with the Provençal abbot is that of assessing families for marriages; the fee is doubled if the bride comes from another village. These sums go to meet the expenses of the local youth (rewards to dancing girls who have been invited to perform for them; more or less long-term loans). This information has been provided by Peter Boratav and is part of a group research project.

[19]André Varagnac, *Civilisation traditionelle et genre de vie* (Paris: Albin Michel, 1948), p. 172.

[20]Z, III, E, Series B-B1, Carry-le-Rouet, Dc of 1738 (sheet 245), 1740 (sheet 263), 1741 (sheet 267).

[21]Frédéric Mireur, *Inventaire sommaire des archives départementales du Var,* introduction, p. lxx.

[22]Robert Latouche, *Histoire de Nice des origines à 1914,* 2 vols. (Nice, 1951).

[23]Register of community debates for Saint-Zacharie, in Mailloux, *La Quinzoutite,* p. 10; for the year 1619 the new standard-bearer of the young people received "the flag that the community has purchased, along with its cord and tassels."

The young men who were part of an abbot's "retinue" would decorate their hats with ribbons of a color chosen by their abbot.[24] We know that the dues levied by the Youth Abbey were merely a continuation of the very old practice by which villages would levy such communal dues as the *pelote,* initally a fee imposed upon all newlyweds. This payment rapidly came to be considered a compensation for the harm done to the community by the creation of a household in which one partner came from outside the village. (If the outsider was a woman, it meant that the female segment of the population had lost a potential husband; if the newcomer was a man, the males had lost a potential wife.)

During the seventeenth century popular opinion viewed the pelote as a fee that by unwritten right formed a permanent part of the Youth Abbey's resources and could be spent at the abbot's discretion.[25] Thus, "the aforesaid Collomp, as youth abbot of Saint-André for the year 1650, ought to have paid with his own money, or at least with *the money he received from the pelote, which was rather considerable that year,* the cost of the debauchery in the lodgings of Claude Simon, innkeeper of that place."[26] Despite an order of the Parlement of Provence in 1554 condemning the abuses stemming from the collection of these fees,[27] the improprieties continued and refusal to pay brought harsh reprisals. In 1626 criminal proceedings were initiated against "several inhabitants of La Garde who, in order to compel Durand Aulne to pay the pelote for having married, had removed the outer door of the house and placed it on the ground during the wedding banquet, intending to enter forcibly, and who then had entered the stable and tried to capture some poultry and expel a she-ass stabled there."[28]

On the other hand, in the early twentieth century, the young people of Saint-Jeannet honored the future bridegroom's generosity by lighting a joyous bonfire before his door or that of his fiancée and by aiming salvos at the doorframe of the house.[29]

These charivaris conducted as reprisals for nonpayment of the pelote and also, as we have seen, for marriages contracted outside the village, were under the jurisdiction of the abbot, who directed them. We know that in rural communities they were planned in the chambrettes of the young men in the abbot's circle. A definition of the relationships between the youth abbot and the chambrette is of capital importance. For the period during which such information is available to us from interviews with members of chambrettes, it

---

[24]Until 1681 at Saint-Zacharie these ribbons were donated by the local Benedictine monastery.

[25]X, Iv, Series B, 1039.

[26]X, Iv, Series B, 1030.

[27]An order of the Parlement of 23 December 1554 made it illegal to require the *pelote* from any bridegrooms passing through town or from bridegrooms residing in the city, unless such bridegrooms were willing to pay. Julien's *Commentaire sur statuts de Provence* (Aix, 1778), vol. 1.

[28]X, Iv, Series B,727.

[29]Joseph-Etienne Malaussene, *L'évolution d'un village frontier de Provence; Saint-Jeannet* (Paris: Picard et Fils, 1909), p. 24.

is evident that the preparations for the patron saint's feast day had already become the abbey's chief activity. The abbey was in a position subordinate to the chambrette, but the relationship between the two has thus far remained obscure.

The resources available to the abbey included two other sorts of income. The first came from the group of newlyweds, and the second stemmed from age-old rituals of magical purification and took place at the end of the year. In Provence all newly wedded couples were in a position subordinate to the youth of the community. In Le Lavandou, as soon as his election had been ratified by the *viguier*, the abbot, accompanied by drummers, would present a bouquet to every newly married couple; they would in return give him a sum of money as their means and generosity dictated.[30]

Until World War I a form of the second type of levy was still to be found at Utelle, along the upper gorges of the Vésubie River. During the first day of the new year a banquet was held exclusively for young bachelors. The search for the needed supplies was organized by the three abbots and formed a part of a triple visit to the entire village during the hours of transition between the old and the new year. The abbots, accompanied by a drummer, made the first two rounds on the night of 31 December, the first before midnight to offer wishes for a happy end to the waning year, the second after midnight with wishes for a happy new year. The third visit was paid during the evening of New Year's Day, at which time the abbots collected pigs' ears and tails, pieces of smoked pork, and sausages from the local inhabitants. This meat was carried off skewered on a halberd and was served at the winter youth banquet held in the village inn a few days later.[31]

In addition to these permanent and inherent prerogatives due the leader of the most distinct age group of the community, the abbot had a series of tasks involving preparations for the annual patron saint's feast day. In traditional Provence he shared the responsibility with the town captain, another annually elected officer, whom I will discuss later.

The abbot was given the responsibility of planning the program and making all final decisions about the celebration. His budget came from several sources. Municipal support came in the form of an offical gift by the town council, equal—in the town of Saint-Zacharie, for example—to half the amount received by the town captain.[32] In addition, it was an accepted practice for all families in the village to contribute. For this purpose the abbot and his priors went from house to house to the sound of fife and drum several

---

[30]Davin, *Monographie du Lavandou*, p. 107.

[31]I should like to mention that the ceremony for expelling pestilences that marked the year's end in ancient China was carried out principally by young boys bearing large drums with handles. Among other movements, they would walk three times around the hall of the Imperial Palace and then would lead the various pestilences outside. M. Granet, *Danses et légendes de la Chine ancienne*, rev. ed. (Paris, 1959), 1:301.

[32]Mailloux, *La Quinzoutite*, p. 4.

Sundays before the scheduled feast day. Each family offered them a drink and presented the sum of money that represented its share in the costs of the festivities. In the back country near Grasse, where the Youth Abbey was active until 1914, and in back country near Aix, where it was still to be found around Rousset until 1940, the abbot would, in exchange, give each family a commemorative bouquet.[33]

What form does this very strong and deeply rooted institution take in present-day society?

The name has disappeared, but the officers have remained, transformed into an official association of both sexes called the Feast Committee. Formerly society stressed the abbott, one individual singled out from the rest; today it stresses the "retinue" that accompanies the abbot. Midway between them is the president, who serves as a representative figurehead. However, this annual committee also reveals a grouping of several functions around the activities connected with the summer festival.

Despite these changes, the Feast Committee remains subject to the same rules governing election that the young people observed in the past. At the beginning of the summer the young men and girls meet in the town hall— which has been made available to them especially for this purpose—and designate, by a show of hands, a male president and a female vice-president of the committee. In turn, these two officers select a group of volunteers, who must receive unanimous approval. This complete Feast Committee becomes the undisputed representative of the young people of the village. Whenever the number of young people is sufficiently large to permit it, the entire committee is chosen from the same age group, as were the abbot and his retinue in the past. During the festivities this solidarity is given concrete form in the large cockade of red, white, and blue ribbon with gilded edges that the young men wear on their jacket lapels and the girls pin to their bodices. This cockade is worn by elected members only.

Like the electoral process, the manner of collecting contributions for the festivities also resembles that of the past. On several successive Sundays, committee members "find subscribers" by paying visits to the village families in order to obtain the necessary subsidies. Fife and drum have disappeared, but not the moral obligation for all villagers to contribute to the collection. In 1967, in the upper Verdon Valley, a showy charivari on the night of the village festival—a charivari tacitly approved by public opinion—penalized the attitude of one family, which had been discourteous during the committee's visit and had haughtily refused to contribute to the festivities.

Dancing has always played a decisive role in Provençal festivities. Organiz-

[33]Information provided in 1966 by two former youth abbots from La Colle-sur-Loup and Rousset. Remember that the bouquet of greenery was a magical instrument offering protection against sorcery.

ing and supervising the ball were among the abbot's prerogatives. In sizable urban areas, large enough for the youth of the town to split up into several sociologically distinct groups, or *compagnies,* each *compagnie* was assigned a specific part of the city according to a strict geographical compartmentaliza- tion. Thus, at Draguignan and Nice, the groups described above each had a village square for their dancing. The *Grand Jouvent* of Draguignan danced in the place du Marché, the *Basoche* in the place de l'Observance, the artisans in the places de Portaiguières, du Cros, and Porte-Romaine (today the place aux Herbes), and the *Bassaquets* in the Marché Neuf. In like manner, at Nice the noble ball was held at the Loggia; merchants danced in front of the bishop's palace, artisans celebrated in the place Saint-François, while fishermen and agricultural workers danced in the place de la Condamine, high up in the old city. At Mons-du-Var, peasants and artisans each held their ball in 1777.[34] Each abbot was supposed to supervise his territory and see that only members of the appropriate social class attended that particular ball. At Nice, social distinctions could be disguised by the omnipresent mask during Mardi Gras, for any person in costume and wearing a mask could dance at the ball of his choice.

Location and social class went hand in hand, and so did the cultural level of the entertainment, which governed even the composition of the orchestra. The aristocracy danced to the sound of violins, the bourgeoisie to the drum and flute,[35] and the common people to the small drum and fife.[36]

In a contract signed before a notary, each of these youthful subgroups hired a staff of fiddlers for the festive period.[37] In addition to wages, the contract established the conditions for the fiddlers' upkeep: room and board were rotated among the members of the local youth. Each day the abbot designated the person who was to provide hospitality for the fiddlers; he might make his decision known to the individual concerned by sending him a bouquet. In the cities, in view of the sizable expenses involved, receipt of a bouquet was often considered a rather dubious honor.[38]

---

[34]V, Gf, Series B, 1299.

[35]V, Iv, Series B, 296, sheet 213. This document reveals that the community feared the activities of the "Great Youth," who, during the Mardi Gras celebrations of 1633, broke up the ball being held on the place de l'Observance by the Basoches, "who were dancing without harming anyone" to the sound of a drum and flute. "The Prince of the Great Youth came, accompanied by several others, who took their drum and flute from them and, not content to stop at that, beat and bloodied several of the children attending the aforesaid ball." The King of the Basoche lodged a complaint and the leaders of the ball held at the Observance were vindicated.

[36]Y, G, 1390, dealing with a lawsuit dated 1645 in the seigneurial court of Bezaudun, a suit by J. Jaume, F. Fouque, and Jacques Odoul, drummers and fifers, who sought the sum of 50 sous owed them by the youth abbot, Jacques Martin.

[37]Various contracts found in the notarial archives of 26 January 1611, the study of Notary Segond; and of 6 January 1617, study of Laugier, in Mireur, *Inventaire sommaire,* p. lxx.

[38]The bouquet was called *malegrâce* [unkindness] at Draguignan. In the seventeenth century members of the Basoche were so afraid of receiving a bouquet that they stayed away from work and gave up their legal studies. See the thought-provoking study, "Le Royaume de la Basoche," by Mireur, *Inventaire sommaire,* introduction.

I should like to point out that until 1940 in Upper Provence the local orchestras hired for the patron saint's feast day by the Feast Committee were always fed and lodged in the homes of the village youth, even in those localities that could boast a hotel. Since 1945 they have been housed in local inns.

In addition to planning the ball, whose organization was his exclusive right, the abbot played a leading role in organizing the games played each year during the festivities. He also presided over the horse races, the winners of which received a prize; but here he worked closely with the town captain. I shall discuss their joint work later.

Today games are still played; they are organized by the Feast Committee, as are the arrangements for raffles and the intercommunal matches of *boules* [bowls] that have replaced the horse races.

As a corollary to the role played by the Youth Abbey as magical mediator for the community, certain villages would turn to the girls and choose *abbadesses* [abbesses] to serve the same functions. Abbesses still played a rather important ceremonial role in village festivals during the nineteenth century. At Lambruisse, "that day the abbots and the abbesses preside over the festivities, both in church and at the ball." Throughout the procession the abbesses wore on their heads two enormous cakes decorated with bouquets, which the abbots presented to the priests for a blessing; then these cakes were broken into pieces and distributed to the townsfolk.[39] Elsewhere, at Saint-Zacharie, festivities were organized in such a manner that the girls were given the privilege of opening the ball. However, the attributes of the abbess were neither as powerful nor as ubiquitous as those of the abbot, and I have been unable to delineate the abbess's precise role. In particular, I am unable to define the relationships that existed between the abbess and the young girls elected yearly to incarnate the magical functions of the May Beauty.

An excerpt from the chronicles of César de Nostradamus, nephew of the author of the *Centuries*, provides us with a sixteenth-century description of this temporary royalty, the May Beauty: "It is a very old custom to choose the prettiest and youngest girls of the various neighborhoods and to bedeck them with crowns of flowers, garlands, jewels, and silken garb upon thrones and raised seats, as if they were young goddesses placed in niches commonly called *mayes*, and to whom all passersby, at least all respectable ones, are invited and obliged to contribute a few coins in return for a kiss."

The May Beauty, like the youth abbot, had a surrounding escort that sollicited donations for her in the vicinity of her *maye: Dounas quaucaren à la bello Maïo qu' a tant bono graci coume vous* [Give something to beautiful May, who shows as much good grace as you do!]

Rituals intended to hasten vegetative growth, performed by the annual

---

[39]J.-J.-M. Feraud, *Géographie historique et biographique des Basses-Alpes* (Digne: Repos, 1849), p. 101.

cortege of beautiful maidens that until 1939 enlivened the main thoroughfares of Provençal cities and villages on May evenings, are still to be found in Lorraine and Champagne, where the Queen of May, magical promoter of the growth of wheat, parades annually.[40] Such is also the case in the Valais region, where the *Majorèches*[41]—a group of pretty girls between the ages of fifteen and eighteen—on the morning of May Day process through the meadows around the village, bouquets in hand, and exert their beneficial powers by tramping upon the grass in order to make it grow high.

NEWLYWEDS

Newlyweds serve as a link between the young people and the heads of households.

As a sort of corollary to the respect paid the May Beauty, an honorary status—evident in certain religious confraternities of women—was granted to the brides of the year in Provence. In Martigues at the end of the seventeenth century the two youngest brides by right served as prioresses in the Confraternity of Saint Margaret. They were entrusted with the upkeep of the side altar devoted to that saint and, on Saint Margaret's Day (20 July), the confraternity would meet and "go in a procession from the house of the prioress to the church, preceded by the banner of the confraternity and by violins."[42]

We have seen how at Le Lavandou the entire group of newlyweds was obliged to pay dues to the abbot; but at Utelle, on the eastern borders of Provence, the ritual of the *cepoun* shows the position occupied by the newly married couples of that year, midway between the village's young people and the heads of families. Despite the drastic population decline that almost emptied the old free city of Utelle in a mere fifty years, the inhabitants of the city continue this customary ritual, which takes place each year on 16 August, the feast day of Saint Roch, their patron saint.

In the village square a competition is held between bachelors and married men. This contest centers on a block of wood, an emblem of virility; it is presided over by the youngest bridegroom of the year, who directs the game and at the same time acts as wine steward. At six in the evening the orchestra stops playing for the ball and cedes its prerogatives to a more traditional band composed a fife, small drum, and bass drum. The married men of the town then bring to the outskirts of the dance floor the *cepoun*, a block of hard pear-tree wood that is stored from one year to the next in the blacksmith's shop. The same block can be used for thirty or forty consecutive years. Around it stands a guard of two, four, or six married men. The youngest bridegroom of the year, perched atop the block of wood, receives bids from the married men who wish to lead the farandole that ends the ritual. The

---

[40]Varagnac, *Civilisation traditionelle*, p. 122.
[41]Personal inquiry in the Valais region, autumn 1967.
[42]Z, III, G, 301: Tp of 1688 to 1733 (sheet 78).

money goes to the married men of the town. The winner of the auction is made temporary leader of the heads of households. Then the competition begins and the married men leap over the cepoun, while any bachelors who attempt to join them are repelled by fisticuffs. At more or less regular intervals the small drum that has been keeping up a rhythmic beat in the background stops. This is the signal for all combatants to stop, toast one another, and drink on the spot the wine that has been provided as a compulsory donation by the youngest bridegroom, supervisor of the game.

In a second phase of this game, the young men of the village attempt to spirit away the cepoun being guarded by the married men and to take it out into the countryside. This triggers a general melee that in the past was marked by true aggressiveness, giving each man involved a chance to settle all the quarrels of the previous year. The confrontation continues for an hour and ends with a farandole danced by married men, though a few bachelors are allowed to catch hold at the end of the snakelike line of dancers. The father who had earlier made the highest bid leads the dance, halberd in hand.

First I would like to point out that although this ritual is a central element of the village festival, it is strictly limited to males and is actually a ritual belonging to male society. It is the exact antithesis of the Men's Festival held at Marquens,[43] in the department of Aude [the region around Carcassonne], in which the bridegrooms are hazed by the unmarried men.

In addition, the ritual itself seems to me to juxtapose three elements of different origin and antiquity: (a) the survival—in this case in the form of the cepoun[44]—in Provence of an old phallic cult;[45] (b) the trace of practices, to be found in several French provinces, involving economic aid given collectively to young couples by the more economically stable heads of households—here this aid takes the form of the gift and the countergift, since in return for the money collected for the bids, the young couples must furnish the conciliating wine, produced by the family vineyard; (c) and lastly, the confrontation among various age groups—bachelors, newlyweds, and older married men—similar to those found in the sixteenth-century games played for Mardi Gras.[46] The local group of married men asserts itself as such in the face of the dynamism of the village youth who, as we have seen, make their own demands upon the village community as each new year is ushered in. In this sense the supper cepoun serves to counterbalance the new year's banquet for bachelors.

The halberd held by the married men leading the final farandole places the

---

[43] Varagnac, *Civilisation traditionelle*, p. 268.

[44] The cepoun was originally the block upon which a previously sawed log was split with an ax. It is always selected from a tree with very hard wood, usually the wild pear. It is stored at the blacksmith's shop, and the links between the forge and virility are obvious. I should also like to point out that some villages gave the *capitaine de bravade* the nickname "Cepoun."

In Calabria, however, the log—*il ceppo*—placed before a girl's home during the night was a public sign of love.

[45] Roubin, *Chambrettes des Provençaux*, p. 19.

[46] Varagnac, *Civilisation traditionelle*, p. 182.

age group of the married men of Utelle within its setting in Provençal society as a whole,[47] for throughout Provence that society is organized about an annual official, the town captain, who is to the citizen–head of household what the abbot is to the village youth.

THE TOWN CAPTAIN AND THE *BRAVADE*

Indeed, although the village community transferred to the town captain the responsibility for collecting the tribute paid by newlyweds, it entrusted the assembly of heads of families with the responsibility of protecting the community. Emancipation from seigneurial authority occurred very early in Provence, where numerous free cities were to be found in the thirteenth and fourteenth centuries. These cities used the *compagnie du guet* [company of watchmen] to assure their safety. In the sixteenth century the head of this local militia bore the title *capitaine de ville* [town captain]. He was entrusted with guarding the city day and night against its enemies and was authorized to "take the men needed for the defense of the locality . . . and needed to make up the watch."[48]

A community debate indicates that at Vence this watch service was to be assured *per homines* and not *per pueros*—by grown men and not by adolescents.[49] Those making up the watch were mature men, citizens and heads of families, indissolubly linked by the strength of the communal pact that guaranteed collective security for all. In addition, the local watch was mobilized whenever any important event occurred in the town, and each deployment of the municipality's strength in this manner may be considered a *bravade*.[50]

The bravade formed an integral part of any festivity, but it could also be organized to celebrate the entrance into the town of an honored guest—an outsider arriving or a local dignitary returning home—in other words, each time circumstances called for the whole series of rituals dictated by hospitality. Indeed, the fact that a visitor was per se considered sacred resulted in a double and contradictory requirement; on the one hand the gates must be thrown wide to greet him, yet on the other hand the townspeople must be

---

[47]The halberd of the farandole dancer at Utelle seems related to the halberd involved in the *offerte;* these offerings to assure prosperity represented the first fruits and were made during the midnight mass on Christmas Eve, that is, during the holiday season that occurs during the winter solstice. On the end of a halberd the peasants would present the "flowering apple," bristling with coins. This sort of offering has been described in several other Provençal communities during the summer patron saint's day festival. See Fernand Bénoît, *La Provence et le Comtat Venaissin* (Paris: Gallimard, 1949), p. 228.

[48]Saint-Tropez, register of community debates, 24 June 1558 and 18 May 1562.

[49]P. Tisserand, *Histoire de Vence et de son canton* (Paris: Belin, 1860), p. 64.

[50]*Bravade:* the institution described here seems to have gotten its name from the old meaning of the adjective *brave*, as it is still used in the expression *se faire brave*, "to dress up in one's best clothes." For villagers, carrying out a bravade meant appearing in their most festive clothes.

prepared to fend off any surprise attack the stranger may have been planning. Thus, the entire town would mobilize to greet the visitor, who, surrounded on all sides by the local militia and townspeople, was treated with due respect. Therefore the bravade originally was nothing more than an armed reception of a guest, whoever he might be.[51] By the sixteenth to eighteenth centuries the weapons were loaded with blanks.

In June 1506 a bravade with the customary gifts and rituals was included in the official welcome given Louis and Pierre de Villeneuve, joint lords of Vence, upon their return to that city.[52] Likewise, in 1699 Saint-Laurent-du-Var greeted François de Berton de Crillon, its bishop, with "the sound of bells and the firing of six or twelve small mortars." The prelate's description of his entrance into the city is revealing. "Having entered we found several armed inhabitants led by an officer wearing a gorget who, after having saluted us with his short pike, ordered his men to fire their guns in honor of our entry; after which, followed by the consuls and all the inhabitants who had been there to greet us, we went to the parish church, where we were saluted by a second salvo fired by the same inhabitants."[53]

A bravade could be held to honor saints as well as important people or religious dignitaries. At Saint-Jeannet on 16 September 1695, the relics of Saint Dieudonné, a seventh-century pope and martyr, were opened and presented to the town council by the local lord. Such a celebration should have religious overtones; and, indeed, as was fitting, the ceremony was presided over by the grand vicar and the clergy, in the presence of the marquis. However, a *grand bravade* had been organized, and the officers chosen by the town council used three measures of gunpowder in firing off small mortars and muskets.

In addition, musicians, brought from Vence and conducted by a music master, sang a motet while the relics were being opened. The officers carrying out the bravade were given the sum of eleven livres, three of which went to feed those playing the fife and drum.[54]

My discussion of the village festival will indicate the part that music played in the bravade. For the moment we must remember that music formed an

[51]The bravade is the Provençal form of a Mediterranean-wide practice of beginning a show of hospitality with the firing of salvos. In Corsica, a traveler nearing a village would be greeted by rifle shots fired within the village. In Calabria, on the annual feast day of Saint Eufemia of Aspromonte, the statue of the village's patron saint is still paraded between a double row of men who fire their rifles simultaneously into the air (research trip to Calabria in 1956). In Turkey, villages greet important persons or the procession of a bride coming from a different village with rifle shots fired into the air (information supplied by Boratav).

I therefore reject Agulhon's interpretation of Abbé Terris's hypothesis that the bravade began with the Wars of Religion. The ceremony held in Vence in 1506, in which the bravade was clearly already an established procedure, occurred three years before John Calvin's birth. See my review of "La sociabilité méridionale," in *Arts et traditions populaires,* December 1957.

[52]Quoted in Tisserand, *Histoire de Vence,* p. 92.

[53]Y, Tp. Series G, 1250.

[54]Malaussene, *Saint-Jeannet,* p. 332.

integral part of life in Provençal communities and that it accompanied all major ceremonies until the seventeenth century. By the eighteenth century, when, as a result of centralization, royal governors replaced the local militia that had been defending French territory, the title "town captain" became an honorary one that communities preserved as a sign of their former autonomy. Two offices—*capitaine de ville* and *capitaine de bravade*—tended to merge until the latter title, which once had represented the subordinate position, finally replaced the former and became the sole survivor.

The bravade itself, no longer linked to the vital need of defense, lost its connection with daily life[55] and became part of the annual festival, where it flourished until 1914. I shall now analyze the various components of this sort of bravade.

An offshoot of the village militia, the bravade—a parade of armed citizens—reflects the town's social stratification. In villages it was made up of mature men capable of handling a gun. In larger market towns it included several companies.[56] At Aups the town captain commanded the first company, the youth abbot the second, the standard-bearer the third (made up of artisans), and the sub-standard-bearer the fourth (composed of peasants). In coastal communities it would also include a company of musketeers, formed by seamen, and a company of mounted dragoons, drawn from among the artisans. In addition, the bravade was always accompanied by military drums and fifes to do credit to the processions.[57] In the nineteenth century the ghost of the Napoleonic army survived in the military uniforms worn, chiefly those of the sappers and the artillerymen.

We shall now take a rather detailed look at the functions of the town captain, for although this annual official was progressively stripped of his prerogatives, he nonetheless remained an important cog in traditional Provençal society. The man chosen by the heads of families to command the watch was selected on the basis of the respect he had gained in the community, where he had already proved himself. In some instances during the previous year he had been first consul,[58] who was always a married man with a certain social standing.[59] Records of the episcopal visitation to Saint-Laurent-du-Var indicate that as a sign of his office he carried a pike, to which the halberd of the farandole dancer at Utelle can be likened.

In 1549 the town council of Saint-Zacharie proceeded to "nominate a town captain to do the honors at the feast of Our Lady of Mid-August; during which feast he customarily conducts the great solemnities, for the costs of which the treasurer gives him ten pounds of gunpowder, two oil jugs full of wine, and the bread baked with two measures of wheat."[60]

---

[55]P.-A. Février, "Fêtes religieuses de l'ancien diocèse de Fréjus," *Provence historique,* April-June 1961, pp. 174 ff.
[56]Agulhon, "La sociabilité méridionale," p. 103.
[57]Mailloux, *La Quinzoutite,* p. 10.
[58]Agulhon, "La sociabilité méridionale," p. 102.
[59]Ibid., p. 105.
[60]Saint-Zacharie, Dc, B-B1 in Mailloux, *La Quinzoutite,* p. 9.

Early in the twentieth century in Upper Provence, where the bravade was still practiced, the nomination of the town captain was planned in the chambrettes and gave rise to long discussions, for all the members of the bravade belonged to a chambrette. The choices proposed were limited to those who could afford to accept the office, since the names of those who would find it a financial hardship were automatically eliminated.

The town captain had multiple duties: (a) directing the entire bravade for which the gunpowder was destined; (b) seeing that the food supplies distributed by the township to couples in financial difficulty, as well as to all the young men who had helped organize the festival, were properly allocated so that, on that day at least, everyone would have bread and wine on the table; (c) opening the festivities and giving them official recognition. This was done in close cooperation with the youth abbot. For this purpose the town council would give the captain a sum of money and some *joyes*, objects he was to distribute as prizes in the various games and contests. In 1550 the *joyes* purchased by the town council of Saint-Zacharie included three brass basins, two pewter plates, two ribbons, a pair of gloves, a mirror, and two dozen *aiguillettes* [ornamental shoulder knots].[61] Along with the sum of sixteen écus, these were handed over to the town captain in order to show the generosity of the community.

It might happen that during a year of poor harvests or plague this subsidy, the purchase of *joyes,* and the bravade itself would be suppressed; but with the exception of these years of public calamity, a sort of rivalry among the various communities developed and supported this officialdom. The captain was well aware that he had to be a good aedile for the entire village and a generous host to all members of the bravade, for whom a place was ready at his table.

Compared with this very important office, the domestic nature of the group composed of wives and mothers becomes all the more noticeable. Segmentation into a series of households resulted in the absence of an office that corresponds to the one I have just described for men. At the very most the prioress of the Mutual Aid Confraternity might be viewed as an example of the ascendancy of one individual over the rest of female society. All the members of this confraternity, the equivalent of the male White Penitents, would take turns at participating in wakes and funeral processions. But the most prestigious woman of the town was the town captain's wife, a primacy that became evident in the organization of the municipal festival.

The Saint's Day Feast

As we encounter it today, through archival materials and direct observation, the village festival appears to be a rich blend in which history has

---

[61]Mailloux, *La Quinzoutite,* p. 9.

accumulated a succession of geological strata, marked by the expected fault lines, intrusions, and folds.

The Provençal festival really deserves a study all its own.[62] Here I can only sketch a few of the main outlines involving those permanent components that imply a more or less direct involvement of the chambrette-club.

THE VENERATION OF TUTELARY POWERS

The veneration of the saint who protects each community is the cornerstone of the village festival as we know it today. Very often distinct from the patron saint of the parish church, the patron saint of the village festival is honored by a chapel built upon a hill or plateau outside the village. In most cases veneration of this saint replaced an ancient pagan cult dedicated to the fertility of the local fields. Systematic excavations would provide clearer knowledge about these sacred spots that the original Ligurian populations must have rendered holy with human sacrifices and whose present-day names are often derived from the name of the pagan god.

In some instances, in the sixteenth century a chapel within the town proper began to serve as the rallying point on which the current celebration centers. Whatever the location in terms of the plan of the town itself, in every region of Provence the cult of the tutelary saint involves two ceremonies: a high mass and a procession through the town. Everyone in town is familiar with this ritual, and the community zealously follows the strict rules established by local custom. Confronted with such traditions, for self-preservation the clergy frequently had to arrive at a modus vivendi. Indeed, the clergy, seen by the village community as the integrating factor in the saint's day festivities, took care to oblige every inhabitant—in other words, first and foremost the members of the bravade—to participate actively at the side of the priests during the ceremonies held in the church.

During the solemn worship service the members of the bravade used to form two rows along the central aisle, face to face. At the elevation of the host, a salvo was fired by a detachment stationed outside the door of the sanctuary. The exit of the members of the bravade at the end of the service involved a series of maneuvers much dreaded by inexperienced captains who had to utter the proper commands.[63]

The procession was held either late in the morning, immediately after the

---

[62]The study has already been begun. It is one of the topics included in a cooperative study being conducted by a group of ethnologists of which I am a member. It will be based upon material dealing with the entire Mediterranean region.

[63]Indeed, the two rows had to turn and face the high altar, then fall back in a double turn in order to reach the narthex and exit by the central door. The commander had to utter the following commands: "Right face and left face! Right! Left! Right wheel and left wheel! Forward, march!" After a number of vain attempts, one mountaineer of the upper Verdon Valley shouted out despairingly in Provençal, *Anavousen au diable!* "Go to the devil!" Roux, *Légendes, moeurs, et coutumes,* p. 12.

high mass, or in the midafternoon, after the vesper service had been sung. The statue or bust of the saint, or a chest containing his relics, was carried through the town with great pomp and followed a long-established itinerary. Every level and class of the population took part. The blend of civic and apollonian ceremony made the procession seem less a strictly religious act than the sort of procession that might have been seen climbing up to the Acropolis every four years to pay homage to Athena Parthenos.[64]

At the head of the procession came the companies of the bravade, firing off salvos and shooting in cadence as commanded; then came the fiddlers and drummers who were supposed to keep the procession moving. Next came the various town officials, the different confraternities preceded by their banners, the children, and finally the clergy grouped about the image of the saint carried by townsmen. During the intervals between the salvos fired by the men of the bravade, the procession advanced to the beat of the drums.

The prior of Bar and Coursegoule wrote the bishop of Vence in 1737: "They do not believe in God in this area unless they can see him with their very eyes; and, since they have turned the drum into a sort of divinity, there is no use in wondering whether this instrument of the Devil will join the procession. It has never failed to do so. The drum has more friends and protectors here than the King of Kings and Lord of Lords."[65] Fifteen years earlier the bishop had threatened to suppress all processions to the chapel of Saint Barnaby "if people do not mend their ways and do not banish the drum, fife, dances, and cabarets."[66] In 1742 the priest at Collobrières was left to finish the mass in a virtually empty church after he had interrupted the vesper services to protest the salvos fired by the bravade.[67]

Until 1914 several communities in the upper Verdon Valley practiced a form of bravade that was intentionally destructive. At Saint-André-les-Alpes, at La Baume-de-Castellane, and elsewhere, obstacles would be piled up along the path to be taken by the procession, forming a barricade that the men of the bravade would break down to free a path for the marchers. At Saint-André these obstacles were carts placed so as to block the road, and the sappers of the bravade would run ahead of the procession and cut the wagon shafts with their axes, knowing that the captain would pay for their repair or replacement.

Today the religious ceremonies forming a part of village festivities in Upper Provence are still much the same as in the past. The contracts drawn up by the Feast Committee stipulate the work expected of the orchestra: to perform an instrumental piece during the elevation of the host during the mass and to accompany the hymns honoring the patron saint during the procession.

The procession begins at the church and moves through the village, passing

---

[64]The organization of a procession that I observed in Calabria in 1966 during the annual festival was virtually identical.

[65]Y, G, 1417, letter from Prior Ardisson to the bishop of Vence in 1737.

[66]This text refers to a procession of the Holy Sacrament; thus it can be considered even more valid for the great procession of the patron saint, as the following text indicates.

[67]Agulhon, "La sociabilité méridionale," p. 120.

through the square that has been prepared for the ball. Crossing this square from one end to the other, it moves on to the monument to the war dead of 1914–18 and 1939–44, where a memorial service is held as part of the votive rites honoring the patron saint. Immediately after the invocation to the dead, spoken by the mayor, and the response by the townspeople, the hired orchestra performs the "Marseillaise," after which the statue of the patron saint is carried back to its chapel.

COMPENSATING HIERARCHIES IN THE FACE OF ESTABLISHED SOCIAL STRATIFICATION[68]

The tasks assigned the youth abbots have revealed the very marked social stratification of Provençal society. The village festival has provided a chance to view this stratification in action. Indeed, by observing the roles collectively assigned to these various social groups, by studying their arrangement, and by examining the categories of individuals to whom certain privileges are granted, we can see the discrepancy between an individual's official status and his position on the ladder of prestige, the relationship between titles acquired and precedence conferred—in short, the actual organization of power in the town.

Just as the chambrettes revealed the leaders of male society, so the village saint's feast day reveals itself to be a source of competition among households and a source of stimulating incentives for all inhabitants. It gives rise to a whole panoply of intangible rights that have been hallowed by custom, external signs of the high respect the community may confer upon only certain families, not necessarily those of its civic leaders; at the same time the feast day helps create a tangible image of the local hierarchy through the various ways in which it confers precedence. Thus, among high-ranking personages, the festival turns the spotlight on various series of precedences that coincide only partially, and this state of affairs is the source of both tensions and incentives. For example, the office of chief magistrate of the town—consul or mayor—and that of *capitaine de bravade* were never merged; and although a few texts do indicate that in past centuries the outgoing consul of large market

---

[68]The needed study has been begun. It will attempt to define the mechanisms for the periodic redistribution of goods and power that develop on the local level as a result of the annual competition for offices among the various age groups who are responsible for the patron saint's feast day in the northwest Mediterranean and in the Indian communities of the Andes, where these offices came into existence during the Spanish conquest.

It appears that these offices—but probably not their implications for cultural equilibrium as a whole owing to a radically different techoeconomic structure—are similar, whether it is a question of the elective Provençal ceremonies I am discussing here or of the honorary functions of the Peruvian major-domos, captains, and standard-bearers. See Alfred Métraux, *Religions et magies indiennes* (Paris: Gallimard, 1967), p. 241, and William Stein, *Hualcàn: Life in the Highlands of Peru* (Ithaca, N.Y.: Cornell University Press, 1961), p. 256.

towns might be named captain, all the persons I interviewed in Upper Provence stressed the autonomy of the two offices.

In like manner, the last youth abbots and today's presidents and vice-presidents of the Feast Committee, who have the honor of closing the ball by leading the farandole through the village, come from different families than those headed by the leading municipal officials.

Competitive games give everyone a chance to win. This free competition transcends family ties and unites the town in its admiration of the victors. Drawn up after the most agile, the strongest, and the fastest have been determined in public, the prize lists indicate truly popular acclaim. The honor attached to the *joyes* that used to reward success—silk scarves, bridles, or harnesses for the winners of the horse or mule races,[69] and sickles, ropes, tools, or hunting rifles for the winners of the jumping, greasy-pole, or singing contests—also reveals how important the community believed it was to single out its most gifted youths through these contests.

At the same time the village festival stresses the public hierarchy, for the ritual of the *aubade* [literally, "serenade at dawn"] represents the incorporation of all the village notables into the festivities. In the past the aubade took place on the afternoon before the festival and, in order of precedence, began at the church, then moved to the town hall, and finally reached the houses of the officials. In the seventeenth century the itinerary of the aubade at Saint-Zacharie included the Benedictine monastery that donated a major share of the *joyes* and the ribbons worn by the members of Youth Abbey.

Today the aubade takes place on the morning of the festival in front of the houses of the mayor, the adjunct mayor, and certain notables who have made large contributions to the costs of the saint's day festival. A musical salutation offered to the notables of the town by the officials responsible for the festivities, the aubade is led by the entire Feast Committee, accompanied by the orchestra. The latter are instructed to perform an instrumental selection before each of the houses visited. In the past each household honored in this manner would offer money or produce in return for the entertainment. Today various drinks are provided, along with herb, pumpkin, or jam tarts, which are served to all present once the musicians have finished playing. After the drinking has ended, a second piece is played, this time inside the house, before everyone moves on.

While paying homage to the local public and administrative officials in all its activities, the Provençal festival tends to confer a second series of honors based on other values—physical qualities or generosity in making contributions—and by this means it keeps a healthy, competitive spirit alive within the very bosom of the hierarchy that it is thus keeping socially open.

---

[69]Like the blessing of the cattle at Saint-Eloi, the horseraces that were so important to all patron saint's day celebrations are related to the rituals of agricultural fertility transmitted through the horse. Bénoît, *La Provence et le Comtat Venaissin*, p. 255.

REDISTRIBUTION OF WEALTH IN AN
APOLLONIAN CLIMATE

Triste qui pourrit,
Qui échappe rit!
[He who sits and rots is sad,
He who breaks loose is glad.]

The assertion made by this proverb sums up the most obvious function of the village festival: to create a state of mind, born of collective gaity, that permits the coming together of male and female society, which are ultimately united in marriage.

The magical quality of laughter as an antidote against evil charms has long been valued. In addition, countless symbols designed to ward off death are evident everywhere in the decor of the festival. The protective nature of the bouquets distributed by the youth abbots as they made their rounds collecting contributions has already been mentioned. The same protective function is served by the multicolored ribbons tied about girls' arms, cockades worn by the Feast Committee members, and multicolored cockades—replacing the bouquets of the past—that are distributed before the ball begins to all those strolling about in the vicinity of the festivities.

The green trees planted at the main entrances to the village, and even the "green bower" that the committee constructs in the square to turn it into a public ballroom, mark off the boundaries of the area that will be devoted to amusements for several days.

When the decorations are ready, music—small drum and, more recently, an orchestra—opens, and eventually closes, this period of festivities during which a different order of people and things reigns in the town. During this entire period collective feasting occupies an important place and occurs simultaneously on two levels: municipal and familial. We have seen how the distribution of foodstuffs has survived—in the cakes of the abbesses of Lambruisse, for example. On the municipal level, every community holds a banquet that is open to all comers. It generally takes place on the day after the actual festival. I am referring to the *Ailloli,* which in the past was prepared in the village square by the most expert cooks. It was eaten in an empty barn, loaned for this specific event, in which trestle tables had been assembled. Today it is served in the village inn and is included in the festival budget.

Yet at Utelle we see perpetuated the old sort of truly communal meal, eaten in the public square on the morning of the festival by all the townspeople. At dawn on the previous day,[70] the committee obtains from all the families of the town the foodstuffs necessary for a hearty Provençal brunch—tomatoes, leeks,

[70]This may well be a relic of the earlier form of aubade that played a major part in the redistribution of property.

cucumbers, olives, hard-boiled eggs, oil, and bread (the ingredients for a salad worthy of Rabelais' giant, Pantagruel), all of this washed down with copious amounts of local wine. This old custom is clearly one form of the redistribution of possessions that is a main purpose of the village festival, another form being the economic obligations involved in the office of *capitaine de bravade*.

In addition, in each household the arrival of cousins—who in the past would pile the family into a cart and start out from neighboring villages at dawn, but who now arrive in the family car—transforms the family meal into a family reunion. Now that his turn has come to entertain, each host tries to treat his guests to as copious a meal as possible, during which anyone who comes to the door must be considered a potential guest. For the adults the meal and drinks, accompanied by songs and reminiscences about family history, stretch on and on. On the other hand, when the time for the ball arrives, the young cousins, to whom these family reunions offer a chance to get to know one another better, are liberated from the usual household chores—no matter what point the family banquet may have reached—and are permitted to go off and ''dance the first one.''

In this province where, as we have seen, daily life is organized upon the principle of separation of the sexes, the village saint's feast, by putting girls and boys together, multiplies the number of licit meetings and permits courtship. Thus, the festival plays a very important part in the search for a marriage partner. The meetings between young people at the dance are public, as are those occurring at the family reunion; they take place before the very eyes of the community, crowding about the vicinity of the dance floor, which is always open to public scrutiny. These spontaneous meetings are observed, commented upon, and remembered by everyone. In establishing the relationships existing between dancing partners, ''the first'' dance opening the ball is of prime importance and in the past would have been reserved several weeks in advance. This first dance reveals publicly the budding inclination, the seeking-out, the pledge of a couple that is already ''talking.''

In addition, the community presides over the opening of the ball where these interpersonal relationships take place. Until 1870 the township played an especially coherent role at Saint-Zacharie.[71] After dinner, on the evening of 14 August—the eve of the Feast of the Assumption of the Virgin—the young men would meet in the square before the town hall. The abbot, with his banner, would take his place at the head of the farandole. To the beat of the small drum, he would pass through the village streets, collecting along the way the girls who were waiting on their doorsteps. Meanwhile the married couples would go directly to the ''green bower.'' Once the line of farandole dancers had returned to the square, the town captain would present his wife to the first consul, who would tie ribbons about her arm and open the dancing with her.

[71]Mailloux, *La Quinzoutite*, p. 5.

On the afternoon of 15 August, the actual day of the Feast of the Assumption, once the *joyes* had been distributed to the winners of the various games, the abbot would present his fiancée or a girl of his choosing to the second consul, who would attach ribbons, kiss her, and open the ball with her.

On the evening of the next day, the young people of the village would once again dance the farandole through the town, accompanied by flags, torches, and drums.

Thus, the farandole forms the link between two normally disjointed components of the village youth. This mingling of values involving hierarchy and prestige at an authorized time, together with this reorganization of the entire village order—which, though temporary, is vital for its future—under the stimulus of music and dancing, constitutes the basic continuity underlying the village festival, the one event of the calendar year during which townspeople can best compensate for the habitual segregation of the sexes.